NEW-FOUND VOICES
Third Edition

New-Found Voices

Women in Nineteenth-Century English Music

Third Edition

DEREK HYDE

Ashgate

Aldershot • Brookfield USA • Singapore • Sydney

© Derek Hyde, 1998

Published by
Ashgate Publishing Limited
Gower House
Croft Road
Aldershot
Hants GU11 3HR
England

Ashgate Publishing Company
Old Post Road
Brookfield
Vermont 05036–9704
USA

British Library Cataloguing-in-Publication data.

Hyde, Derek
    New-found voices: women in nineteenth-century English music – 3rd ed.
    1. Women musicians – Great Britain – History – 19th century
    2. Music – Great Britain – 19th century
    I. Title
    780.8'2'0941'09034

Library of Congress Cataloging-in-Publication data.

Hyde, Derek.
    New-found voices : women in nineteenth century English music / Derek Hyde. —— 3rd ed.
    Includes bibliographical references and indexes.
    ISBN 1-85928-349-7 (alk. paper)
    1. Music—England—19th century—History and criticism.
    2. Women musicians—England—History—19th century. 3. Women composers—England—History—19th century. I. Title.
ML286.4.H93 1997
780'.82'0942—dc21   97–33014
                        CIP
                        MN

ISBN 1 85928 349 7

Printed on acid-free paper

Typeset in Sabon by Intype London Ltd and printed in Great Britain by Biddles Limited, Guildford

Contents

Acknowledgements

The music extracts from the works listed are printed by permission of:

Edwin Ashdown Ltd	'Liebeslied' by Dora Bright
Breitkopf & Hartel, Wiesbaden	'Hey Nonny No' by Ethel Smyth
J. Curwen & Sons Ltd, London	'March of the Women' by Ethel Smyth (Words by Cicely Hamilton)
Novello and Company Ltd	'Four Songs: Anacreontic Ode' 'The Dance' by Ethel Smyth
Universal Edition (Alfred A. Kalmus Ltd)	'The Wreckers,' 'The Boatswain's Mate' by Ethel Smyth

Acknowledgement is also made to Ash Parochial Church Council for permission to quote from the Vestry Minutes of 1853 and 1858.

Preface

When researching material for this book in the 1970s there was, generally, little printed material on the role of women in music. The last two decades have seen, and are seeing a blossoming forth of women's studies, of studies in gender and music and the publication of much new material on women composers of the past. In revising the book for this third edition I have incorporated references to this material where appropriate and looked afresh at the varied contribution of women artists, composers, teachers and writers in nineteenth-century England. Their achievements are considered against a backcloth not only of music history but also of the societal position of women generally in the nineteenth century.

My interest arose initially from purely practical considerations. As conductor of a women's college choir I found it increasingly difficult to discover original music, particularly of the past, for female voices. Whilst looking into this lost repertoire I became particularly interested in the whole question of the neglect of the female in music, and nineteenth-century England, with its opening up of opportunities in music and for women generally, provided the focus for this study.

I am indebted to Emily Lowe, formerly Professor of Music at Eastern Michigan University for help over many years with repertoire; to Dr Arnold Bentley for his most valued criticism and advice and to Dr Kenneth Pickering for his practical assistance in the preparation of the text. To Lucy Ross for her patient work in preparing the typescript, Dr Dalwyn Henshall for the printing of the music examples and to Lawrence Dean, music librarian at Canterbury Christ Church College, I am indeed most grateful.

Finally, and not least, to Margery Hyde for her support and encouragement over many years I do record my thanks.

DEREK HYDE

Introduction

'Women have arrived at excellence in every art in which they have striven ... If the world has long remained unaware of their achievements, this sad state of affairs is only transitory.'[1] So wrote Ariosto at the beginning of the sixteenth century when Italy was awakening to the artistic potential inherent in women, as evidenced at the aristocratic courts of Northern Italy.[2] The first published composition by a woman composer was in Venice in 1566 and the first dictionaries of music published in 1732[3] both list a female composer – Elisabeth-Claude Jacquet de la Guerre; yet the accepted musical canon in Western music today contains no evidence of women composers. What silenced the musical propensity of women and reduced their contribution to the peripheries of Western art music?

The growth and interest in women's studies has revealed a wealth of music composed by women throughout the ages: many reasons are advanced for its neglect until very recent times. What is certain is that wherever the opportunity arose, whether in convent,[4] court or the home, three areas where it was deemed acceptable for women to compose and make music, there was no shortage of ability. Herein lies the first reason for the neglect by the musical world at large: this was music-making in the closed or private world. It was not acceptable for women to appear in the public domain as musicians. As performers, they grudgingly gained acceptance in the late eighteenth and (increasingly so) nineteenth centuries, but as composers in competition with men they were operating outside their allotted sphere: theirs the private or domestic world, the 'Angel in the House' of Coventry Patmore's poem.

A canon of musical taste, once formed, tends to be exclusive and also self-perpetuating[5] and from the nineteenth century onwards in Europe, male compositions of musical weight and seriousness

1

formed the staple ingredient, reflecting the artistic mores of the age. Debarred very largely until the twentieth century from participation in the performance of this largely orchestral repertoire, it is not surprising that women's musical inspiration related to less imposing music of the salon or home, in which they could participate. It is an interesting conjecture as to whether this was by nature the sort of music they were most suited to write or whether they were conditioned into it by societal factors. For example, was, Mendelssohn's insipid 'Songs without Words', taken up largely by the middle-class piano-playing young ladies of England, an example of the acceptance by women of male conditioning? Existing in a male-dominated society it is indeed difficult to define what is essentially 'feminine'; ' . . . because women have been nurtured in a male-dominant society they have internalized and appropriated many of the assumptions and conventions that could be dubbed female.' (Citron: 1993, p. 8). This indeed is the inherent problem in referring to 'male' and 'female' music as such, particularly so in the latter part of the twentieth century which seems as much concerned with discovering with greater confidence what might be termed the feminine in the masculine and the masculine in the feminine. Our mixed sexual beginnings are conditioned by social gendering to emphasize one or other of these preferences. If, in musical terms, the nineteenth-century stereotype definition of feminine as being 'tuneful', 'unpretentious' and small-scale, and masculine as being 'powerful', 'aggressive' and large-scale,[6] is accepted, then one is mainly concerned with the extent to which these elements hold sway in a composition, since some or all of them contribute to the ebb and flow of music. For example, the first movement of Brahms' Fourth Symphony is made up of many lyrical themes interspersed with more powerful and aggressive ones which leads to a rich and satisfying musical experience: lyricism or aggressiveness are not the preserve of either sex. It seems, therefore, misleading to associate gender with any one particular type of music and to argue that ' . . . phallic violence underlies Beethoven's Ninth Symphony'[7] (Citron: 1993, p. 223) is to find in the intangible a very specific and personal response that has more to do with sexual politics than music. In what terms would one describe Ethel Smyth's aggressive and bombastic Overture to *The Wreckers* one might ask? In fact, in dealing with later twentieth-century music which is more often concerned with texture rather than melody, rhythm rather than harmony and meditative rather than climactic music, it is difficult to see how gender issues as expressed in music have much relevance. One is inclined to agree with the conclusion which Marcia Citron arrives at when she says

> ... that there are no stylistic traits essential to all women nor exclusive to women, but certain tendencies, perhaps related to subject positioning or socialization, seem to manifest themselves in many works by women. Such tendencies are also available to men. The absence of any specifically female style is another indication not only of the difficulty of applying absolute meanings to music but of the fact that women have been socialized largely by male norms. (*Citron: 1993, p. 11*)

By far the most crippling influence in the past that has detracted from female creativity in European music has been the male-dominated Christian religions and lack of sexual and economic freedom. Whilst the study of the role of women in nineteenth-century English music is more concerned with the increasing involvement of women in all facets of music-making and music education, many of the issues that are more pressing in feminine music studies in the latter part of the twentieth century have their origins in the historical and societal aspects of the nineteenth century.

The events and cross currents of any chosen period of history are diverse, though often related, and the nineteenth century, which witnessed the transformation of society from an agricultural to an industrial one in several European countries (though firstly and most intensely in England), presents a bewildering spectrum of reformist movements united in their aim to better society. Mary Wollstonecraft had drawn attention to the position of one very large section of society in the closing years of the eighteenth century. Her *A Vindication of the Rights of Woman* (1792) had focused attention on the subservient role and restricted opportunities that women in England suffered from, and had thereby set the long debate going,[8] a subject which women novelists found particularly close to their hearts. There was no simple solution to a social problem of such complexity, lacking as women did the opportunities for education and consequent economic independence, legal and property rights, enfranchisement and not least, a means of escape from the fatigue of an excessive number of pregnancies. The nineteenth century saw progress – amazing progress when one considers how distant was the starting point – on all four counts. It produced exceptional women in many fields of endeavour, women who, by their example, revealed the enormous potential and capabilities lying dormant and untapped. Elizabeth

Fry, Harriet Martineau and Florence Nightingale, in the first part of the century, more than exemplified the practical achievements women were capable of in their chosen fields of prison reform, economics and nursing. They were the pioneers, challenging ingrained predispositions, and by their prominence, began the slow process of changing both men's and women's attitudes to feminine roles. To a lesser extent, prima donnas and actresses who contributed to this gradual metamorphosis, often by their more liberated behaviour, challenged the rigid moral conventions which were outwardly subscribed to by society in general.

The practice of music and its enjoyment underwent great changes in the nineteenth century also. No longer the preserve of a rich minority, music began to embrace all sections of the community, and in so doing, became caught up in commercial promotion and consequent debasement. As a social activity it was pre-eminent: singing occupied a privileged place in the curriculum of the emerging state schools, and home entertainment was centred on music-making with the family and friends. In the more public domain the new choral societies attracted large numbers of enthusiastic men and women to experience the new-found delights of singing oratorios: industry saw the benefits of works' bands and encouraged the brass band movement, whilst the church, particularly the evangelical churches, found in hymn-singing a solace and strength that was as rewarding and stimulating as the best delivered sermon. In the popular Music Halls, music contributed very largely to the common bond of identification that united both audience and performers, mainly in the singing of popular ditties. Music was regarded by social reformers as a universal panacea and by most educationalists as a force for moral good. The moral goodness of music, particularly as expressed in the oratorio and the 'serious' ballads, may account for the very large number of women who took to music in the nineteenth century. Music came close to godliness.

It is the confluence of the movement towards the greater freedom for women and the general movement towards the greater dissemination of music, both developing side by side in the nineteenth century, that is the subject of this book. The one strengthened the other and it was therefore no historical accident that it was the nineteenth century that first witnessed the emergence of professional women musicians in any appreciable number. Their contribution was distinctive in its fresh outlook and diverse in its variety. As they forged access into a hitherto predominantly male domain they were in the van of the movement towards greater freedom and opportunity for women. One or two effectively bridged both worlds, but most women musicians contributed to the women's movement by establishing their own professional identity and independence.

Entering into a male-dominated world of music some women musicians were inclined to make an attempt to upstage the male. This tendency is pinpointed in Osbert Sitwell's remark about Ethel Smyth, the first outstanding English woman composer. 'Poor Ethel', he said, 'she would look exactly like Richard Wagner if she were only more feminine.' (Lutyens: 1972, p. 53). Like sheep in wolves' clothing, these pioneer women musicians needed to prove themselves in men's eyes, and in their capacity to organise, in their attention to practical details, their energy, determination and sheer stamina, they were indeed most formidable. The prima donnas, however, relied more strongly on the generally accepted feminine characteristics and were undoubtedly, in social terms, the most successful group of women musicians.

It was opera and oratorio more than any other musical genre that brought the female musician into prominence. In Europe, the church, with its male-dominated priesthood, had found no place for the female in its musical liturgy. The girls' choirs that had been a feature of the early church were banned from the fourth century onwards, the combination of the prevailing ascetic ideal[9] and Pauline doctrine being too powerful a scourge. Certainly to this day there is little evidence of female organists or choristers in English cathedrals though it is worth noting that music certainly flourished in the convents, particularly those of the Benedictine order, where male influence was negligible.

Although there were women to be found amongst the Troubadours and Trouvères it was not until Renaissance times that opportunities arose for women to be associated with music at the courts where, especially in Italy, there were orchestras with women players and women composers writing specifically for them. Francesca Caccini, the most outstanding of the late Renaissance female composers, and the first woman to compose an opera, was but one of many female composers active at this time. Tarquinia Molza actually directed the court musicians at Ferrara, as did Louise Couperin, at a later stage, at the court of Louis XIII and Antonia Bembo at the court of Louis XIV. Under the enlightened patronage of women such as Isabella d'Este, the long-subjugated female creative talents surfaced for a brilliant, but short appearance.

The delight in part-singing was not restricted to men: madrigals were specifically written for women singers, particularly for those women singers whom Isabella d'Este had gathered round her at Mantua, notably for Tarquinia Molza, Laura Peparara and Lucrezio Bendidio. Examples of madrigals with prominence given to a trio of female voices can be found in both Luzzaschi and Monteverdi. There are over fifty examples of three-part English madrigals, many of these being for female voices. Obviously women were encouraged to sing madrigals: what was sanctioned in the privacy of the home was not sanctioned publicly until quite some time later.

Boarding schools for girls made their first appearance in England in the seventeenth century. Renaissance idealism, particularly with regard to the intellectual attainments to which women might aspire, was forgotten, and an education which relied on the 'accomplishments' was thought the most suitable for girls. Thus music, though seen as a leisure pursuit for girls, became an indispensable part of the curriculum in the many girls' boarding schools which flourished particularly in and around London. A certain Mrs Perwick's Academy opened in Hackney in 1643 at which 'No fewer than sixteen masters were employed to teach the girls singing and music [a nice distinction this!] ... the school had its own orchestra of lutes and viols.' (Kamm: 1965, p. 69). This was an exception not only in the breadth of its music provision, but also in the opportunities afforded for concerted music-making. Most often, music meant individual singing lessons taught mainly by continental musicians. Many were the scandals associated with these schools and their music teachers: Tom D'Urfey's *Love for money or, the Boarding School* (1691)[10] was based largely on observable fact, as was no doubt, at a later stage, the character of the disreputable music teacher, Don Basilio in Rossini's *The Barber of Seville*. Handel, however, was above reproach and was appointed to teach the daughters of the Prince of Wales. It is to one of these girls' boarding schools and to the enterprise of its director that the first English opera, *Dido and Aeneas*, by Henry Purcell, owes its origin.

Undoubtedly the most famous and influential music schools of the eighteenth century were to be found in Venice where the standard of performance at the four charity schools for orphaned girls, both vocally and instrumentally, was a revelation to musicians who came from all over Europe to hear the performances at the conservatorios. In 1704 Vivaldi was appointed violin teacher at the Pietà and for the next thirty-six years was associated with it, either as Maestro de' Concerti (from 1716), or for a period when Gasparini was away, as Maestro di Coro. The influence of the Venetian Conservatorios was considerable: not only had they revealed the vocal and instrumental skills that could be acquired by orphaned girls in state-financed schools where music was made a priority, but they had also further encouraged the growing appreciation of the female artist. Composers of repute found the writing of music for female voices an attractive proposition and works such as Pergolesi's *Stabat Mater*, commissioned by the nuns of the convent of San Luigi di Palazzo in Naples, reflect not only the musical standards of these establishments, but also composers' growing awareness of the unique tonal qualities that female voice part-music affords.

The emergence of the new art-form, opera, itself an outcome of the Renaissance and its discovery of Greek drama, had a profound effect upon the course of music history. In the operatic aria, with its increasing emphasis on virtuosity, can be found one of the important elements that led to the development of the instrumental concerto. The new-found delight in vocal display was pandered to by the castrati and the new, female, prima donna, the latter presenting, in time, the first great challenge to men's monopoly of Western music in the public domain.

From the beginning of the seventeenth century the castrati appeared in increasing numbers, dominating both church and theatrical performances. They sang both soprano and alto parts and took the female roles in opera. It has been estimated that by the eighteenth century approximately 70 per cent of all male soloists were castrati. Pope Innocent XI, known as 'Papa Minga' because he was inclined to say 'no' to everything, banned women from the stage in Rome in 1676 and by implication, elsewhere in catholic Europe.[11] His successor, Pope Innocent XII, actually had an opera house pulled down, so strong was the Church's disapproval of women on the stage. 'The disapproval of female theatrical performers and the coupling of their name with that of prostitution and licentiousness was an ancient tradition ... [which] seems to have had considerable foundation in fact.' (Heriot: 1927, pp. 23–24). Thus the Church unofficially condoned the abhorrent practice of castration which, though illegal, became a thriving Italian industry. The Papal Choir maintained castrati until late into the nineteenth century,[12] and set the example for Italian church choirs. France virtually banned Italian singers from its courts and theatres, and thereby the castrati, because of this practice. It was the only country in civilized Europe that did not fall under the sway of these fêted and usually quite brilliant singers. The French writer De Brosses commented: 'It is not worth while forfeiting one's effects for the right to chirp like that.' (Heriot: 1927, p. 14) and in it one certainly recognizes that characteristic blend of Gallic rationality and wit.

Throughout the eighteenth century, women singers gained in popularity and though the behaviour of many of them cannot be said to have greatly improved their reputation – the words 'virt-uosa' and 'prostitute' being often regarded as synonymous – they eventually brought about the downfall of the castrati. With the decline in interest in the stylized and highly artificial world of Metastasian-type Italian opera, and the increasing attractions of the more realistic ballad operas in the vernacular, the prima donna emerged victorious, and the nineteenth century saw her complete ascendancy over her rivals. Adulation and often immense wealth were the rewards which, in turn, encouraged behaviour that would not have been tolerated by society had they not been so venerated. The prima donnas were often noted for their sexual freedom, their independence of thought and action, and in some cases for a certain theatricality of dress. It was La Maupin, a singer of late seventeenth-century France, who took to dressing and behaving as a man; and the first woman to wear breeches on the stage in England was Lucia Vestris, an opera singer and theatre manager of the early nineteenth century. Taken up by high society, a significant proportion of prima donnas married into the aristocracy and had access to very influential members of the State. Both consciously and unconsciously they made a large contribution to breaking down dismissive attitudes to the female and through success as musicians achieved very often a remarkable mobility of class.

The social position of women in nineteenth-century England improved as the century progressed: indeed, Ellen Moers, in her book *Literary Women*, goes further and says 'There were many active Victorian feminists . . . which made the nineteenth century the greatest period of female social progress in history.' (Moers: 1989, p. 19). One would certainly concur that in numerous areas the nineteenth century produced outstanding women and that the sum total of their work did constitute, by the end of the century, a major achievement, which made it inevitable that the twentieth century would be engaged in a reorganization of society to accom-modate the changing role of women.

By the end of the nineteenth century, women had forged an

entrance into nearly every branch of music; but entrance is one thing, equality of opportunity is another. In some areas, for example solo performance, something approaching equality was emerging, whereas in others, for example as orchestral players, women were still disregarded. It is to be expected, therefore, that nineteenth-century women musicians would be generally supportive of women's rights agitation, engaged as they were in overcoming prejudices. Several took a very active part in the wider issues of female liberation and developed the skills of pamphleteer, writer and lawyer.

If one hesitates to ascribe to the artist the power to influence and change deep-seated convictions, one must only call to mind Harriet Beecher Stowe's *Uncle Tom's Cabin* (1851), and the overpowering effect it had on popular feeling with regard to slavery and its abolition. However much Virginia Woolf may have criticized nineteenth-century women for using literature as a means of airing social grievances, there is no doubt that many long-needed social reforms gained impetus from their writing. It is no accident that revolutionary movements soon give birth to their protest songs or arousing anthem: the Women's Suffrage Movement in England was no exception. In the protest songs of Eliza Flower connected with the agitation for the 1832 Reform Bill and the repeal of the Corn Laws in 1846, the feminist Marches of Alicia Needham and Ethel Smyth, nineteenth-century women used music as a means of protest.

It is, then, in the writings of Caroline Norton (1808–1877), poet and musician, and in the writings, letters and law suits of Georgina Weldon (1837–1914), a singer and composer, that one encompasses a wide spectrum of social protest, as a result of which laws and attitudes were changed. Notwithstanding Mary Wollstonecraft's *A Vindication of the Rights of Woman* (1792) and John Stuart Mill's cogently argued *On the Subjection of Women* (1869), women in England were not encouraged to develop their minds or their abilities,[13] but were expected to sacrifice all on the altar of marriage. Though in effect a greater form of bondage than that of dutiful daughter, marriage at least afforded respectability, and in return for a meek submissiveness, a degree of material comfort and safeguard. Both Caroline Norton and Georgina Weldon suffered for their indiscretions, the former with Lord Melbourne, the Prime Minister, and the latter with Charles Gounod. Through their separate agitations over many years, during which they fought against prejudice and complacency with tremendous determination and skill, long-needed reforms were eventually made in the Marriage Laws and the Lunacy Laws – there being, it is stressed, no connection between the two.

Caroline Norton was a society beauty, as were her other two sisters, Lady Dufferin and the Duchess of Somerset; indeed, collectively they were known as the 'Three Graces' on account of their beauty. Caroline was immortalized by Meredith in his novel, *Diana of the Crossways* (1884) where she is but thinly disguised as the heroine. As a musician she composed many songs, the most famous being *Juanita*, which went into fifty editions and became one of the most popular ballads of the mid-nineteenth century. A granddaughter of the playwright Sheridan, she inherited some of his literary ability and had established a reputation as a writer by 1830 with her novels which reflect a strong social concern. Her unhappy marriage to George Norton and consequent indiscreet behaviour with Lord Melbourne developed into a major scandal of the period, for her husband instituted legal proceedings. As a result she found herself in a similar position to that which Marie d'Agoult was in when her romance with Liszt had finished, that is, she was socially ruined and without access to her children. It was as a result of her agitation and lobbying that the Infants' Custody Bill was passed in 1839, which gave women estranged from their husbands, some degree of legal access to the children of the marriage. However there were many loopholes in the Bill which her husband soon took advantage of, and she continued in her efforts to get effective legislation, publishing *English Laws for Women in the Nineteenth Century*. Many of the recommendations contained in this pamphlet were eventually incorporated in the Marriage and Divorce Laws of 1857, which represented a big step towards the Married Women's Property Act of 1882. This gave women full legal status allowing them to proceed in a court of law as a 'femme sole'.

Georgina Weldon also moved in aristocratic circles: she was a much more active musician than Caroline and differed from her also in that her writings, which include many articles, letters, pamphlets and an autobiography, make no claim to literary merit. Her liaison with Charles Gounod was the beginning of the notoriety that surrounded her, dating from 1871 onwards. Her behaviour became more unpredictable and unconventional and led to an attempt by her husband to get her certified insane. Immediately following the Married Women's Property Act of 1882 she served a series of litigations, being now a free agent to do so. She exposed the appalling state of the existing Lunacy Laws, handled the cases herself, and in so doing proved an excellent lawyer in seventeen High Court actions. She won grudging respect from several lawyers, even though she satirized them mercilessly in the famous Music Hall acts she undertook to help pay for the litigations. She served two periods of imprisonment for libel, which she claimed she enjoyed: she was irrepressible.

Her major contribution was in drawing attention to the abuses of the existing Lunacy Laws, and in so doing, preparing the ground for their reform. She was the most radical of the women musicians and she included the Copyright Laws, prison reform and the commercialization of music amongst her targets. She lived to see the women's Suffrage Movement in England, though she was never asked to speak at its gatherings: there are perhaps class distinctions even among radicals. She exposed hypocrisy with a zealousness that was most unladylike, and did not pull her punches, often thought to be a little below the belt and therefore ungentlemanly.

Ethel Smyth's contribution to the Women's Suffrage Movement is detailed elsewhere in the text but she also belongs to this group of women composers who were actively involved in the Women's Movement and who also suffered imprisonment for her convictions.

It was not only as professional musicians that women emerged in greater numbers in the nineteenth century. As amateur singers in the large oratorio choruses particularly, they supplanted the boy trebles and male altos: the soprano, contralto, tenor and bass four-part chorus dates in England from the mid-nineteenth century. The advent of women into the various branches of music teaching often brought with it a challenging of traditional methods as was the case with Sarah Glover and the teaching of notation. In so many ways women brought new attitudes, a burning desire to get things done: they were pragmatists, impatient and full of energy. The emergence of women musicians in the nineteenth century was but an aspect of the greater dissemination and practice of music that both the French Revolution and the Industrial Revolution brought in their wake. To the former can be ascribed the transference of the patronage of music from the aristocracy to the emerging middle class, and to the latter, not only the technology for the production of cheaper pianos and the printing of cheap music, but also the creation of an urban civilization for which music afforded a means of entertainment and of escape. By the end of the century, music, in its ever increasing variety of forms, had become a most profitable business. Its new vast public, part-educated through *Tonic Sol-fa* choirs, the new schoolrooms where music had an important place, and the church, exerted considerable influence upon the quality and nature of the music provided. The mass production of industry was mirrored in the mass production of music, much of which was debased and pandered to the cheapest tastes. It was at the beginning of this age of commercialized popular music for the masses that women musicians entered the field. It was both the best and worst of times.

Notes

1   Lodovico Ariosto (1516) *Orlando furioso* (Turin: Einaudi 1971) ed. Caretti (translation Anthony Newcomb) quoted in *Courtesans, Muses, or Musicians? Professional Women Musicians in Sixteenth-Century Italy* by Anthony Newcomb (Bowers and Tick, 1986, p. 90).

2   For a discussion of the extent of women's involvement in composing and music-making in the courts and convents during the sixteenth to eighteenth centuries see *The Emergence of Women Composers In Italy 1566–1700* by Jane Bowers (Bowers and Tick 1986, pp. 116–162). Their involvement, first as singers then as composers, though small in comparison with men musicians of the period, can be assessed by the variety of genres and the number of compositions published by these first professional women musicians. Over twenty women composers had their music published, some in large quantities.

3   Evrard Titon du Tillet (Paris) and Johann Gottfried Wather (Leipzig) produced dictionaries in 1732 listing Elisabeth-Claude Jacquet de la Guerre. See Preface (ix) *Women Composers in Musical Lexicography* by Julie Anne Sadie (Sadie and Samuel 1994, p. ix).

4   The long tradition of women's music in the convents suffered severe repression in the late sixteenth and seventeenth centuries. In 1686, Pope Innocent XI declared that 'music is completely injurious to the modesty that is proper for the [female] sex' and issued an edict severely restricting its practice and tuition (Bowers and Tick: 1986, p. 139).

5   In her thought-provoking discourse *Gender and the Musical Canon* (1993) Cambridge, Marcia Citron examines the formation of the repertorial canon and deplores the exclusion of women from it, creating as it does ' . . . a narrative of the past and a template for the future.' (Citron: 1993, p. 1).

6   See Derek B. Scott's article *The Sexual Politics of Victorian Musical Aesthetics* (Scott: 1994, pp. 91–114).

7   See McClary: 1991, pp. 128–129.

8   It is acknowledged that there were 'feminist' writers before Mary Wollstonecraft. These include Judith Sargent Murray (1751–1820) whose essay 'On the Equality of the Sexes' was published in the

Massachusetts Magazine in 1790 and, more influential on Mary Wollstonecraft, Catherine Macaulay whose 'Letters on Education' was published in the late 1780s and was reviewed by Mary Wollstonecraft in the November edition of the *Analytical Review* in 1790. (See Rossi: 1973, pp. 16 and 29.)

9   Marriage was not made a sacrament of the church until 1550.

10 A Restoration comedy of intrigue in which Mr Semibrief, the singing master, and Mr Coopee, the dancing master, seduce two of their pupils.

11 There were many exceptions to the ban, which was not consistently observed. Indeed, there were occasions when women singers actually appeared on the stage in Rome, disguised as castrati, who were themselves disguised as women! Confusion of identity was often further increased by the tendency of some castrati to go about their normal business dressed as women (see Heriot: 1927).

12 Allessandro Moreschi (1858–1922) is credited with being the last of the Papal castrati. He retired in 1913, though not before making some recordings of his singing.

13 In 1839, 49.5 per cent of women marrying in England were illiterate.

1 The New Concert Artists

More so than in any other sphere of music women first came under public scrutiny as concert artists and inevitably led the way in the breaking down of social taboos that had prevailed for centuries regarding public display by women. It was, strangely enough, the respectability of the oratorio and the sanctimonious approval this art-form received that made it possible for women soloists to be taken seriously and respected. It is, then, to the soprano and contralto soloists of the nineteenth century that we must first turn our attention.

Nineteenth-century England was, contrary to the often-quoted tag,[1] the land *with* music. Nearly every celebrated musician, both composer and performer, came to London. The Philharmonic Society Concerts, begun in 1814, Italian opera at the King's Theatre, and the long-established provincial Choral Festivals were the regular musical events throughout the century to which were added a whole variety of Ballad Concerts, 'Pop' Concerts, Promenade Concerts, Musical Entertainments and Music Hall. The three charts (see Appendix 1) show the extent of the foreign competition that English sopranos and contraltos had to contend with in their rise to recognition. The singers included in the charts were all celebrities and it will be noted how many foreign singers either made their homes in England, or at least remained in England for a significant period of their careers. The large number of female singers active in London and the provinces is the phenomenon of the nineteenth century: England worshipped the female singers in a way previously unknown.

Huge sums of money were paid to the 'stars' right from the beginning of the nineteenth century. In the year 1806, the famous

Italian soprano, Angelica Catalani, earnt over £16,000 from her London engagements; Jenny Lind received £20,000 for her American tour of 1850–1852 and by the end of the century, Adelina Patti is reputed to have amassed a million pounds from her singing career, which spanned almost half a century. Particularly noticeable is the accompanying philanthropy that several women singers indulged in. Selina Storace bequeathed upwards of £11,000, including two substantial legacies, to what has since become known as the Musicians' Benevolent Fund: Jenny Lind provided money for hospitals in Liverpool, London and an Infirmary for children in Norwich, and also endowed the Mendelssohn Scholarship at the Royal Academy of Music. Clara Butt raised large sums of money for the Red Cross during the 1914–1918 war, one concert alone raising £9,000, and Marie Lloyd, the star of the Music Hall, is reputed to have provided the money for 150 beds nightly for the destitute in London during the height of her career. Indeed, her generosity accounted for most of her enormous earnings.

Valued so highly by society, it is not surprising therefore that some of the singers were known for their 'temperament'. They took amazing liberties with the music, showing little of the respect that has since been accorded to the printed page.[2] Antoinette Sterling disliked piano interludes, seeing in them distractions from the singer and expunged them whenever she thought necessary, and no composer, even the revered Handel, was exempt from added interpolations designed to show off the voice. Though they may have come from humble origins the successful prima donnas were nothing if not regal, and it seems entirely fitting that Adelina Patti, the 'Queen of Song', should have lived in her own castle in Wales.

The first English prima donna, that is the first English singer accepted on the stage in Italy, was Cecilia Davies (1750–1836). She had arrived in Italy after a period at the court of Maria Theresa in Vienna where, along with her sister, Marianne, she had been teacher to the children. Marianne was not only a singer, flautist and harpsichordist but also an armonica player,[3] and whilst at the Viennese court the two sisters performed a work specially written for them by Hasse, which had an accompaniment for armonica. On her return to England, 'L'Inglesina', as the Italians had nicknamed Cecilia, met with great success in Italian opera in London in 1773 and at the Three Choirs Festival in 1774. She was eclipsed a few years later by the most celebrated of eighteenth-century English sopranos, Selina Storace (1766–1817) who, as a girl, had studied at one of the Venetian Conservatorios, the Conservatorio dell'Ospedaletto, under Sacchini. In May 1786 she had played the part of Susanna in the first performance of Mozart's *The Marriage of Figaro* in Vienna. The composer wrote for Selina a scena and aria, 'Ch'io mi scordi di te', which is entered in Mozart's manuscript catalogue as being 'For Signora Storace and me'. There is no evidence to prove that he was on more intimate terms with the singer as has sometimes been suggested: it would appear, however, that there was a close friendship between them. In 1784, Selina had made a disastrous marriage to an Oxford doctor of music, called Fisher, who was banished from Austria by the Emperor for his ill-treatment of her. On returning to England in 1787 she built up an impressive career: in 1791 she performed at the Handel Festival in Westminster Abbey and from 1801 to 1808 was engaged at Covent Garden, where her talents as an actress as much as those of a singer were appreciated.

Contemporary with Selina Storace at Covent Garden in the early years of the nineteenth century was Maria Dickons (c. 1770–1833), an English soprano whom the music historian, George Hogarth, described as rivalling the great Catalani. In 1807 she took part in Thomas Arne's *Artaxerxes* and in 1812 played the Countess in *The Marriage of Figaro*. She retired in 1818 having made her debut in 1787. Harriet Abrams (1760–c.1825) was a composer and pupil of Arne; as a soprano she sang at the main London concerts in the latter part of the eighteenth century, often with her sister, Theodosia. A third sister, Eliza, also a singer, completed the trio which often sang at the Ladies' Catch and Glee Concerts.

When Haydn heard Elizabeth Billington (1765/68–1818) sing in London in 1791 he was overwhelmed and described her as a great genius. She was certainly a great beauty,[4] her portrait as St Cecilia was painted by Reynolds, and she attracted no less a person than the Prince of Wales, becoming, so it was thought, his mistress. She had been very well trained musically, both she and her mother having received instruction from J.C. Bach. Her all-round musical ability can be judged from the fact that she made her first public appearance as a pianist, accompanying her brother, a violinist, and that she published several of her compositions for this combination. It was not until her return from Italy in 1801, where she had been friendly with Emma (Lady) Hamilton, that she reached the height of her success. Her second marriage, to a Frenchman called Felican, resulted in separation on account of his brutality: he had previously implicated her in his false claim to be an officer for which he had been publicly flogged, and it was suspected, but never proved, that

Elizabeth met her death in Venice in 1818 at his hands.[5] The years 1801–1811 saw her in constant demand at the Concerts of Ancient Music and at Covent Garden. She was able to insist, as a condition of her engagement, that her brother be appointed to lead the orchestra at £500 an appearance. It was she, rather than Mrs Dickons, who was the true rival to Catalani.

The scandals and notoriety surrounding Elizabeth Billington, as recorded in the *Memoirs of Mrs. Billington from her Birth*, published by James Ridgway in 1792, were more than equalled by those surrounding the English contralto Lucia Elizabeth Bartolozzi, known under her married name of Madame Vestris (1797–1856). The *Memoirs of the Life of Madame Vestris, Illustrated with Numerous Curious Anecdotes*, privately and anonymously printed in 1830, claim that she too had an affair with the Prince of Wales and that her mother had sold her into prostitution.[6] What is certain, however, is that she had a rich, though largely untrained voice, and that allied to her beauty and real ability as an actress, she had an attractive, almost magnetic personality. Although she made her debut in 1816, it was in Stephen Storace's (the brother of Selina) *Siege of Belgrade* (1820) that she really came to the fore. Between 1820 and 1830 she appeared in operas, musical comedies and concerts, at one of the latter introducing the song *Cherry Ripe*. In 1830 she leased the Olympic Theatre and became theatre manager, later acquiring the lease on Covent Garden and the Lyceum Theatre. From her detailed knowledge of French theatre she was able to transform the moribund Olympic Theatre into one unrivalled for the excellence of its vaudeville.[7] Many of her theatrical reforms, particularly her meticulous attention to costume and scenery, were of lasting effect.[8] Her enactment of male parts and the wearing of breeches attracted audiences and gave rise to certain scurrilous verses. The first verse refers to her performance as Macheath in *The Beggar's Opera*:

> What a breast – what an eye! What a foot, leg and thigh!
> What wonderful things she has shown us;
> Round hips, swelling sides and masculine strides –
> Proclaim her an English Adonis!

and the second, to her performance of the titular part in Mozart's *Don Giovanni*:

> The profligate youth she depicts with such truth
> All admire the villain and liar;

> In bed-chamber scenes, where you see through the screens,
> No rake on the town can come nigh her.

At Covent Garden, operas and Shakespearean plays were well produced by Madame Vestris and at the Lyceum Theatre the same attention to detail that had characterized her work at the Olympic Theatre was evident.

Three other English singers established enviable reputations in the first few decades of the nineteenth century. These were Catherine Stephens (1794–1882), who became the Countess of Essex and who made frequent appearances at Covent Garden and provincial festivals during the years 1814–1835; Eliza Salmon (1787–1849),[9] who came from a family of musicians and who made her Covent Garden debut in 1803, subsequently singing at the Concerts of Ancient Music and the Three Choirs Festival; and anny Ayton (b.1806–   ), who, after studying in Italy, shone on the English stage from 1827 to 1832 in Rossini operas.

Sarah Mountain (1768–1841) and Anna Marie Tree (1801–1862) were both noted for their performances as Polly in *The Beggar's Opera*: the latter was the sister of Ellen Tree, the actress, and has certainly a claim to fame, at least in nineteenth-century terms, in that she was the first singer to render Bishop's 'Home Sweet Home', which occurs in his opera, *Clari* (1823).

During this period, roughly 1780–1830, several foreign sopranos held sway for various periods of time. The two who most dominated the scene were Gertrude Mara (1749–1833), who was more successful in oratorio and concerts than on the stage, and Angelica Catalani (1780–1849), the highest paid singer during these years. She was noted for her sheer virtuosity and hence excessive, and often tasteless, love of ornamentation.

In describing an evening's entertainment at Vauxhall in 1769 and comparing the styles of singing between two ladies Mrs Vincent and Miss Brent, Oliver Goldsmith, in his essay *Parallel between Mrs. Vincent and Miss Brent*, reflected the growing public interest in styles of singing. It became a matter of great debate in the following century which saw a profusion of singing methods and singing schools, each conflicting with the other in aims and methods. George Bernard Shaw in his musical writings of the 1890s rarely missed an opportunity to fulminate against the style of vocal training at the Royal Academy of Music where Manuel Garcia reigned supreme. Vocal technique tended to become an end in itself and it was this alienation from musicianship that particularly annoyed Shaw.

The most influential style in England in the nineteenth century was the Italian opera vocal training afforded by Manuel Garcia (1775–1832), who founded his singing school in London in 1823 and whose method was continued by his son, Manuel Patricio Rodriguez Garcia (1805–1906), as the aforesaid Professor of singing at the Royal Academy of Music from 1848–1895. The latter's two sisters, Madame Malibran and Madame Pauline Viardot became famous singers and Pauline Viardot eventually took up the post of Professor of singing at the Paris Conservatoire.[10] Whilst the Garcia method was responsible for the development of some of the outstanding voices of the nineteenth century it was not necessarily the most suitable for ballad singing or concert arias. Two English singers successfully developed their own methods: in 1872 Helen Sainton Dolby set up her Singing Academy in London at which many English singers were trained. Her most distinguished pupil, though only for a short time, was the American contralto, Antoinette Sterling. In the same year, Georgina Weldon published her *Hints on Pronunciation and Singing*, which was the key to her system of training. She aimed at simplicity, the avoidance of showy tricks and meaningless display and encouraged her pupils, largely children, to put the music first. Jean de Reszke, the leading tenor of the period, propounded these ideas of a purer style of singing, with due attention to vowels and diction. In a similar way, Antoinette Sterling was concerned with clarity and simplicity. 'More Heart, less Art' was her motto, and as she was mainly a ballad singer – indeed, one of the greatest ballad singers – her views on ballad singing are worth recording:

> People think ballads are easy to sing. As a matter of fact they are the most difficult of all music to render with true effect. The ballad is simple in words, melody, and accompaniment. There is nothing to help out the singer . . . It is a question of art, interpretation and personality combined. (*Sterling Mackinlay*: 1906 p. 82)

Antoinette Sterling was at her most persuasive when singing unaccompanied and it was in this intimacy which she was able to create with her audience that much of her success lay. This was also true of Jenny Lind who soon discovered that in the simple singing of a ballad she was at her most effective.

In 1836, the management at the King's Theatre (Italian Opera) forbade their star performers contracted to them to sing at the Philharmonic Society Concerts as had always been the practice in the past. This proved of great benefit to English singers, since the Society had to look to native talent to fill the gaps and many more opportunities arose for English singers to be heard. The 1830s witnessed the beginning of the Victorian age, an age which saw in music a great moral force for social improvement, and as we move into the middle years of the century the public persona which the singers presented grew more respectable. They sang of the bliss of domesticity, of the evils of alcohol (Antoinette Sterling signed the pledge and spoke at Temperance Meetings), of Christian charity and love of country. The important place that music was assuming in the newly industrialized society is reflected in the more serious approach of the artists themselves.

In 1834 the following poem appeared in the July issue of the Athenaeum:

To Clara N

The Gods have made me most unmusical,
With feelings that respond not to the call
Of stringèd harp or voice – obtuse and mute
To hautboy, sackbut, dulcimer, and flute;
King David's lyre, that made the madness flee
From Saul, had been but a jew's-harp to me:
Theorbos, violins, French horns, guitars,
Leave in my wounded ears inflicted scars;
I hate those trills, and shakes, and sounds that float
Upon the captive air; I know no note,
Nor ever shall, whatever folks may say,
Of the strange mysteries of Sol and Fa;
I sit at oratorios like a fish,
Incapable of sound, and only wish
The thing was over. Yet do I admire,
O tuneful daughter of a tuneful sire,
Thy painful labours in a science, which
To your deserts I pray may make you rich
As much as you are loved, and add a grace
To the most musical Novello race.
Women lead men by the nose, some cynics say;
You draw them by the ear – a delicater way.

It commemorated the London debut of sixteen year old Clara Novello (1818–1908) and was written by Charles Lamb.[11] Clara, who was destined to become one of the greatest of English sopranos, had actually made her professional debut at the Three

Choirs Festival the previous year, having studied singing in Paris. She was the fourth daughter of Vincent Novello, all-round musician, editor and publisher and one of the founder members of the Philharmonic Society, at whose house Charles and Mary Lamb, Shelley, Keats and Leigh Hunt were frequent visitors. Her mother acted as her business manager and arranged several successful continental tours. In 1837 Mendelssohn invited Clara Novello to sing at the Gewandhaus Concerts, and both he and Schumann were impressed not only by her voice but by her musicianship. In a letter from Mendelssohn to Sterndale Bennett dated 11 November 1837 he wrote, 'Clara Novello is creating a tremendous furore. The public is quite beside itself when she sings with such perfect intonation, such ease and such reliable musicianship. Half Leipzig is in love with her.' (Novello: 1910, p. 66). It was thus an English soprano who 'introduced' to German audiences the arias of Handel which were relatively unknown in Germany at that time. To many it was a revelation. During the decade 1850–1860 she sang at all the principal oratorio festivals in England and was the only female soloist at the opening concert at the new Crystal Palace in 1854. Subsequently she 'opened' halls at Leeds and Bradford. In 1855 she sang at a Philharmonic Society concert conducted by Wagner and at the height of her career retired to Italy to support her husband, Count Gigluicci, in the struggle for Italian independence.

Contemporary with Novello was Mary Shaw (1814–1876), a contralto who, after studying at the Royal Academy of Music, made her London debut at the Amateur Musical Festival at the Exeter Hall in the same year as Clara Novello, in 1834. The next four years saw Mary Shaw taking leading parts at provincial choral festivals: at Liverpool in 1836 she sang the contralto part in the English premiere of Mendelssohn's St. Paul. As a result she was invited to sing in Leipzig under Mendelssohn's direction and he spoke most highly of both her and Clara Novello. After further successes in Italy and at Covent Garden she retired in 1843. This early retirement was caused by the mental breakdown of her husband, the strain of which so affected Shaw's voice that she was no longer able to sing in tune.

Another outstanding English singer of these middle years of the century was the contralto Helen Sainton Dolby (1821–1885). As was the case with both Clara Novello and Mary Shaw, Sainton Dolby's career benefited considerably from the help of Felix Mendelssohn who obtained engagements for her with the Leipzig Gewandhaus Orchestra. In addition he dedicated his *Six Songs*, op. 57 to her and also wrote for her the contralto solos in *Elijah*. Her English debut, after studying at the Royal Academy of Music, had been in 1842 and from then until 1870, when she retired, she was the leading contralto in Europe. Lowell Mason, the American musician and journalist, was particularly struck by the degree of dedication that she brought to her singing. Commenting on her performance at the Norwich Festival in 1852 he referred to her ' . . . most becoming appearance . . . The voice, the countenance, and the whole demeanour seemed to correspond.' (Mason: 1854, reprinted 1967, p. 282). He considered her the best living contralto and undoubtedly she was one of the outstanding women musicians of the nineteenth century.

Four other English singers achieved a high degree of success during the period 1830–1870, notably Louisa Pyne (c.1832–1904), who was a popular soprano at the Philharmonic Society's concerts, indeed so popular that she became the recipient of the Society's highly-treasured Gold Medal; Ann Bishop,[12] the second wife of Henry Bishop (at least for eight years until she eloped with a harpist); Susan Sunderland (1819–1905), who was known as the 'Yorkshire Queen of Song' and was the leading female soloist in the North of England for a good quarter of a century; and Helen Lemmens-Sherrington (1834–1906) who, after studying at the Brussels Conservatoire, established herself from 1856 as one of the leading English sopranos.

The element of exhibitionism, never far from the surface in Victorian times, can be seen in the preoccupation with freaks of nature of one kind or another. In the sphere of music this interest took the form of searching out child prodigies and one reads with horror of the debut at a Plymouth theatre of Louisa Vinning (1836–1904) aged two and a half years. A year later, the Duke of Wellington took her to sing before the Queen and at the grand age of four years she made her London debut as the 'Infant Sappho', accompanying her singing with harp. What is amazing is that she survived this early exposure to become a highly respected oratorio singer in later life.

It was during the mid-nineteenth century that several female duos became popular. Whether it was Mendelssohn who encouraged their existence by writing duets, or whether he wrote for existing ensembles is hard to determine; however, the 'Misses Williams' (Ann and Mary) sang in the first performance of *Elijah* in 1846, and the Cole sisters Charlotte and Susanne made their debut in 1849. A third duo, Sophie and Fanny Robertson, also became well known.

English women choral singers are also indebted to Mendelssohn for it was he who commented, in 1837, that in England we should follow the German custom of employing females for both the soprano and alto parts in four-part choirs. Sopranos had been gradually supplanting boy trebles in non-liturgical choirs in England since the second Birmingham Festival of 1778 when women choral singers were brought from Lancashire[13] to sing the soprano parts in this Festival, and later, at the Concerts of Ancient Music, in London. That contraltos had made little headway in their attempt to oust male altos can be seen from the disposition of the voices at the Norwich Festival of 1852: forty-one sopranos, thirty-four boy trebles, five contraltos and forty-seven male altos. At the Birmingham Festival of the same year, the upper part was sung entirely by sopranos but the alto part was sung entirely by men. The singing came in for some stern criticism from Lowell Mason in his *Musical Letters from Abroad*, particularly the harshness of the alto part and the fact that these singers were often under the note. He had recently been most favourably impressed by a four-part choir at the chapel of All Saints in Munich where the soprano and alto parts had been sung by female voices.

The realization of the value of girls' and women's voices for church choirs had been taken up in Switzerland by Nageli in the early nineteenth century, who found that girls' voices between the ages of twelve and sixteen were more flexible and reliable than boys' voices. His work with girl choristers had been highly praised and did much to remove the prejudice against girls singing in church choirs. However, the opposition to girl choristers in English parish churches was much more entrenched[14] than on the continent and girl and women choristers were only slowly assimilated. One might suspect that cloaked behind arguments proclaiming the purity of boys' voices compared with those of girls was, and is, a more profound reluctance on the part of the church to allow participation by women in the liturgical rites on an equal footing with men. The all-male liturgical choir is still the norm in English Cathedrals.[15]

In an article, 'The Choir of St. James, Marylebone' in the *Illustrated London News* of 20 August, 1892, the Rev. H.R. Haweis, noted writer on music (and morals), argued very forcibly for mixed male and female choirs in parish churches. Quite realistically he saw ' . . . a new and remunerative sphere for female labour. . . .

exactly suited to that enormous middle class of unemployed girls who have cultivated, often, musical tastes and nothing much to do, yet sometimes only half enough to live on.' (Haweis: 1875, p. 242). He argued that with girls and women one could select those who could sight-read, that there would be no changing-voice problem, and for good measure he added that weekly rehearsals could be held in daytime, thus avoiding 'consumption of gas'. The case is perhaps weakened by his blistering attack upon choirboys and one is left with the distinct feeling that his espousal of female choristers resulted from his lack of success with boys. He complains of 'The dirty nails, the "messy" ways, the interminable sweet-sucking and dog's-earing of Psalters, the sniggering and whispering and stretching and kicking and fidgeting and sleeping, the ruins of hassocks, surplices, and choirstalls, the endless labour of training . . .' (Haweis: 1875, p. 242). It is impossible to make any generalizations about the introduction of girls and women into parish choirs since it varied considerably in different parts of England. For example in Flora Thompson's *Lark Rise to Candleford* she describes an Oxfordshire parish church of the 1880s where girls formed the choir: 'Below the steps down into the Knave stood the harmonium, played by the Clergyman's daughter, and round it was ranged the choir of small schoolgirls.' (Thompson: 1939, p. 227). What is certain, however, is that the impetus came from the introduction of women singers into the non-liturgical four-part choirs based upon the German practice.

In the professional field certainly, the onslaught by women singers onto the English stage began in earnest during the years 1830–1870. Foreign singers who commanded a large public in England included Alboni, Grisi, Lind, Lucca, Marchesi, Murska, Nilsson, Pasta, Patti, Scalchi, Sontag, Titiens, Trebelli, Viardot; the Irish soprano Catherine Hayes, the Scottish contralto Janet Patey, and the Welsh soprano Edith Wynne. Each was hailed as the greatest until eclipsed by the next visitor. Perhaps the only safe comment that can be made regarding the various claims of these singers is that of Robert Elkin when he describes Marietta Alboni as being ' . . . generally regarded as the greatest (certainly the stoutest) contralto of the century.' (Elkin: 1946, p. 48). Photographs constitute evidence: words describing singers do not.

During the last thirty years of the nineteenth century English women took to professional singing in large numbers. There were several reasons for this but probably the most influential was that there were large sums of money to be earned: the 1880s, in particular, seemed to offer a golden lining to all types of musical ventures. For singers there were the lucrative fields of Music Hall, Operetta, Ballad Concerts, 'Pop' Concerts, Oratorio, Opera, provincial tours, American tours and tours to the far-flung Empire. Singing had long been a socially acceptable 'accomplishment' for girls and the step to professional ballad or oratorio singing, both associated in the Victorian mind with a certain moral worthiness, was not too large a one to contemplate. Even so, that had its attendant dangers as the writer in the *Girl's Own* of 1883 says:

> The calling of a musician is a fair and legitimate calling for a woman . . . as a teacher . . . as an organist. In the career of the public singer too she may do much noble work for God and man if she treats it in all earnestness and soberness, keeping firm hold of the Almighty hand; she may help to keep the moral tone of the nation high and pure . . . If, however, she resolves to follow this path in life, she must put on, before she treads it, the whole armour of Christ . . .' (*King: Girl's Own* 1883, p. 823)

A further inducement, which would not have gone unnoticed, was the proportion of singers who married into the aristocracy: Marietta Alboni, Giulia Grisi, Pauline Lucca, Christine Nilsson, Clara Novello, Henriette Sontag and Catherine Stephens had all married Earls, Counts or Barons, whilst Adelina Patti's first husband had been a Marquis and her third, a Baron. Indeed, success as a singer offered fame, wealth and social rank, barriers of race and class being swept aside in the adulation afforded to the singer. Early retirement offered further lucrative opportunities, those of teaching and of writing one's 'Reminiscences'.

The lower rungs of the ladder to success were provided by the provincial choral societies and *Tonic Sol-fa* choirs which were springing up in every new town. Here, amongst this enthusiastic choral activity, the aspiring singer could acquire a very practical grounding; here also, her future audience was schooled in the best possible way, that is from the discernment acquired through practical participation. It is usual to speak of an English musical renaissance in these latter years of the nineteenth century and the performance of Parry's *Prometheus Unbound* at the Three Choirs Festival in 1880 has served as the starting date for this revival. The real renaissance was founded in the schoolrooms and the choral singing movements: above all, it can be seen in the identification of music with all classes of the community in a way hitherto unknown in England: 'Supreme art is not a solitary phenomenon, its great achievements are the crest of the waves; it is the crest which we delight to look on, but it is the driving force of the wave below that makes it possible.' (Vaughan Williams: 1963, p. 50).

The year 1870 saw the debut of Georgina Weldon (1837–1914) in London. For many years she had charmed society ladies, and men particularly, with her voice which Gounod described as 'the voice of both sexes', but had not taken the decisive step of becoming a professionally trained singer. She triumphed in Paris in a performance of Gounod's *Gallia*, specially written for the reopening of the Conservatoire, and was successfully received at Philharmonic Society and Promenade Concerts in London.

It was particularly as an oratorio singer that Anna Williams (1845–1924) was pre-eminent and as such premiered many of the works of Parry and Stanford. She came to prominence by winning the first prize at the National Prize Meeting Festival at the Crystal Palace in 1872 and subsequently studied in Italy. She was appointed to both the Royal College of Music and the Royal Manchester College of Music as Professor of singing but her many engagements precluded her from actually teaching at the latter institution. Her most noted pupil, the contralto Muriel Foster (1877–1937), made her debut at the Popular Concerts in 1899 and acquired a European reputation after her performance of the Angel in Elgar's *Dream of Gerontius* at Düsseldorf in 1902. Like her teacher, she excelled in oratorio and in recognition of her achievements was awarded the Philharmonic Society's Gold Medal.

Several singers, like Anna Williams, retired from singing to teach and became as distinguished for the latter as for the former. These include Helen Lemmens-Sherrington (Professor of singing at the Brussels Conservatoire, at the Royal Academy of Music and at the Royal Manchester College of Music), Giulia Warwick (Professor of singing at the Guildhall School of Music), Agnes Larkcom (Professor of singing at the Royal Academy of Music) and Marie Brema (1856–1935; Professor of singing at the Royal Manchester College of Music). As a contralto Brema made her debut in 1891 and enjoyed a successful career in opera. In 1894 and 1896 she sang at Bayreuth in *Lohengrin* and *Parsifal* and followed these successes with many other operatic roles which included Brünhilde in *Die Götterdämmerung*. She was therefore able to impart a great deal of practical experience as teacher in the opera school at the Royal Manchester College of Music.

Another singer who made a successful operatic career was the soprano Fanny Moody (1866–1945), who was the original English

Tatiana in Tchaikovsky's *Eugene Onegin* and, unlike many of her contemporaries, had a fine dramatic gift. Both Mary Davies (1855–1930) and Liza Lehmann (1862–1918) preferred the concert to the operatic stage, building their reputations as ballad and lieder singers respectively. Mary Davies enjoyed great popularity in the last two decades of the century at the London ballad concerts and when she retired, in 1900, she contributed much to the development of higher education in Wales and to the Welsh Folk Music Society. Liza Lehmann had studied the interpretation of Schumann's songs with Clara Schumann, who accompanied her in Schumann lieder at a concert in 1888, three years after her London debut. She included the songs of Purcell, Arne and Hook in her repertoire, having copied them out from manuscript sources at the British Museum, and thus, as a singer, stands rather apart in her dislike of Victorian ballads and their substitution for genuine art-songs. In 1894 she retired from singing and began her notable career as a composer.

It was the Great Exhibition of 1851 that demonstrated most powerfully the changes being brought about by steam power. For the first time large numbers of people were able to take advantage of the excursion trains to London and at once the size of the country seemed to shrink. The railways made it possible for London-based singers to undertake extensive provincial tours and several women singers formed their own opera companies and made successful provincial tours, followed by more adventurous tours of America, Australia and South Africa. The most enterprising was undoubtedly the soprano Emily Soldene (1840–1912) who took her light opera company on its first provincial tour in 1871.[16] Its success, and the success of her adaptation of Offenbach's *Genevieve de Brabant* at the Islington Theatre, London, which ran for over a year, encouraged her to take the Soldene Opera Bouffe Company to America, and in 1879, to Australia. As a producer she was, like Madame Vestris, concerned with detail and spectacle: she realised that a bevy of pretty girls, even if they served no particular dramatic function, attracted audiences, and made sure that her company recruited the best looking girls. In 1879 she produced Bizet's *Carmen* at Leicester, and its enthusiastic reception encouraged her to produce further performances in Liverpool, Glasgow and Dublin. Considering that *Carmen* had been a failure when first performed in Paris in 1875 and that it had hardly had time to establish itself in the professional repertoire, the enterprise shown by Emily Soldene was quite remarkable. It was not until

1883 that the opera was revived in Paris after its disastrous first performance.

Though the most notable, Emily Soldene was not the first in the field. In 1867, Florence Lancia, fresh from her studies in Italy, toured the country with her own opera group and others followed suit. Blanche Cole (1851–1888), who had made her debut at the Crystal Palace in 1869, formed her own company and made a provincial tour in 1879, and Georgina Burns, who had played the titular part in Goring Thomas's *Esmeralda* (1883) formed a company, in conjunction with her husband, that toured throughout the United Kingdom. She very successfully revived, in English, Rossini's *La Cenerentola*. In 1896, the soprano Amy Sherwin formed an opera company and took it to South Africa – indeed, there seemed to be no limit to the size and scope of the undertaking. In all this activity one is aware of a tremendous vitality flooding into the highways and byways of the musical life of the country.

The absorption of foreign stars went on unabated during the years 1870–1900: no longer, however, did it seem quite so necessary to be Italian to acquire a reputation as a singer. Indeed, the English speaking countries produced many of the great singers of these years; from Australia came Nellie Melba and Ada Crossley; from India, Alicia Gomez; from Canada, Emma Albani and from America, Emme Eames, Lilian Henschel, Emma Nevada, Lilian Nordica, Antoinette Sterling and Ella Russell. The European contingent consisted of Therese Titiens from Germany, Pauline Lucca from Austria, Rosa Calvé and Mary Roze from France, Jenny Lind and Christine Nilsson from Sweden, Marcella Sembrich from Poland, Ilma de Murska from Croatia, Blanche Marchesi and Soffia Scalchi from Italy, Edith Wynne from Wales, Margaret Macintyre and Janet Patey from Scotland. But one surpassed them all, the Spaniard Adelina Patti who made her last appearance, aged 72, in 1915, for the Red Cross war fund, fifty-three years after making her London debut. She was rightly called the 'Queen of Song'.

No survey of nineteenth-century women singers in England would be complete without reference to the Music Halls. Here there was less homogeneity in the constitution of the audience than there was in the largely middle-class ballad audience. Indeed, Laurence Senelick[17] describes five types of Music Hall ranging from the aristocratic variety theatres, through the bourgeois halls of the suburbs to the working class halls of the poor. In all of them the performer-audience relationship was the most important factor and only artists with a genuine empathy for their differing audiences were successful. Outstanding for her artistry and rapport was Marie Lloyd (1870–1922), whom many claim was the greatest of all the Music Hall artists: 'It was, I think, this capacity for expressing the soul of the people that made Marie Lloyd unique . . . it was her understanding of the people and sympathy with them . . . that raised her to the position she occupied at her death . . . I have called her the expressive figure of the lower classes.' (Eliot: 1975, p. 173). Her social significance should not blind us to her great musical ability of which George Bernard Shaw spoke on several occasions. She made her debut in 1885 and was the star attraction of the Music Hall from 1890–1914. Some found her racy and coarse, whereas to others she afforded a welcome antidote to Victorian stuffiness. 'The delicacy of her indelicacies was exquisite', said one writer,[18] and it was perhaps her consummate artistry that always carried the day.

Lottie Collins (1866–1910) also found a champion in George Bernard Shaw who admired artistry wherever he could find it, even in her performance of 'Ta-ra-ra-Boom-de-ay' which was Miss Collins' main claim to fame. She was in greatest demand during the years 1892–1896 whilst Jenny Hill and her cockney songs caught on in the early days of Music Hall, which can be said to have taken shape in the 1860s. Jenny Hill was perhaps the most genuine working class artist of the women performers, having known what it was to be destitute. Both Vesta Tilley (1864–1952) and Ella Shields were famous for their song routines incorporating male impersonations, particularly in the song 'Burlington Bertie'.

There were many women artists such as Katie Lawrence, Nellie Farren, Kate Vaughan, Nellie Power, the sisters Leamar, and others too numerous to mention, who all contributed to 'the very stuff of social history', as Rudyard Kipling described the Music Hall song. Certainly it represents a mass culture, but it would be too great a simplification to describe this as working class. The songs in no way represented the voice of the people as did, say, the eighteenth-century broad-side ballads. It was a culture provided for, not by, the working class.

If one were writing a fairy-tale ending to this survey of nine-teenth-century English women singers one would be tempted to describe a singer who most fully represented the high idealism of the age, who rose from fairly humble origins to become the embodiment of all that was noble, patriotic and virtuous. She would combine the excitement of world tours, the pageantry of ceremonial occasions with the humbler joys of marriage and family.

She would sing the songs that went to the heart: she would be, in short a national heroine.

In 1892 such a person made her debut in Sullivan's *Golden Legend* and a few days later confirmed her sensational first appearance with an outstanding performance in Gluck's *Orfeo*:

> The principal performer, Miss Clara Butt, a comparatively raw recruit from Bristol, far surpassed the utmost expectations that could have been reasonably entertained ... If Miss Butt has sufficient strength of mind to keep her eyes, ears and mind open in the artistic atmosphere of the Royal College of Music, without for a moment allowing herself to be taught (a process which instantly stops the alternative process of learning), she may make a considerable career for herself. (*Shaw*: 1932, Vol. 2, p. 211)

Her deep, rich contralto voice made her famous overnight: the Prince of Wales made it understood that Clara Butt (1873–1936) was to be invited to any social function to which he was invited: the Queen invited her to sing at Balmoral: she sang at the German Court, completely captivating the Kaiser with the beauty of her voice, and a year or so later, undertook a triumphant tour of America and Canada. Her provincial tours with the attractive baritone, Kennedy Rumford, captivated English audiences, and when the love duet which they sang became genuine expressions of their own feelings for each other a fairy tale was in the making. In the year 1900 their marriage took place in Bristol Cathedral; although St Paul's Cathedral had been offered (a most rare consideration for anyone not of Royal blood), it was declined. The people of Bristol took a half day's holiday, the Queen sent a present and special excursions ran to bring all the famous singers and society from London. A year later Butt paid a nation's homage to its dead Queen by singing 'Abide with me' at the Memorial Service for Queen Victoria. Elgar wrote the *Coronation Ode* for her for the coronation of King Edward and the Philharmonic Society presented her with its Gold Medal. In 1907, with her husband and three children she set sail for Australia where a triumphant reception awaited her, which was repeated in 1911 when she sang in South Africa. During the First World War she raised huge sums of money for the Red Cross by organizing concerts throughout the country and in 1920 she was made a Dame of the British Empire in recognition of her services, an honour which as a woman musician she shared with Ethel Smyth.

Such were the main events of her life.[19] No English singer before, or since, captured the public's imagination to the extent that Clara Butt did. She was the perfect embodiment of the aspirations of her age which she crowned with glory – and song.

* * *

> . . . an exquisite slave is what we want for the most part, a humble, flattering, smiling, child-loving, tea-making, pianoforte-playing being, who laughs at our jokes, however old they may be, coaxes and wheedles us in our humours, and fondly lies to us through life. (*Thackeray*: 1904, p. 133)

Of all instruments the piano was the one that women identified themselves with more than any other. Its development and availability on a vast scale during the nineteenth century, and the provision of quick-rewarding salon music by a host of composers and others, headed by Mendelssohn, provided a strong incentive to that grossly underoccupied and largely neglected section of the community, the middle-class girl. Furthermore, to play the piano demanded no inelegant posture as did certain orchestral instruments: for example it was considered indecent for girls to play the 'cello, except in the 'side-saddle' position, an attitude that persisted in certain educational institutions well into the twentieth century. Indeed, the mellow candlelight emanating from the two candlesticks held in the brackets of the piano often enhanced the performer's appearance considerably. The piano and the pianist became the focal points in the drawing-room: not to own a piano became socially remiss and not to be able to perform upon one, for a young girl, a mark of lack of breeding.

London became the European centre for piano-making, ahead, as it was, of Europe in its industrialization. London manufacturers were able to use steam-driven machines, circular saws and planing machines from early in the century, and it is therefore not surprising to find that in 1851 there were 180 firms in London producing an estimated 25,000 pianos a year.

The opportunism of the German pianist and teacher, Johann Bernhard Logier (1777–1846), was more than equal to the occasion and his class piano teaching methods, employing up to twenty pupils, mainly girls, playing on as many pianos simultaneously and in time, met with a surprising success, and Logierian Academies sprang up in many English cities. The composer Spohr visited the Logier Academy in London on several occasions and both he and the composer Kollmann wrote articles in praise of the system. In 1821, the Prussian Government invited Logier to Berlin to organise the introduction of his system into Prussia, which he did over the next three years. His method[20] included teaching harmony from the very first lesson and, as the pupils progressed, to use the 'chiroplast', a bracket which he had invented to hold the hands in a good position. He insisted that the finger should remain in continual contact with the key and what was aimed at was a delicate, caressing style of playing. There was much opposition to his system, particularly from private teachers who feared lest they be deprived of their own livelihood, and by more independent-minded critics such as George Hogarth who wrote disparagingly of the incessant discord made by about forty young ladies all playing at the same time. However, so distinguished a musician as Sir Alexander Campbell Mackenzie, Principal of the Royal Academy of Music from 1888 to 1924, records in his autobiography, *A Musician's Narrative*, that as music master at one of the Merchant's Schools for Girls, he taught eighteen piano pupils simultaneously for four hours every morning. Truly, he was a man of exceptional tenacity, but it would seem that it was not so much a matter of preference as one of sheer expediency, the demand to learn to play piano was so great. As the century progressed, mass teaching methods, particularly of vocal reading, became the order of the day.

Whilst at an amateur level women pianists were just as numerous as women singers, there appeared to be fewer full-time professional women pianists than singers in England. The many large Choral Festivals, so much a feature of English musical life from the eighteenth century onwards provided, in addition to London concerts, a regular circuit of engagements which was not enjoyed to the same extent by women, or for that matter, men pianists. Their source of earnings was largely the London concerts and, hopefully, engagements in Germany, particularly with the Leipzig Gewandhaus Orchestra. That there was no dearth of aspiring women pianists is confirmed by the fact that St James's Hall, London was, according to Bernard Shaw, full of young lady pianists giving concerts every afternoon. The association of pianos and young girls was established very early in the century: when Mendelssohn made his debut in London in 1829 he wrote of it to his sister Fanny, saying, 'Old Francois Cramer led me to the pianoforte like a young lady'. Although Spohr had established the new role of conductor with the Philharmonic in 1820, the old tradition of directing from the keyboard was still implied in Mendelssohn's letter, since the work to be performed was his Symphony in C minor, op. 11.

One of the first English women pianists of the nineteenth century to make a reputation for herself was Catherine Bisset (1795–1864), who made her London debut in 1811, and subsequently played in Paris. More outstanding, however, was Lucy Andrews (1797–1878) who made her debut with the Philharmonic Orchestra in the same year as Mendelssohn, playing the Hummel Concerto in B minor. It was she who introduced Beethoven's *Emperor* concerto to England. She married G.F. Anderson, who was Master of the Queen's Band, and was later appointed Pianiste to Queen Victoria, teaching the piano to both her and her children. Another royal appointment was achieved by Robena Laidlaw (1819–1901), who in the 1840s became Pianiste to the Queen of Hanover. Robena had studied in Germany and so impressed Schumann with her playing in 1837 at a Gewandhaus concert, that he dedicated his *Fantasiestücke*, op. 12, to her. She made her London debut in 1834 playing at Paganini's Farewell Concert.

It was in the 1840s that Kate Loder (1825–1904), a former student of the Royal Academy of Music and later Professor of harmony there, came to the fore as a pianist. During the years 1847 to 1854 she made several appearances at Philharmonic Society Concerts performing the Mendelssohn Concerto in G minor, her playing of which Mendelssohn had previously praised. Her growing paralysis did not prevent her from encouraging many young musicians, and her musical enterprise is seen in her organizing a private performance of Brahms's *Requiem* in 1871, three years after its first performance, and the first in England, in which she arranged the orchestral accompaniment for piano duet, playing it with Cipriani Potter.

Encouragement was not forthcoming, however, in 1853 when Costa, who was the conductor of the Philharmonic Society at this time, refused to perform the aspiring Bennett's Concerto for piano in C minor. The matter was brought to a head by the selection of this concerto for her debut with the Philharmonic Society Orchestra by Arabella Goddard (1836–1922), who was told by Costa to select some other work. To her credit she refused to do so and performed the work at the rival Society's concert, the New Philharmonic Society. The affair was reported in *Punch*, 30 April, 1853:

The Embroglio at the Philharmonic

(Done into Verse by a very Old Subscriber and Poet)

Sterndale Bennett was Indignant with Costa
For not playing Bennett's composition faster;
Costa flew into Excitement with Lucas,
For showing him Bennett's Order of Ukase,
Haughtily Resigned the Seat which he sat on,
And contemptuously told Lucas himself to Take the bâton,
Moreover Stipulated this year with the Directors
That Nobody was to read him any more Lectures;
Also, he made it a Condition Strict,
He was Only to conduct what Pieces of Music he lik'd,
Whereby this year Costa doth Prevent
Any performance of Music by Sterndale Benn't:
Likewise excluding the young and gifted Miss Goddard
Whom with Admiration all the Critical Squad heard:
All to be Deplored, and without more Amalgamation
The Philharmonic will Tarnish its Hitherto Deservedly High
    Reputation.

Her debut with the Philharmonic Society came in the first season that Bennett was conductor of the Society Concerts in 1856; it was a notable season in that both Clara Schumann and Jenny Lind made their English debuts. From 1850, when Arabella Goddard made her first London appearance at Her Majesty's Theatre under Balfe, until 1876, she was the leading English woman pianist. Her technique was prodigious, as she had studied in Paris from the age of six under Kalkbrenner, and later in London under Lucy Anderson and Thalberg. Her tastes were catholic: on the one hand introducing the late Beethoven sonatas and yet equally at home in the mindless, showy quadrilles and medleys of the day. Bernard Shaw admired her technique, but had reservations about her dedication:

> She was an extraordinary pianist... there was something almost heartless in the indifference with which she played whatever the occasion required: medleys, fantasias, and pot-pourris for 'popular' audiences, sonatas for Monday Popular ones, concertos for classical ones... She was more like the Lady of Shalotte working away at her loom than a musician at a pianoforte. (*Shaw*: 1937 p. 276)

In 1859 she married James William Davison who was *The Times* music critic for fifty-three years (from 1846–1899); to what extent she benefited professionally from her marriage it is impossible to say. Certainly he guided her taste towards the classical repertoire, but she had already earned a high reputation as a pianist before 1859.

The concept that music is 'about' something fostered the pro-gramme-symphony and the consequent programme-notes of the nineteenth century: it also encouraged the lecture-recital which became increasingly popular as the century progressed. Miss d'Esterre Keeling's lectures on the great composers, Mrs Clarinda Webster's Mendelssohn concert preceded by a lecture on Mend-elssohn, Mrs Lieblich's lecture recitals on Chopin, Miss Constance Howard's three lectures on *Die Meistersinger* illustrated at the piano (all mentioned by Shaw in *London Music*, 1890–1894) are evidence of this sort of activity. One of the earliest and most successful in this field was Mrs John Macfarren (1824–1894), who as 'Jules Brissac' composed variations and romances for the piano. Her lecture/recitals at St James's Hall in the 1860s, with remarks on the works performed prepared by her famous brother-in-law, Sir George Macfarren, Principal of the Royal Academy of Music from 1875 to 1888, attracted large audiences.

It has already been recorded that Clara Schumann made her English debut in 1856; her influence as a teacher was profound. A whole generation of English women pianists studied under her in Germany and became noted for their poetic and thoughtful style of performance. From 1865 to 1888 Clara Schumann was a frequent performer in London, though finding time to teach at Baden-Baden where she lived and later, from 1878, at the Conservatory at Frank-fort o/M. Mary Wurm (1860–1938), Fanny Davies (1865–1936) and Adelina de Lara (1872–   ) were all distinguished English pianists who had studied under Clara Schumann. Of these pianists the most outstanding was Fanny Davies whose long career, spreading well into the twentieth century, was founded on study at the Leipzig Conservatory under Reinecke followed by two years with Clara Schumann at the Frankfurt Conservatory. She became a champion of Brahms's chamber music and in 1885–1886 she played in a trio with Joachim and Piatti in a series of concerts in London. Her interpretation of Beethoven's G major concerto, noted for its sheer delicacy and sensitivity, captivated the Crystal Palace audience at her London debut in 1885. In 1888 she played the work with the Leipzig Gewandhaus orchestra and her continental reputation was assured. She travelled much on the continent and met Brahms, for whose music she had a particular affinity, no doubt due, in part, to Clara Schumann's influence.

However, the English pianist most closely associated with

Brahms was Florence May (1844–1923) who after studying with the composer became his chief exponent in England,[21] although, the first London performance of Brahms's second piano concerto was given by another woman pianist, Adela Verne (1877–1952). The youngest of three musical sisters (Mary Wurm and Mathilde Verne),[22] Adela had studied with Paderewski and had made her Crystal Palace debut at the age of fourteen. She also performed chamber music with Joachim and Piatti and became the leading English woman pianist at the turn of the century. In 1900 she performed at a Promenade Concert under Henry Wood and later toured the USA. Until she had performed it, the Brahms second concerto was not thought suitable for a woman!

Dora Bright (1863–1951) began a distinguished career at the Royal Academy of Music as both composer and pianist. She performed her first piano concerto under Reinecke in Germany and her second concerto at a Philharmonic Society concert in 1892. She pioneered English music and gave a piano recital devoted entirely to it, which was quite a bold undertaking in the nineteenth century. As a pianist, Shaw paid credit to her musicianship but implied that her interpretative powers were rather shallow. In 1892 she married and thereafter, like Liza Lehmann, devoted herself largely to composition. Other pianists of the period who 'surfaced' for short periods of time were Fanny Frickenhaus (1849–1913) who, having studied in Brussels under Dupont, was noted for her introduction of new works, and Katherine Goodson (1872–   ), who after studying at the Royal Academy of Music went to Vienna for a long period of study under Leschetizky. She played at a London concert in 1897, and many others subsequently, and toured with Kubelik from 1902 to 1904.

Several European women pianists made successful appearances in London and some settled permanently, such as the German pianist, Louisa Dulcken (1811–1850), who from 1828 made London her home. Agnes Zimmermann (1847–1925), though German by birth, came to England at a very early age and was trained at the Royal Academy of Music. She made her debut in 1863, playing two movements of Beethoven's *Emperor* concerto at the Crystal Palace, and from then onwards built up a fine reputation for her classical style and purity of tone. Apart from Clara Schumann, the two outstanding European women pianists in the late nineteenth century were Agatha Backer-Grøndahl (1847–1907), a Norwegian pianist and pupil of Bulow, and Sophie

Menter (1846–1918), a German pianist and pupil of Liszt. Both made frequent visits to London and met with much acclaim.

Despite the profusion of Piano Academies[23] that sprang up in London and elsewhere to teach aspiring pianists, and the growing reputation of the Colleges of Music, study abroad under the great European masters (and mistresses) was what English women pianists sought. Many of the great nineteenth century composers were pianists and it was to these, or their pupils, that English women pianists naturally preferred to go.

There were several women organists in the first half of the century who had been appointed as a result of open competition to posts of considerable importance which could be equated with other forms of professional music-making. Ann Mounsey, whose career as a musician will be considered in a later chapter, was one such and commanded great respect as organist at St Vedast's, Cheapside, London. As the century progressed, such organists became fewer, and indeed an opposite trend with regard to musical opportunities is discernible in this sphere of activity when compared with any other. For example, in 1865, a London church, St Luke's, Old Street, advertised for an organist, stating specifically that ladies were not eligible and from about 1870 onwards women organists in the big parish churches declined in number.

Undoubtedly, the spread of the Oxford High Church Movement with its imitation of cathedral practice in parish churches, involving the movement of the organ and choir from the west gallery to the chancel, provides a clue to the decline in the number of women organists. The Oxford Movement, with its emphasis on tradition and cathedral practice, was inevitably out of sympathy with women in the chancel. Whilst the choir and organist were out of sight in the west gallery, Anglican susceptibilities were not aroused, but the new prominence now given to both choir and organist changed matters radically. No longer peripheral, the musicians were now placed just before the High Altar and were seen to be central to the liturgy. It was obviously not thought fitting that a woman should direct so important an aspect of the worship. The cathedral example was quite clear: there had never been (nor has there since been to my knowledge) a woman Cathedral organist in England.[24] Another reason for the decline of women organists in churches put forward by Percy Scholes,[25] was the growing complexity and awkwardness of management of many organs and, as it was thought, the unsuitability of such instruments for the female. In support of this suggestion he cites a demonstration in 1881 at the

London Organ School which was designed to answer such criticisms of the organ and prove that ' . . . all legitimate organ music can be performed even by ladies on an organ with ordinary straight and parallel pedals of ample dimensions.' (Scholes: 1947 p. 731). Considering that within fifteen years women were taking to such 'unfeminine' pursuits as bicycling, golf, hockey and tennis, the argument that women were physically at a disadvantage when attempting to play 'modern' organs was proved fallacious.

But the village churches had to accept whoever they could get: often the vicar's daughter or wife trained what choir there was and played the organ, and many were the years of devoted service, often unsung, certainly unpaid, given by women musicians to village churches. The following two Vestry Minutes from the parish of Ash, near Canterbury, Kent, are worth examining in this respect:

Vestry Minute, 28 March, 1853
That this meeting desire to tender their best thanks to Miss Maude for her kind and able services in playing the organ of the Parish Church gratuitously during the last twelve months and that the Perpetual Curate be requested to inform her of the same.

Vestry Minute, 1858
. . . that [Mr] W. Dixon be allowed £10 as an organist's salary . . .

The status of the village church musician has always been a lowly one: that of the unsalaried female organist, one that was often but grudgingly tolerated.

Several very capable women organists command our attention in the first half of the nineteenth century. In 1837, Elizabeth Stirling (1819–1895), aged eighteen, gave a recital in St Katherine's Church, Regent's Park, which included five preludes and fugues and three trios (all using pedals) by J.S. Bach. Two years later she was appointed organist at All Saints, Poplar, and from 1858 until 1880 was the organist at St Andrew's, Undershaft, London, which post she gained in open competition. She was also a very capable composer, writing for the organ, though more well-known for her popular part song, *All among the barley*. In 1858 she submitted a B. Mus. Exercise to Oxford University which was accepted though not awarded. Elizabeth Mounsey (1819–1905) became organist of St Peter's, Cornhill, London in 1834, again in open competition, and remained there until 1882. She was but fourteen years of age when appointed, having secured eighty-eight votes as against her next closest rival, a Mr George Smith, who gained twenty-five votes. Her duties included teaching the Charity School children psalmody on Saturday mornings.[26] Mendelssohn, himself a fine organist and the enthusiastic advocate of J.S. Bach's organ music, admired Elizabeth Mounsey's skill, and twice played at St Peter's, in 1840 and 1842.

It was in 1840 that the first C-c organ was erected in England, and this was at St Peter's, which, no doubt, was the source of attraction for Mendelssohn. Elizabeth was also a guitarist and wrote music for guitar, piano and organ. Her sister, Ann Mounsey (1811–1891), has already been referred to: it was at St Vedast's Church, Cheapside, London, that she established her reputation as an organist, which post she held for fifty years. Like her sister, Ann also composed pieces for the organ.

Two daughters of famous musical fathers, Eliza Wesley (died 1895) and Olivia Buckley (1801–1847), the latter the daughter of J.L. Dussek, were organists of London churches. Eliza, whose brother, Samuel Sebastian Wesley was one of the greatest nineteenth-century organists, was organist at St Mary Patten's for most of her life: Olivia, also distinguished as a harpist, pianist and composer, was organist at Kensington Parish Church, 1840–1847. Ann Stainer, the sister of John Stainer, was for fifty years organist at Magdalene Hospital Chapel, Streatham.

It is not surprising that some women organists discovered abilities as choirmistresses and developed further these skills. For example, Margaret Fowles (1846–1907), was organist and choirmistress at St Michael and All Angels, Ryde, Isle of Wight, and from 1874 onwards, having founded the Ryde Choral Union, conducted it in performances of oratorios for the next twenty years. Similarly, Mary Deacon (1821–   ) was for twenty years organist at St Mary's Church, Leicester and for ten years at two Congregational churches. In 1842 she began singing and accompanying at local concerts and training a choir for oratorio performances, at which she was most successful. In 1896 she was presented with a portrait and a purse of money in recognition of her achievements. She placed the money in trust and thereby founded the 'Deacon Prize' for local students. Mrs Mary Layton who, as organist to nonconformist churches in London, became in 1872 the first woman Fellow of the Royal College of Organists, also distinguished herself as a conductor, particularly of women's voices.

Some professional singers also became conductors and choirtrainers. Jenny Lind gave valuable assistance to her husband, Otto Goldschmidt, when preparing the Bach Choir for its first complete performance in England of Bach's *B minor Mass* in 1876, by training the female section of the chorus. Mary Paton, the Scottish soprano, trained a church choir at Chapelthorpe, Yorkshire in the 1840s and 1850s, and Georgina Weldon prepared and conducted a choir of two hundred and fifty voices which gave six successive concerts in St James' Hall, London, in 1873. Indeed, women conductors began to attract attention in the latter years of the century. Emily Lawrence, a former pupil of the Royal Academy of Music, conducted ladies' choral societies in both Rugby and Wembley: on a more professional basis, Caroline Holland's Choir gave annual concerts in London from 1883 onwards, introducing new works by Grieg and Rheinberger. Shaw was full of praise for her enterprise and the standard of performance. The most notable woman conductor, however, was Clara Novello Davies (1861–1943), who for nearly sixty years (from 1884) conducted the ladies' choir named after her, which set standards in female voice part-singing. In 1893 the choir won first place at the Chicago World Fair, and a year later sang before Queen Victoria. Its fame was not diminished over the years and in 1937 it was invited to perform at the Paris Exhibition.

It was, however, the ladies' orchestras, conducted most often by women, that attracted attention in the closing years of the century. The Czech violinist Wilma Neruda, later Lady Hallé, had been one of the first women to make a successful career as a violinist, and her many performances in England had done much to make the violin fashionable for girls ' . . . at a time when the harp or the piano were considered the only proper instruments for women.' (Elkin: 1946, p. 48). Wilma Neruda had made her London debut in 1849, but her real influence in England dates from her regular appearances from 1869 onwards. In 1901 she was made violinist to Queen Alexandra, thus getting the seal of Royal approval. The Colleges of Music, particularly the newly-established Royal College of Music, were notable for their encouragement of violinists: 'All the violins were in the hands of students: fourteen lasses and ten lads; and they played capitally, the influence of King Cole at South Kensington appears to have developed fiddling at the College in an extraordinary degree.' (Shaw: 1937, p. 328). In a performance of Schumann's *Genoveva* in 1893 at the Royal College of Music, thirty-four out of the total of fifty string players were women, which reflected the growing enthusiasm amongst women for the violin.

Women's orchestras were at first received with amused tolerance;

a certain 'whatever will they get up to next?' attitude seems to permeate the following report: 'The novelty of last season was Mrs. Hunt's Orchestra – a resident orchestra of ladies performing in a professional way and conducted by a lady.' There is then a long, detailed description of the costume, of the blue silk skirts, blue cloth coats, lace cravats, black velvet cocked hats and rosettes of blue and white worn by the performers. Most of the performers, it appeared, had some connection with the Guildhall School of Music who provided strings, flute and cornet. Two gentlemen accompanied the orchestra playing clarinet and drums. The report concludes with a paragraph which sets the social climate in which these ladies' orchestras developed: ' . . . all have society manners and refinement, thus enabling them to receive the little attentions from their aristocratic supporters which make ladies feel at home.' (*Musical Herald* 1889, February). It was in 1882 that Viscountess Folkestone, later Countess Radnor, founded a ladies' orchestra which raised £850 for the worthy cause of the founding of the Royal College of Music. It was an orchestra of strings only and grew to about seventy players. It attracted high praise as did the work, *Lady Radnor's Suite*, which Hubert Parry wrote for it.

Indeed, amateur ladies' orchestras were springing up not only in the provinces; in 1882 a string orchestra was formed in Dundee and an orchestra of nearly one hundred women players drawn from Hampshire and Wiltshire, conducted by Rev E.H. Moberly, began annual concerts in London. It was in 1893 that Shaw wrote of a concert given by the 'English Ladies Orchestral Society' at Chelmsford in which both wind and percussion parts were played by women. Aware of this growth in amateur music-making the editor of *The World* prevailed upon Shaw to go to Bow instead of the regular circuit of professional concerts:

> When I got into the concert room I was perfectly dazzled by the appearance of the orchestra. Nearly all the desks for the second violins were occupied by ladies: beautiful young ladies. Personal beauty is not the strong point of West-end orchestras, and I thought the change an immense improvement until the performance began, when the fair fiddlers rambled from bar to bar with a certain sweet indecision that had a charm of its own, but was not exactly what Purcell or Handel meant. (*Shaw*: 1937, p. 64)

Particularly with regard to singers, but also apparent in the above quotation and elsewhere, one is aware of the fact that feminine beauty, allied of course to musical ability, was often a determining factor in the degree of public and critical acclaim afforded to women artists. Whilst lack of it might not be held against a woman artist, its presence certainly was a very great help. Above all, traits perceived as masculine were strongly resented in women, and even though to achieve international recognition, a high degree of determination and toughness was necessary, women were expected to present an acceptable image of femininity. One cannot help feeling that in the following criticism, Shaw's animosity was aroused not so much by the standard of musical performance as by other factors:

> A very remarkable performance was that of Brahms' violin concerto by Miss Wietrowetz at the Philharmonic last Thursday. It was not by any means musically satisfactory; for Miss Wietrowetz is powerful, impatient and, like all modern women, somewhat contemptuous of manly gentleness. I confess I am afraid of Miss Wietrowetz. She is so strong and wilful that even her playing gives me a humiliating sense of being ordered about – positively of being hen-pecked. Joachim is called by courtesy her master; but I suspect that what really happened was that Miss Wietrowetz bought a fiddle; took it to his house; and said, 'Here, show me how to play this if you please. Look sharp'; and that he meekly obeyed. (*Shaw*: 1932, p. 279)

It is amusing, but it is hardly fair.

Whilst Shaw's attitude to the emerging women musicians was, on the whole, enlightened, championing as he did Ethel Smyth and generally treating women equally with men in his assessments of their musical abilities, there is sometimes just the suggestion, or veiled hint, that his tongue was in his cheek. It may have something to do with class issues: nearly all the women musicians came from middle or upper class homes and it was the Music Hall artists, such as Marie Lloyd and Lottie Collins who, coming from working class backgrounds, commanded his whole-hearted support. Certainly when writing about these artists one senses that he was determined to see them in the best possible light, commending their virtues with unstinting praise.

The ostentation of certain American artists he roundly condemned in passages of devastating Shavian wit. Advertised as 'Mrs. Shaw: the American Lady Whistler' he began by asking 'If she be Mrs. Shaw, how can she be Lady Whistler?' and then proceeded to inform the readers that Mrs Shaw is an American lady who whistles. A 'serious' account of her concert then followed:

Mrs. Shaw is a tall, dark, pleasantly-favoured woman with a good deal of cheek, not too chubby, but just slack enough to allow plenty of play to her lips ... After the manner of the countrywomen, she travels with enormous wreaths and baskets of flowers, which are handed up to her at the conclusion of her pieces. And no matter how often this happens, she is never a whit the less astonished to see the flowers come up. (*Shaw*: 1937, p. 205)

London concert life was a very heterogeneous affair in the 1890s, the serious and over-serious rubbing shoulders with the worst of Victorian exhibitionism: Shaw took on a daunting task and fearlessly exposed the pretentious and the sham. Of the 'Ladies Amateur Harp, Mandoline and Guitar Band' (thirty-two girls in all, three playing harps; four, violins; six, guitars; and nineteen playing mandolines) he was not encouraging: 'It is disquieting to find that there are nineteen people in England who can play the mandoline: and I sincerely hope the number may not increase.' (Shaw: 1932, Vol. 3, pp. 115–116). What a field day he would have had in 1856 had he been *The Times'* music critic who experienced a performance of Schumann's *Paradise and the Peri*, ostensibly conducted by Sterndale Bennett but with Clara Schumann ' ... posting herself on the orchestral platform, in front of the conductor to whom every now and then she gave indications which he had to try and communicate to the players and singers.' (Elkin: 1946, p. 59). This interference was certainly not calculated to put performers at their ease: how Shaw would have revelled in this teutonic, and feminine, overkill! Needless to say the performance was not a success and did Schumann's cause no end of harm in England. It was nearly ten years before any other music by Schumann found its way into the Philharmonic Society's programme.[27]

Several English women violinists distinguished themselves as soloists, though none rivalled Lady Hallé in performance or popularity. They included Emily Skinner (1862–1901), a pupil of Joachim, whose string quartet of ladies established a good reputation; Isabella Donkersley, who led a string quartet at the Royal College of Music; Nellie Carpenter, a pupil of Sarasate, wife of the 'cellist Leo Stern, and who first performed Dvorak's 'cello concerto; Leonora Clench, Kate Chaplin, Frida Scottra, Lilian Griffiths, Beatrice Langley and Mary Cardew. Several of these violinists were brought to the fore by Mr August Manns at his Crystal Palace concerts in the early 1890s.

Apart from the piano and violin, young ladies showed a strong preference for the flute and harp. The popularity of the former had much to do with the brilliant performances by Cora Cardigan who, having studied under R.S. Rockstro, toured the continent as a recitalist. The flute was considered 'A most suitable instrument for women, because it can display their powers in rapidity of fingering, in producing sympathetic and refined tone, in strengthening lungs and in performing the high-pitched brilliant music which is so attractive to them, whether as vocalists, pianists or instrumentalists generally.' (*Music Herald* 1889, July). Both Florence Hudson and Clara Eissler were noted for their ability as harpists; the latter gave recitals with her sister Marianne, who was a violinist. At a concert in 1890 organised by a Mr John Thomas, Shaw noted that there were twenty harpists, all young ladies. Whilst women harpists found entry into professional orchestras easier than any other women instrumentalists, presumably because of the lack of manly associations with the instrument, women string players infiltrated only gradually. At the Handel Festivals held at the Crystal Palace women soon made a place for themselves in the orchestra. In 1891 there were but eight women engaged in the orchestra; in 1900 there were sixty-eight, and in 1903, one hundred and ten, which included three double-bass players.[28]

However, the struggle for women instrumentalists to be accepted in the professional orchestras was (and still, is) a twentieth-century one in which Henry Wood played quite a large part, bringing women into the Queen's Hall Orchestra and retaining them after the 1914–1918 war. The late nineteenth century saw a burgeoning forth of amateur orchestral activity by women on a scale previously unknown. Women had fully entered the professional world of music-making as singers and pianists. The scale of amateur activity and the professional training being enjoyed at the Colleges of Music made it inevitable that these two avenues would not remain the only ones available for professional music-making by women.

Notes

1   England was known in Europe in the nineteenth century as the 'Land ohne Musik' (Turner: 1941, p. 7).

2   When Weber was rehearsing excerpts from his opera *Der Freischutz* in London in 1826 with the Scottish soprano Mary Paton, he frequently had to admonish her for adding to what he had written.

3   Not to be confused with the harmonica. The Musical Glasses were very popular in England in the eighteenth century, several noted performers upon them being women. Ann Ford published in 1761

her *Instructions for Playing the Musical Glasses*, she herself being a celebrated performer, and on account of her beauty, the subject of a painting by Gainsborough. It was a certain Benjamin Franklin, who modified and improved the method of performance and who renamed the Musical Glasses to that of the 'armonica' in the 1760s. Marianne Davies was friendly with the Mozart family in 1773 and it is very probable that it was her playing of the armonica that attracted Mozart to the instrument. In 1791 he wrote his Quintet for armonica, flute, oboe, violin and 'cello for a blind girl armonica player, Marianne Kirchgessner.

4 Not all female singers were renowned for their beauty. Benedetta Pisaroni, an Italian contralto who sang in London in 1829 was indeed very ugly, her face having been disfigured by smallpox. She sent her portrait ahead warning the management of the theatre that her actual appearance was worse than the portrait might suggest! The fact that she was successful in her career lends strength to the argument that women musicians were accepted on their merits as musicians.

5 For further details see *Queens of Song* by Ellen Creathorne Clayton.

6 See also *Gossip of the Century* (Volume 2) by Julia Clare Byrne.

7 Planché wrote *Olympic Revels* for her.

8 See *The Witch of Wych Street* by Leo Waitzkin.

9 Salmon became an alcoholic. There is an amusing (?) account of her swaying about, holding the music upside down and generally disconcerting Sir George Smart, the conductor, at a concert in 1824, after which she had to be physically escorted from the platform. See Rev. J.B. Cox's *Musical Recollections of the last half century*.

10 Another Garcia-trained singer, Mathilde Marchesi, became Professor of Singing at the Vienna Conservatory in 1854.

11 Not the only singer to be the subject of a poem. Congreve's Ode *On Mrs. Arabella Hunt, singing* was occasioned by the beautiful voice and great beauty of Arabella Hunt, whose portrait was painted by Kneller. She was the seventeenth-century singing-mistress of Princess, later Queen, Anne and favourite of Queen Mary. Several of the songs of both Purcell and Blow were written for her (*British Women*: 1983, p. 214).

12 She made her debut at a Philharmonic Society concert in 1831 and later embarked upon world-wide travels, singing in Australia, Russia, India and America, giving 260 concerts in the space of four years and survived shipwreck in the Pacific to end her days in New York.

13 Affectionately known as 'The Twelve Lancashire Witches' at the Concerts of Ancient Music where they became a regular feature.

14 'Female choristers are undesirable, if only on the score of decorum and propriety.' (Letter from the Organist and Choir-master, St Barnabas Church, Bradford in the *Musical Herald*, March 1889.)

15 There is a useful summary of arguments for and against women in church choirs, and whether they should be robed, in the *Musical Times* for 1 September, 1889. The writer, who is anonymous, argues that the Roman Catholic church actually forbids the use of women in the choirs where men are also engaged, and on this score alone, women could not be admitted to any cathedral choir. The writer

claims also that the 'childish treble' is a more elevating sound than any that can be achieved by the voice of a woman in church.

16   See *My Theatrical and Musical Recollections* (1897), Emily Soldene.

17   See *Politics as Entertainment – Victorian Music Hall Songs*, (Victorian Studies, Vol. XIX, No. 2, December 1975).

18   C.B. Cochran, quoted in *They were Singing* (p. 201) by Christopher Pulling.

19   For fuller details see *Clara Butt* by Winifred Ponder.

20   Friedwick Wieck adapted Logier's system to his own use, retaining the idea of teaching harmony simultaneously with that of the piano, and thus both Clara Wieck (Schumann) and Robert Schumann can be said to have benefited from Logier's method.

21   In 1905 she published *The Life of Johannes Brahms* (2 volumes) which became one of the standard works on the composer. A second edition was published in 1948.

22   The family name was changed from Wurm to Verne in 1895.

23   Many of these were founded by women, for example the Kensington Musical Academy founded by Margaret Gyde, the Anglo-German School of Music at Norwood, founded by Emily Upton, the Scientific Training School for Music funded in 1894 by Louisa Thomas, the Aberdeen Music School by Clarinda Webster, the Piano School begun by Amina Goodson (herself a pupil of both Liszt and Clara Schumann) in 1905, and another Piano School, opened in 1909, with a special children's branch by Mathilde Verne. Amongst the latter's pupils were the future Queen Mother, Lady Elizabeth Bowes Lyon, and the future concert pianist, Solomon.

24   The *Musical Times* in 1907 reported that there were no less than ten women cathedral organists in the Irish Anglican cathedrals.

25   *The Mirror of Music*, Vol. 2.

26   As stated in an article on Elizabeth Mounsey in the *Musical Times*, November, 1905.

27   Clara Schumann made her amends with the performance of Schumann's Piano Concerto in 1865: from then onwards Schumann's music became increasingly popular in England.

28   Percy Scholes: *Mirror of Music*, Vol. 2.

2 Creative Outlets and the Victorian Ballad

In 1823 the first twenty-one students, aged between 10 and 14 years, began their studies at the newly-founded Academy of Music in London. Of this number, ten were girls.[1] It was a boarding establishment, strictly segregated with a woman Superintendent to look after the girls, where morals and religion along with a general education were inculcated in a daily music curriculum extending from 7 a.m. to 9 p.m. The selection for places was by public examination and the fees initially were fifteen guineas per annum, which was very reasonable. A further sixteen students were enrolled later in the year and these included Fanny Dickens, sister of the author, Charles. In 1830 a royal charter was granted so that it became the Royal Academy of Music and though it had many struggles ahead of it, gradually its national reputation was established for the serious study of both the performing and composing of music. From its inception women professors were engaged and the original staff for singing included three women. As the century progressed, women professors of harmony, pianoforte and singing distinguished themselves, though they always had to contend with certain prejudices against them:

> The best-trained female teachers had a long tussle for recognition. My own conviction of their worth and desire to help met with constant opposition from an unexpected quarter: the rooted objection of young women to be instructed by members of their own sex! Strange logic! Were not the pupils' future interests identical with those whose capabilities they refused to acknowledge? These obstacles were over-ridden poco a poco, and the present list of female teachers contains the names of thirty-seven full professors and thirty-five 'subs' in active service. (*Mackenzie*: 1927, p. 236)

As proof of this prejudice one can cite the fact that when the Academy was reopened in March, 1867, after a few months' closure for reconstruction on the appointment of Sterndale Bennett as Principal, none of the women professors were reappointed. The matter was soon put right, but it is evidence of the unwarranted prejudice against women musicians. That stated, one must look to the other side and give credit to an institution which from the outset afforded a musical training for women, and it was very largely the work of this institution which accounts for the number of well-trained women composers and performers active in England in the middle and late nineteenth century. Of the many women composers to be discussed in the following pages, sixteen received their musical training at the Royal Academy of Music.

Opportunities for studying music were greatly enlarged in the last two decades of the century with the opening of the Trinity College of Music in 1872, the Guildhall School of Music in 1880, the Royal College of Music in 1883 and the Royal Manchester College of Music in 1893. The soprano, Jenny Lind, was one of the first professors at the Royal College of Music and Arabella Goddard one of the principal piano teachers. At the Royal Manchester College of Music women students and teachers were much in evidence: in 1897 there was a total of 151 students of whom 112 were women; the staff included several women teachers. Composition was also a very popular study for women at the Manchester College of Music: 'Curiously most of the student composers of those days (1910) from Dr. Carroll's class, seem to have been women.' (Kennedy: 1971, p. 51).

Something of the role that women played in the Royal Academy of Music can be deduced from the programme for the official opening of the new Academy of Music in 1912, when the final work was the performance of a fifty-part motet, *Sing unto God*, for ten five-part female choruses, specially composed for this hundred-strong choir by Frederick Corder. The orchestra of eighty-eight players contained forty-nine women in all departments except brass and percussion – the last stronghold of the male musician? Listed amongst its distinguished students are the names of Dora Bright (pianist and composer), Mary Davies (soprano), Kate Loder (composer and professor of harmony at the Royal Academy of Music), Clara Macirone (composer, pianist and professor of pianoforte at the Royal Academy of Music), Charlotte Sainton Dolby (singer, composer and teacher) and Maude Valérie White (composer).

In Frederick Corder's *A History of the Royal Academy of Music* some interesting and amusing sidelights are thrown upon the moral rectitude of our nineteenth-century ancestors. When the father of a student complained about his daughter taking a small part in an opera, Lord Burghersh, Chairman of the Committee of Governors wrote: 'Should there be any objection on the part of their Parents to their Children appearing on the stage they will be allowed to remain unseen, attended by their Governess at the Wings, but giving their assistance.' (Minutes of 30 July 1830). The stage and its associations were still regarded by respectable nineteenth-century Englishmen with great distaste, a place of loose moral standards. A minute of 1831 records that: 'The Committee having received a Report of the manner in which Harmony lessons in the Female Department were conducted by Dr. Crotch[2] which was extremely unsatisfactory, they resolved that his future attendance on the Female students should henceforth be dispensed with.' Poor Dr Crotch: one injudicious kiss led to his resignation. Not that all the female students themselves were models of propriety and industry, as these three minutes record:

> *21 February, 1833:* The Revd. Mr. Hamilton having directed Miss Wallace to attend the Committee this Day with her Mother, to explain to them the circumstances of her having written a very improper letter to Master Lavenu . . . Misses Wallace, Hopkins and Roberts were severely reprimanded for such improper conduct. (This concerned the passing of love-letters between students.)

> *Minute Book for 1828:* The Governess having reported that the young ladies are in the habit of looking out at the windows in their practice rooms: ordered – that those windows be painted.

> *Minute Book for 1843:* Six lady students ordered to be removed for lack of ability or industry.

As the average age of the students began to rise it became increasingly difficult to maintain order and in 1855 the boarding establishment was abolished.

Finally, as an example of the female students being put to good 'political' ends, this Address to Queen Victoria on the occasion of her wedding deserves to be recorded:

Feb. 6th, 1840.

TO HER MOST GRACIOUS MAJESTY QUEEN VICTORIA, QUEEN OF GREAT BRITAIN AND IRELAND.

MAY IT PLEASE YOUR MAJESTY,

We, the Female Resident Students of your Majesty's Royal Academy of Music, beg to offer our humble congratulations on your Majesty's approaching Nuptials, which event may God grant as conducive to your Majesty's happiness and welfare as it is hailed with delight by your Majesty's devoted subjects. We, the Members of an Institution existing by and under your Royal Favour . . . beg humbly to approach your Majesty with an earnest prayer, that your Majesty will be pleased to permit us to adopt a bridal favour, as an insignium of your Royal patronage, to be worn on that day when one universal Chorus of Joy will be reverberated throughout your Majesty's Dominions . . . (*Corder*: 1922, p. 56)

The desired 'political' result was achieved: the Prince Consort did become a subscriber to the Royal Academy of Music and did show an interest in it by attending many of its concerts.

It was from the 1840s onwards that some of the female students began to attract attention as composers: 'Miss Bendixon's Overture 'Undine' is an extraordinary production for a young lady: it abounds with passages which would not disgrace even Mendelssohn himself, who was present and applauded it very much.' (*The Illustrated London News*, 25 May, 1844, on a concert given by students of the Academy). One might argue, as Ethel Smyth did later, that such praise is belittling, the 'for a young lady' appendage suggesting condescension. Be that as it may, what is important is that women were able to write music for orchestras and choirs and had a fair chance of hearing what it sounded like. No progress can be made as a composer until one can hear performed what one has written. The imposing number of symphonies, concertos, overtures, operas, operettas, masses, oratorios, cantatas, anthems, part-songs, chamber music, piano and organ music composed by English women in the nineteenth century arose largely because for the first time ever, opportunities like those at the Royal Academy of Music existed which, through the experience gained from the involvement in music-making, encouraged and fed the creative urge. That the majority of these compositions never rose above the pedestrian is not surprising or even important: they were produced in an age when length and gravity of mood were artistic canons of taste and when the new and ever-growing public demand resulted in an impoverishment of quality. Compared with the music of many of their male counterparts in England, they are neither better nor worse, though often equally dull. The fact that many were published should not be regarded as any yardstick by which they should be judged except one: that technically, they 'worked'. The compositions are often a testament to the good tuition received, and homage to Handel, Beethoven and Mendelssohn. Commenting on the early compositions by students (both male and female) at the Academy, Frederick Corder says: 'The uncommon thing about them is that while their musical ideas are of the dullest, the technique of the writing is surprisingly good – in fact, irreproachable. In this they differ diametrically from amateur efforts in general.' (Corder: 1922, p. 42). Whilst it is true that the assimilation of models can swamp originality, thus often producing yet another teacher of harmony and composition, the truly original voice will nevertheless emerge. It was the later nineteenth century that produced Ethel Smyth, Liza Lehmann and Maude Valérie White in England, and Augusta Holmès[3] and Cécile Chaminade in France, where individual musical personalities are recognizable. Compared with today, when we are fed on a diet of the accumulated masterpieces of the past, and have therefore little patience for the 'prentice work as an artistic experience, the nineteenth century was apt to hail everything of serious intent as a masterpiece, so athirst was the age for the overwhelming experience. How it would have applauded the Imperial Choir at the 1924 British Empire Exhibition of 10,000 voices. The nineteenth century more than tolerated every musical novelty and encouraged the often uncritical production of new works.

Since personal experience and participation in music-making is essential if one is going to compose music, the invention of the upright piano and its wholesale introduction into middle class drawing rooms from about 1830 onwards must be seen as a very important factor in the high output of piano music and songs that were composed by women. The piano provided the musical liberation of countless women, particularly as the accomplishments of singing and playing were encouraged wholeheartedly by fathers, suitors and husbands. Whilst Haweis saw virtue in the piano in that ' . . . it makes a girl sit upright and pay attention to details' (Haweis: 1875, p. 506), he showed more insight when he spoke of its therapeutic value: ' . . . the piano . . . has probably done more to sweeten existence . . . to young women in particular, than all the homilies on the domestic virtues ever penned.' (Haweis: 1875, p. 112). The piano brought the musical experience, the creative input so to speak, into countless homes and it is for this reason that there was a much higher proportion of amateur women composers writing songs and piano music than in any other branch of composition. Such, however, was the demand for songs and reasonably simple piano music that all composers, whether trained or not, wrote them. Thus songs, pianoforte music and part-songs (a fairly close third), form the common base of the compositions in most of the female composers studied.[4]

It has been suggested that women composers preferred the smaller and more intimate musical forms than large-scale structures because this was their socially determined sphere of activity. Gender stereotyping through genre has its pitfalls and aptitude, opportunity for performance and promotion would seem to be as much determining factors of genre as ideologically-determined norms. Most of the women composers surveyed in this chapter wrote mainly songs and piano pieces because these encompassed very largely their active musical experiences. However, one can point also to composers such as Ethel Smyth, Augusta Holmès and Cécile Chaminade who, amongst others, successfully composed in the larger-scale structures of opera, symphony and concerto. In so doing they were certainly regarded as exceptional and thereby invited comparison with male composers who had until then been largely unchallenged in these areas of composition.

*   *   *

Of the extended orchestral music written by English women composers in the nineteenth century nothing remains in the repertoire today; indeed, very little of it was published. The three Overtures for full orchestra and one for military band, 'Themistokles', by Mary Moody,[5] published by Novello & Co. in the 1880s, reflect a composer who is able to sustain ideas on a large canvas and one who handles the full orchestra with some degree of assurance. Dora Estella Bright (1863–1951) first attracted public attention in the 1890s with her two piano concertos which she performed both in London and Cologne, and her *Fantasie* for piano and orchestra (1892) which was the first orchestral work by a woman to appear on the programme of the Philharmonic Society. The honour of being the first woman to conduct that august body of musicians fell to Ethel Smyth in the early years of the twentieth century. As a pupil of Ebenezer Prout at the Royal Academy of Music, Dora Bright had been outstanding at composition, being the first woman to win the Lucas medal for composition in 1888. Marie Wurm (1860–1938), studied at Stuttgart and later, after winning the Mendelssohn scholarship, in England under Sullivan, Stanford and Bridge. In 1887 she had an overture performed in Berlin and, as befitted a pianist and one that had studied under Clara Schumann, composed her own piano concerto. One of the earliest piano concertos in nineteenth-century England written by a woman was that of Caroline Orger (1818–1892), later known under her married name as Caroline Reinagle, which was performed in the Hanover Square Rooms in 1843. Alice Mary Smith (1839–1889), later known as Mrs Meadows White, wrote many large-scale works. She was a pupil of Sterndale Bennett and George Macfarren at the Academy and in recognition of her achievements was made an Associate of the Philharmonic Society. Among her orchestral works is a Symphony in C (1863), the Endymion Overture, performed at the Crystal Palace in 1871 and a Clarinet Concerto of 1872. Another pupil of George Macfarren, Oliveria Prescott (1842–1919) produced two symphonies, a piano concerto and an overture. She was for a time amanuensis for the blind Macfarren, from which activity she no doubt gained insights into the construction of large-scale works. Whatever else these women composers lacked they were not wanting in confidence and undertook the large-scale forms as a matter of course. George Macfarren, who taught several of these women composers, was obviously a man who could inspire confidence and who was able to bring students into contact with music as a living art-form, and not reduce composition to a pedagogical study of musty rules.

* * *

Most of the large-scale choral music produced by English women in the nineteenth century found publishers – it was, after all, the age of the oratorio, and the accessibility of the scores therefore allows for some assessment of its musical worth. It will be noted that many cantatas are for female voices reflecting, no doubt, the growing demands from women's and girls' choirs. The oratorio, *The Nativity*, by Ann Mounsey (1811–1891), later Ann Sheppard Bartholemew, was performed at the Hullah concerts in 1855. Duplication of text in several places with the two most potent influences in English choral music in the nineteenth century, namely Handel's *Messiah* and Mendelssohn's *Elijah*, is unfortunate since *The Nativity* contains some good moments and reveals a composer of considerable skill. It will be pertinent at this point to trace Ann Mounsey's career since it reflects another means, outside the

Academy, by which it was possible for women musicians to develop their abilities.

Both Ann, and her sister Elizabeth Mounsey (1819–1905) were organists to London churches, the former for nearly fifty years, and the latter at St Peter's, Cornhill from 1834 until 1882. Ann's teachers were Samuel Wesley, Thomas Attwood and Johann Logier, and she so impressed Spohr when he visited England and Logier's Academy in 1820 that he included one of her harmonization exercises as an example in his autobiography.[6] To her skills as talented organist and pianist were added those of composition and concert organization. During the years 1843–1848 she organized a series of sacred concerts at Crosby Hall and it was here on 8 January, 1845, that Mendelssohn's 'Hear my Prayer' was first performed, the piece having been commissioned for one of these concerts. It was her husband, William Bartholemew, whom she married in 1853, who translated the texts of Mendelssohn's oratorios and choral works into English and who became a close friend of Mendelssohn. Ann's high esteem in the professional world of London musicians can be gauged from her election as an Associate Member of the Royal Philharmonic Society in 1834 and as a Member of the Royal Society of Musicians in 1839; in 1845 she composed six songs for the Royal Society of Female Musicians, which had been founded in 1839. In 1855 she was commissioned to write a short *Choral Ode* to mark the occasion of the laying of the foundation stone of the Midland Institute by Prince Albert. Thus her compositions arose largely out of her active engagement in music, and these include music for the liturgy, a collection of hymn-tunes (jointly edited with her sister), piano music for her pupils and part-songs. It was as a result of being a professional musician that opportunities, and the stimulation to compose, originated: the practical involvement in music-making being the overriding necessity for all young composers. It was this involvement that few women were able to experience in the early nineteenth century.

As a result of her association with Mendelssohn she was able to contribute in a small way to Lady Wallace's translation of Elise Polko's *Reminiscences of Mendelssohn* by commenting on the correspondence between Mendelssohn and her husband. The letter quoted below is from Mendelssohn to Mr Bartholomew although this letter was occasioned by Ann Mounsey's request to the former for a work for her concerts at the Crosby Hall:

Berlin, January 31st, 1844

My dear Sir, – I send you the sacred solo (*Hear my Prayer!*) which you wanted me to write for your concerts at Crosby Hall, and beg you will keep the mss. as a token of my sincere gratitude and respect.

You have been so often kind to me, that I am almost ashamed of the trifle I offer in return, . . . (*Polko*: 1869, App. 1)

For Ann Mounsey, it was a very treasured manuscript which she later donated to the South Kensington Museum.

Three settings of the Mass by English women composers were published in the last decade of the century: the most celebrated, that by Ethel Smyth, is considered in a later chapter. Elizabeth Nunn (1861–1894) published her setting of the *Mass* for soloists, chorus and orchestra in 1893, the same year in which Ethel Smyth's *Mass* was performed, and the setting by Mary Grant Carmichael (1851–1935) was published in 1900. The latter can be dismissed immediately, being in hymn-tune style and of little musical worth. The *Mass in C* by Elizabeth Nunn is of a very different order and invokes comparison with that of Ethel Smyth's as an extended work in which the vocal and instrumental textures are well contrasted and one in which contrapuntal writing is to the fore. The fugue, *Et vitam*, is particularly impressive and the whole work is indicative of a composer who could write on a large scale. But for her premature death at the age of thirty-three, who knows what she might have achieved? One other setting, a student work by Maude Valérie White (1855–1937) was performed, though not published, at the Royal Academy of Music in 1881.

After studying at the Academy, Rosalind Frances Ellicott achieved considerable success as a composer. In addition to the performance of her orchestral works she had several works performed at the Three Choirs Festival, the cantata *Elysium* in 1889 and *The Birth of Song* in 1892. In the latter there is some accomplished sustained vocal writing with independent orchestral accompaniment: her father, the Bishop of Bristol and Gloucester Cathedrals, was no doubt helpful to her in getting a foothold at this oldest of English choral festivals, but certainly her cantatas are as worthy of performance as many others performed at festivals during these years. Of the several choral works by Alice Mary Smith the *Ode to the North-East Wind* is the most attractive. Written for chorus and orchestra, it is a modest work and refreshing because it is not striving after effect. It was popular with the new choral societies for whom it was well tailored. Her large-scale cantata, *The Passions*, was performed at the Three Choirs Festival in 1882, and though competently written, suffers from the inevitable inflation that plagues so many festival compositions.

In Clara Angela Macirone (1821–1914), a student and then professor of piano at the Academy, we encounter a musician of obvious talent and wide-ranging ability. She was the first woman composer to have an anthem sung in English Cathedrals. *By the Waters of Babylon* belongs very definitely to the verse-anthem tradition begun by Orlando Gibbons, and found favour in both Canterbury and Ely Cathedrals. Her *Te Deum and Jubilate* was performed in Hanover Chapel, London, and her *Benedictus*, a solo song with piano, was praised by Mendelssohn. It is well suited to the voice with some interesting key shifts. She became a Fellow of the Royal Academy of Music and an Associate of the Philharmonic Society. In later life she turned to the teaching of music in schools and also wrote articles for periodicals including *The Argosy* and the *Girl's Own Paper*. Oliveria Prescott also taught at a London Girls' High School and had the distinction of having her unaccompanied setting of Psalm 126 sung in St Paul's Cathedral. The anthem, *The Righteous live for evermore* (1876), for choir and organ is a fair example of her style, which is unpretentious and rather limited harmonically, though containing some imitative writing and use of contrasting textures. The choral works of Ethel Boyce are noteworthy for their craftsmanship and good choice of text. In *Young Lochinvar* (1891), a ballad for baritone soloist, chorus and orchestra, the words are taken from a poem by Sir Walter Scott and in the more extended and harmonically more adventurous *The Lady of the Brown Rosary* (1890), a cantata for soloist, chorus and orchestra, the words are taken from a poem by Elizabeth Barrett Browning.

Several women composers wrote extensive works for female voices and Charlotte Sainton Dolby's cantata *Florimel* (1885), though owing something to the arcadian world of Sullivan's *Iolanthe* (1882) and *Princess Ida* (1884) contains some sensitive writing for female voices. However, by far the most worthwhile of the many works for female voices is the short Intermezzo by Liza Lehmann (1862–1918), *In Sherwood Forest* (1910), which captures something of the magic of Oberon's court and the fairy world without the triteness so often encountered in music for female voices when setting such subjects. In a similar way, Vaughan Williams's *In Windsor Forest* avoids such pitfalls; indeed, Liza Lehmann's setting has much in common with Vaughan Williams's later work, in her use of flattened sevenths and arresting minor key harmonies (Example. 1).

It is when one comes across cantatas for female voices such as *The Ten Virgins* (1893) by Emily Lawrence (1854–), an ex-Academy student, that one can understand how music of this kind, though not specifically this piece, prompted Gustav Holst[7] to state: 'I find the question of getting music for girls' schools perfectly hopeless. I get reams of twaddle sent me periodically, and that is all the publishers seem to think is suitable for girls.' (Holst, I: 1938 p. 27).

* * *

It is not in the oratorios and cantatas of nineteenth-century England that the most interesting choral music is to be found, for they show a too-ready acceptance of past conventions for them to be anything more than empty façades, a testament to an age of high aspirations but cheap means of production. It is in the part-songs that more often a musical personality emerges, freed from striving after greatness and content to stand on their own merits. The nineteenth-century part-song, the poor relation of the Elizabethan madrigal, served the same purpose in providing the means for concerted domestic music, and often brings us close to the hearts of the Victorians. In its homophonic style it bears a close relationship to the hymn tune: 'O who will o'er the downs so free?' by R.L. de Pearsall, perhaps the most characteristic of Victorian part-songs, comes from the same stable, metaphorically speaking, as the hymn tunes of Stainer, Elvey, Barnby and Dykes.

That the madrigal wasn't quite forgotten we owe to minor composers such as Pearsall and the efforts of the Madrigal Society. Indeed we find that in 1882 Helen Heale (1855–) won the Madrigal Society Prize with her 'Mourn, oh rejoicing heart', which begins well with effective use of discord. She had been taught by Hullah and later turned her energies to arranging music for female voices, including oratorios. Three excellent part-songs by women composers that deserve to be remembered today are 'Blow, blow thou winter wind' by Ann Mounsey (Example. 2), the haunting ballad-style 'The Sun shines fair on Carlisle Wall' and the lightly flowing, ballet-style 'Autolycus' Song', both by Angela Macirone. Equally well-written, though suffering from a ridiculous text, is 'The Bee' by Ann Mounsey.

* * *

Example 1 *In Sherwood Forest (Liza Lehmann)*

Example 2   *Blow, Blow Thou Winter Wind (Ann Mounsey)*

It is to Thomas Reed (1817–1888) that the establishment of operetta in England owes its inception. Together with his wife, he set out to provide theatrical entertainment untainted with the bad reputation that such entertainment had to the Victorian mind. In 1855 he rented St Martin's Hall in Long Acre, London, and provided entertainment of high artistic and moral standards. Included in his performers were Charles Dickens (readings), Mrs German Reed (impersonations) and the ballad singer, Charles Santley. In 1858 he rented larger premises enabling him to enlarge his company and perform short musical plays: it was out of these that English operetta was born and his 'Gallery of Illustrations', as it was called to avoid theatrical associations, was continued after his death, by his son until 1895. Both Gilbert and Sullivan contributed, separately, to these entertainments, though the two most successful names associated with them were Frederic Clay and Alfred Cellier. It was in the 1880s that Gilbert and Sullivan established their reputation; *H.M.S. Pinafore* (1878) was the first really successful work which was followed by *The Pirates of Penzance* (1879), *Patience* (1881), *Iolanthe* (1882), *Princess Ida* (1884), *The Mikado* (1885), *Ruddigore* (1887), *The Yeoman of the Guard* (1888) and *The Gondoliers* (1889) – the last of the operettas to meet with public acclaim. From the 1880s Sullivan's influence was all pervasive: prior to this, operetta had been very much a French preserve, begun in the works of Adam (1830–1850) and brought to fruition in Offenbach (1855–1880s), Lecocq (1870–1880s) and Messager (1890 onwards). In Offenbach's *La belle Hélène* (1864) the definitive work was written, and it became the model for both him and subsequent composers. Operetta was very much a nineteenth-century product and several women composers in England tried their hands at it with varying degrees of success.

The slight, yet effective *Grass Widows* (1875) by Virginia Gabriel, described as a 'Musical Comedietta in one act' has a witty libretto by George March and is written for three characters, two women and one man. The influence of Offenbach is much to the fore: the overture is lively and the various solos and duets are tuneful and unpretentious: it could well make a good companion piece to *Cox and Box*.[8] In *The Follies of a Night*, an operetta in two acts with libretto by J.R. Planché, Virginia Gabriel is less well served with a silly and over-contrived plot. However, she does again capture the style very well, though the ensemble writing is not of a high order.

In the operettas of Annie Fortescue Harrison (1851–1944), later known as Lady Arthur Hill, the influence of Sullivan is discernible. *The Ferry Girl* (1883) was performed at German Reed's 'Gallery of Illustration' and *The Lost Husband* (1884) at the Opera Comique Theatre. The latter requires three characters, two men and a woman, and is quite a lively and effective piece. The plot is a light-hearted attack on marital domination, beginning with the wife bullying the husband, but the roles change after Gasparino's advice: 'What! a woman beat her husband? ... In every well-regulated household, where the husband and wife are really fond of each other, it is just the other way; the husband beats the wife. Take my advice, try it.' Though light-hearted, it is an example of comedy pinpointing a social problem that was fairly common.[9] The libretti for both operettas were written by Lady Arthur Hill.

Another successful operetta, *His Last Chance* (1891) by Ethel Harraden was performed at the Gaiety Theatre, London: it contains some tuneful music but is flawed by a weak libretto, written by her husband. A similar weakness spoils *The Wooden Spoon* (1892) an operetta by Hope Temple (1859–1938), who had studied under Messager in Paris and later became his wife. The work is scored for a quartet of voices which combine in a madrigal for the finale; harmonically, as in her songs, she writes with an engaging freedom. She certainly helped in the writing of Messager's *Mirette*: it was perhaps ungallant of Messager to let this information slip out after the work had proved unsuccessful!

By far the most successful of these operettas[10] was *Sergeant Brue* (1904), composed by Liza Lehmann, which had a successful run at the Strand Theatre. The patter songs are modelled on Sullivan (Examples 3 and 4) and the choruses are straightforward and tuneful. It has the light touch, though lacks his variety of rhythms. Sullivan's influence is obvious in the chorus, 'Hail! the Solon of the Court' reminding one of 'All hail, great judge' from Sullivan's *Trial by Jury*.

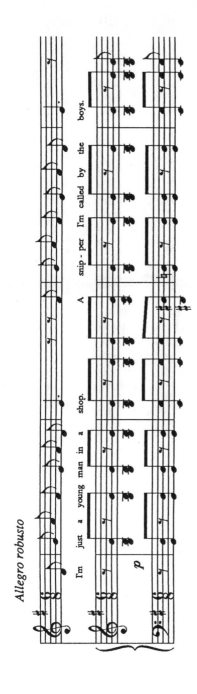

Example 3 *I'm Just a Young Man in a Shop (Liza Lehmann)*

Example 4 *The Bobbies Beano (Liza Lehmann)*

62

The composition of operas was not neglected either by women composers: the most substantial of these, apart from Ethel Smyth's *The Wreckers* which is discussed in a later chapter, were the two operas composed by Florence Skinner (Mrs Stresa) whose *Suocera* was performed in Naples in 1877 and *Maria Regina di Scozia* (1883) in Turin, San Remo and London. In the latter Rossini's influence is very much in evidence in the florid vocal lines which abound in lively rhythms and short catchy tunes; however, the work as a whole is not without merit. The composer, though English by birth, was resident in Italy.

A much more earnest affair is France Allitsen's *Bindra, the Minstrel*, a rescue opera of the *Fidelio* type. Musically, it resembles an oratorio with its solemn chorus writing, rather than an opera. A light romantic opera in three acts founded on Goldsmith's novel, *The Vicar of Wakefield* (1907) by Liza Lehmann uses some traditional tunes but has relatively little ensemble. Lyrical qualities rather than dramatic ones tend to predominate; even so, its success so impressed W.S. Gilbert that he offered Liza Lehmann one of his libretti. The offer was declined.

* * *

The most popular form of composition undertaken by women, apart from song writing, was pianoforte music. The nineteenth century saw the piano elevated into the most popular of all instruments and Mendelssohn's *Songs without Words* provided the model for the short lyrical piece of limited, but effective pianism. It was also the heyday of the virtuoso, of Liszt, Pachmann and Rubenstein, and a whole host of lesser lights, both male and female, and for these there was no dearth of showy but musically empty pieces. They were usually variations, or decorations of well-known tunes: the pattern for these having more recently been set by Mendelssohn with his *Fantasia on the Last Rose of Summer*, but the tradition dates back to the virginalists. There was great public demand for this empty display music and this appetite was fully catered for.

Jules de Sivrai (1834–1907), a pseudonym for Jane Jackson, afterwards Roeckel, wrote some very popular piano pieces of this ilk as well as many transcriptions, which include Beethoven and Mendelssohn symphonies. She had studied under Clara Schumann and was capable of writing well for the piano as her Nocturne, dedicated to 'Miss Smythe', suggests. She also wrote pieces like the *Balkans*, a sort of soundtrack (without the film) of a battle scene, complete with shouts of 'Allah' amidst the 'heavy cannonade'. The bulk of her output was showy variations on operatic arias or tunes, like 'Robin Adair' – facile though pianistic. Another woman composer who wrote in a similar vein was Mrs John Macfarren (1824–1895), whose pieces appeared under the pseudonym of Jules Brissac. She was the wife of Sir George Macfarren's brother, having studied under her future brother-in-law at the Academy. The 'Pearl of Erin' and 'Polka Glissante' give a fair indication of the style by the titles alone.

Middle-period Beethoven and Schubert are the models for the several sonatas written by women composers and most do not achieve any degree of personal conviction: the rather earnest, self-consciously academic first movements tend to discourage the listener, though occasional later movements can be rewarding. The Scherzo of Elizabeth Chamberlayne's first sonata is a case in point, which is an attractive movement, and the final movement of Caroline Orger's Sonata in A has a Mendelssohn-like brilliance.

It is, however, when we turn to the smaller piano pieces that a much more personal note is struck, and amongst this vast literature can be found some attractive and worthwhile piano pieces by women composers. In Maude Valérie White's *Pictures from Abroad* (1892) are several pieces of character, for example, No. 2 (of 14) *In the Carpathians* with its overlapping phrases. Equally attractive is her *Barcarolle* of 1883. Similarly well-varied and interesting are the *Ten Piano Pieces* (1892) by Liza Lehmann which have a refreshing clarity and economy. The first of *Three Valses de Sentiment* from this collection is a good example of her style (Example 5). A real feeling for keyboard style is also apparent in the piano music of Dora Bright: *Liebeslied*, no. 2 of *Three Pieces for Piano* (Example 6) shows that Elgar was not alone in his ability to write the sentimental, yet memorable drawing-room piece. This vein was exploited to the full in the very popular piano music of Cécile Chaminade (1857–1944), the French pianist and composer who, after her first appearance in England in 1892, became a frequent visitor. Her music is, however, outside the scope of this study.

The *Six Pedal Fugues and Eight Other Movements for Organ* (1857) by Elizabeth Stirling contains an impressive fugue on the hymn tune *O Worship the King* with the melody elongated in the pedal part against the fugue proper on the manuals. It builds to a forceful climax and is worth playing today. Elizabeth Stirling was the first woman to pass the B. Mus. degree at Oxford and though her Exercise was accepted in 1856, the degree was withheld

Example 5 *Valse Sentiment No. 1 (Liza Lehmann, Ten Piano Pieces)*

Example 6 *Liebeslied (Dora Bright, Three Pieces for Piano)*

since women were unable to graduate. Another piece for organ, the *Andante in F* by Elizabeth Chamberlayne makes good use of the instrument's possibilities but is musically less interesting. Other works for solo instruments include various fantasias for harp by Elizabeth Anne Bisset (1800–), and guitar solos by Elizabeth Mounsey, who had given guitar recitals in the 1830s.

Several string quartets and many piano trios, quartets and quintets were written by women, but fewer published. Mostly undertaken as composition exercises, they no doubt achieved a performance or two but they need not, however, detain us here.

*   *   *

If there was one sphere of musical activity in which nineteenth-century women in England achieved a degree of equality with men it was most certainly in the writing and composing of the lyrics and music of the drawing room ballad, the popularity of which invites comparison with that of today's more evanescent 'Pop-Song'. Indeed, a magazine of the 1870s, *Musical Jottings*, devoted much of its space to the discussion of the currently popular ballads and served very much in the same way as 'Pop Charts' do today. Whilst Sullivan's *The Lost Chord* (1877) topped the popularity charts, selling over half a million copies by the end of the century, many women composers enjoyed great fame through the performances and sales of their songs. Several of their songs are still known and sung today, for example, Lady Arthur Hill's 'In the Gloaming' (1877), which sold 140,000 copies in its first twenty years of existence. Others include 'Because', by Guy d'Hardelot (1858–1936), a French-born composer whose married name was Mrs Rhodes, 'Come back to Erin' by Mrs Charlotte Alington Barnard, better known as Claribel (1830–1869), Amy Woodforde-Finden's 'Pale Hands I loved' from *Four Indian Love Lyrics* and 'Anne Laurie' by Alicia Ann Spottiswoode (Lady John Douglas Scott, 1810–1900). Many other songs by women enjoyed widespread popularity in their day, such as 'Juanita' by the Hon. Mrs Caroline Norton (1808–1877) but have since been neglected. Not only were women responsible for the music, often under the cloak of male pseudonyms or *noms de plume*, but also for many of the lyrics, such as those by Eliza Cook and Adelaide Proctor, the latter being responsible for the lyrics of Sullivan's *The Lost Chord*. Occasionally the lyrics strike a pertinent note, revealing something of the discontent felt by some women beneath the respectable Victorian veneer, as do these lines by Harriet Grote[11]:

> Full many a sorrowful and tragic tale
> Enfolded lies beneath the semblance frail
> Of wedded harmony and calm content.
> How oft the heart in aching bosom pent,
> And careworn thoughts are borne abroad unseen,
> Veiled in the aspect of a cheerful mien.
> By the sad mourner of a home unblest,
> A faith dishonoured, and a life opprest.

Sentiments such as these were not usually expressed in public and it would be wrong to suggest that the lyrics, both by men and women, rose much above the level of doggerel. However, to survey the vast output of published ballads by English women in the nineteenth century is to realize something of the tremendous creative release that this activity afforded.

The drawing-room ballad was composed for both public and domestic consumption and here was a form of music-making that women could experience at first hand in their homes, unlike the performance of most other forms of music which was largely male-dominated and not of easy access to women. For the first time ever, a large number of English women were involved in the performance of music without any social restrictions: indeed, women were as much the performers as men. Like Victorian women novelists who made a strength out of their restricted domesticated existences, using their detailed observations of the domestic scene as a basis for much of their writings, so the drawing room ballad allowed women full participation in their own homes both as performers and as creators. These circumstances go a long way to account for the large number of women ballad writers that we find in the middle and late nineteenth century.

Another factor was the close relationship that existed between composer and performer. Several of the women composers were, or had been, singers of high repute and both Liza Lehmann and Charlotte Sainton Dolby, two popular song-writers of the second half of the nineteenth century, had made their names on the Continent and in England as singers. Liza Lehmann retired from singing to compose and later, teach, and Charlotte Sainton Dolby retired to set up a Vocal Academy in London in 1872 which was soon much acclaimed. Even if women only sang the ballads in the privacy of their homes as a recognized feminine 'accomplishment', the drawing room ballad encouraged middle-class women to be fully identified with music-making and this was a new development. As a social activity and as an integrating factor this music-making in the home was of great importance, its value probably far outstripping the intrinsic value of the music itself. Undoubtedly the songs reflect the mores of middle class society, its preciosity, sentimentality, conventionality and hypocrisy, but the limitations of the culture which produced these songs should not entirely prejudice one's appreciation of the songs' musical charms. The ballads are melodious, and like some of the 'Pop Music' of today are expressive within their narrow limits.

The financial rewards for composers of ballads were often great since there was an avid public in Great Britain as well as in America, indeed, wherever English was the spoken language. True, it was usually the publisher who made the large fortune since it was the usual practice for the publisher to buy the song outright for a nominal fee. The song, 'Kathleen Mavourneen', was reputedly bought by the publisher D'Almaine for ten pounds and realized from its sales over fifteen thousand pounds. Singers identified themselves with certain songs and made them famous. It was the celebrated soprano Antoinette Stirling who made Sullivan's *The Chorister* popular: similarly, Clara Butt's rendering of Frances Allitsen's 'There's a Land', in the year of the Queen's Jubilee (1897) with topical verse added by Miss Agnes Sibley (a girls' school Headmistress), brought to the public a song which hitherto had not achieved much success. It was Madame Vestris, who as a singer brought 'Cherry Ripe' before the public, who began the practice of demanding a royalty from the composer for including particular songs in her repertoire. The 'Royalty Ballad' with publishers paying singers to promote songs led, of course, to the debasement of many singers' musical discernment and eventually to that of the general public. Today's commercial 'plugging' of songs is not dissimilar.

The traditional ballad, belonging to the folk tradition and of considerable antiquity, shares few characteristics with the nineteenth-century drawing room ballad. The former relied on an oral tradition for its dissemination and dealt with romantic, tragic and historical subjects in a detached way, the main point of the ballad being to tell a story dramatically. As such the ballads represented the truly popular songs of the people. The ballad as literature inspired not only Burns and Scott, but also Wordsworth and Coleridge, whose *Lyrical Ballads* were influenced by the broadside ballads and the German romantic poets. In nineteenth-century England it was Keats, Matthew Arnold and the pre-Raphaelites, particularly Swinburne, who wrote poetry in the style of ballads. Musically, a similar move away from the folk tradition is to be found in the ballad operas of Arne, Dibdin, Shield and Hook during the eighteenth century, where theatricality, prettiness and artificiality came to the fore. By the beginning of the nineteenth century the native ballad, though still popular, particularly the journalistic broadside ballad, was beginning to be swamped and merged with the semi-operatic composed ballad of the theatre. It is largely from the theatrical ballads of the eighteenth and early nineteenth centuries that the drawing room ballad of Victorian England took its origins.

Thus the spontaneity of the original folk tradition, with its fusion of poetry and music expressed in unaccompanied modal melody, was lost: in its place was substituted art-song which owed much to the ballad opera tradition. The piano did duty for the theatre orchestra, providing a rich chordal accompaniment to the exaggerated emotional stance of the singer. The main topics of the drawing room ballad writers were love unrequited, often viewed from the female point of view, ballads of a descriptive nature and ballads with a moral purpose, exposing evils such as gambling or the horrors of the lunatic asylum, or providing a moral uplift through conventional religion to a brave new world.[12] Above all they were topics from which a certain morbid sentimentality could be extracted, for example 'The Old Armchair' or 'Woodman, Spare That Tree'. In most of the songs the virtues of domesticity were extolled, and none so popular or successful in this respect as Henry Bishop's (later knighted for his efforts) 'Home, Sweet Home',[13] which sold over 300,000 copies in its first year of publication, and was sung, particularly by Madame Albani, throughout the world. It is recorded that she sang the song in South Africa, Australia, India, Canada and Europe. Aware that the songs would be sung in the presence of, or by, ladies in middle-class homes, the authors of the lyrics were at pains to avoid anything that might offend nineteenth-century 'good-taste'. Often the songs engender an emotion quite out of keeping with the rather innocuous nature of the text: convention, unlike that of eighteenth- or twentieth-century England, preferred the dichotomy of outward respectability and inward turmoil. Thus, the nineteenth-century drawing room ballad had nothing of the earthy, direct nature of the genuine ballad: it had been rescued from the street and brought into the cosy warmth of the drawing room.

There is no doubt that the use of the word 'ballad' to describe these nineteenth-century songs is a very loose one, based largely on the fact that they were popular songs of a narrative or descriptive nature. A very large number of these drawing room ballads do fall into the category defined by W.H. Colles, of a ' ... composition of the slightest possible degree of musical value nearly always set to three verses (neither more nor less) of conventional doggerel.' (Grove: 1954, 5th edn). It was the unworthy importance attached to these songs in the Victorian age which was the most reprehensible feature, thereby equating songs of such transience and little worth with the art-songs of major nineteenth-century composers. Sydney Northcote, in his book *The Ballad in Music*, reminds us of the fact that Sullivan was appointed Professor of Pianoforte and Ballad Singing at the Crystal Palace School of Art, and this underlines the importance attached to these ballads in their day. Undoubtedly, the reputation of English singers of this period rested upon their singing of the drawing-room ballads rather than any other type of song. The art-songs of Sullivan such as 'Orpheus with his lute' and those of Stanford and Parry do represent a more exalted form of English song, but in no way did they compare in popularity with the drawing room ballads.

It was as a result of a suggestion made by Charlotte Sainton Dolby to the publisher, John Boosey, that ballad concerts sponsored by music publishers began. The first one of this nature was in 1867 at St James's Hall and this venture was soon followed by other publishers. In consequence a veritable flood of ballads swept, like a tidal wave, outwards from the metropolis into nearly every middle-class drawing room in the country: commercialism and popular music joined hands and strode optimistically towards the golden lining of the twentieth century.

Women played a large part in this movement; for example, Brown and Stratton's *British Musical Biography* in 1897 lists approximately sixty nineteenth-century women composers whose work had met with some degree of recognition and success. Whilst these represent but a small proportion of the total number of women composers, it is certainly indicative of the growing respect for women in this sphere of activity. Obviously there were hundreds of women composers active in nineteenth-century England: in the *Musical Times*, February 1900, there is a report of a paper read by Dr A.A. Harding at the annual conference of the Incorporated Society of Musicians on *Woman as a Musician*. He is reported to have stated that there were in existence four hundred and eighty-nine women composers. Whatever his source of information (and none is given), it is evident that in composition of one kind or another middle- and upper-class women in England had found a willing audience for their innate talents.

In an article in *The Illustrated London News* (10 September 1892), Mrs Renwick Miller, writing in 'The Ladies Column' cited the case of Fanny Mendelssohn who was regarded, when a young girl, as having more musical talent than her younger brother, Felix. She states that Felix, in later life, was not averse to passing off some of Fanny's compositions as his own; one of them, a song, became in fact a favourite of Queen Victoria. Whilst Felix was encouraged to regard music as his career, Fanny was told that for her it could be nothing more than an ornament and that her real calling was that of housewife. The writer concludes that until Germany gives more encouragement to women there will be no great women composers, the assumption being the common one that only Germany was capable of producing great composers.

In another article in the *Musical Times*, February 1887, entitled *Women as Composers*, the anonymous writer argued that women were not capable of abstract thought and that, as composers, they were more likely to succeed in song-writing and opera,[14] where words provided the prop. It is possible that the success women achieved as ballad writers might have contributed to this view, but later events make such statements untenable, particularly as a result of the wider musical experience enjoyed by women since that time. However, there is no doubt that women as writers of lyrics and musicians produced a large share of the voluminous number of songs printed in England in the latter half of the nineteenth century.

Although the Victorian ballad belongs to the latter half of the century, in particular the last three decades, its roots can be found much earlier – indeed, its prototype is generally held to be the song 'The Death of Nelson' from the opera *The Americans* (1811). The dramatic rendering of it by the celebrated tenor, Brahams, led to many imitations. The publishing of Moore's *Irish Melodies* between 1807 and 1834 no doubt prompted the *Scottish Minstrels* by Carolina Baroness Nairne in the 1820s. This collection contained eighty songs of her own, the most famous being 'Caller Herrin' and 'Wi a' hundred Pipers an' a'. This remarkable collection of songs became very popular in Scotland: it is unfortunately outside the scope of this present study. In the same spirit of nationalistic antiquarianism Lady John Douglas Scott wrote 'Annie Laurie' and noted down the song 'Loch Lomond' from the singing of a young lad. Lady Dufferin (1807–1867), wrote 'The Irish emigrant' as well as providing verses to Irish folk melodies such as *Oh, Bay of Dublin*. Songs extolling Ireland's beauty and the colleens left behind became legion, the most famous being 'Kathleen Mavourneen', and thus the influence of Moore's *Irish Melodies* can be traced throughout the century.

Perhaps the most popular of all early ballads was 'Alice Grey' (1835) composed by Mrs Philip Millard. It is a simple strophic song with fine melodic shape and was one of several composed by her that caught the public's fancy. Its popularity lingered for many years. There was, however, one song that all singers sang in the middle years of the nineteenth century, both the words and the music being written by Caroline Norton. This song was 'Juanita' with its simple, yet attractive refrain (Example 7) which captured the public's imagination.

Example 7   *Juanita (Caroline Norton)*

The songs of Eliza Flower (1803–1846), were well known in her day, the most ambitious set being *Musical Illustrations to the Waverley Novels* which she published in 1831. Her nationalistic, 'Now pray we for our country' was arranged for many different groups as it was so popular. In the writing of political or protest songs she certainly antedates both Alicia Needham and Ethel Smyth, her first group being concerned with the 1832 Reform Bill. These were 'The Gallant Grey', 'The Gathering of the Unions' and 'The Barons bold on Runnymede'. The next group was associated with the agitation that led to the repeal of the Corn Laws in 1846 and for this she wrote 'Four Free Trade Songs'. All are singable, though not subtle, as for example 'The Gathering of the Unions' (Example 8). Her ballad writing is best seen in 'When thou were here' and something of the extent of her output can be gauged from the fact that a whole concert devoted to her sacred music was given at the Crosby Hall, London, in November 1845. Her sister, Sara Flower, later Mrs S.F. Adams, was a contralto and wrote the words of the hymn 'Nearer my god to thee': she also wrote the words to the 'Four Free Trade Songs'.

Whilst women's influence can be seen in the early Victorian ballads, it was not until after 1850 that their presence was really felt. It was from this time onwards that women composers began to produce an enormous number of songs that, in some cases, rivalled the most prodigious output of men. Their songs were

Example 8   *Gathering of the Unions (Eliza Flower)*

Example 9 *Nightfall at Sea (Virginia Gabriel)*

popular until Edwardian times, particularly those of Virginia Gabriel, Charlotte Sainton Dolby, Claribel, Dolores (Ellen Dickson), Miss M. Lindsay (Mrs J. Worthington Bliss), Lady Arthur Hill, Cristabel, Frances Allitsen, Maude Valérie White and Liza Lehmann. Gradually we see the dedicated amateur composer being replaced by the professionally trained musician.

Of Virginia Gabriel it was said:

> ... Her songs were always melodious, several became great favourites; she was a pupil of Molique[15] and would have achieved some solid, enduring work had she not allowed enthusiasm to override discretion; she possessed the 'fatal facility' which has militated against the lasting success of many composers of higher rank. (*Santley*: 1909, p. 50).

She was a talented composer and of her large output of songs, 'Nightfall at Sea' was one of her most popular. It has a characteristic flowing vocal line which has shape though cliché-ridden (Example 9). Harmonically, there are some effective chromatic touches and in the freely varied strophic form there is evidence of careful construction. Perhaps 'Resignation, Heaven-Born' sums up her strengths and weaknesses for it has real passion when identifying with Lady John Manners' poem:

> How hard to sit with placid brow
> And smile at simple jest
> When raging in the bosom throne;
> The Demon of unrest.

where the richly chromatic music mirrors the unrest of the words. Yet when duty calls for 'resignation' the music capitulates to the soft option of facile sequences and easy flowing lines. Another example of this 'fatal facility' can be seen in 'A Life Scroll' (Example 10).

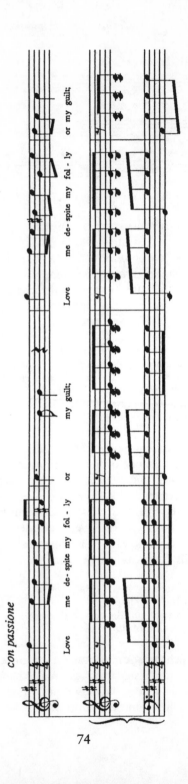

Example 10 A Life Scroll (Virginia Gabriel)

There is no doubt that her fluency accounted for much of her immediate success, but it also led to a lack of self-criticism and the consequent writing of songs of very inferior quality such as her insensitive 'Out in the Streets' where suicide is contemplated to a lilting triple rhythm. The songs, as a whole, inhabit a restricted and fairly predictable area.

Charlotte Sainton Dolby was the most celebrated all-round female musician of the age, achieving fame both on the Continent and in England as a contralto, and great success as a song-writer and teacher. Messrs Moutrie and Son, musical publishers, offered a series of photos of 'Musical Celebrities' and it is interesting to note that Charlotte Sainton Dolby was the only female thus honoured. Her songs, particularly 'The White Cockade', 'My Love stands upon the Quay' and 'When one is old and grey' became very popular. In its telling of a story in music, with a battle scene depicted in the middle section, 'The White Cockade' comes close to the genre of the true ballad and it may well have been this element which captured the public's attention.

Claribel wrote about sixty songs, mostly for Charlotte Sainton Dolby and all have a rather restricted emotional range and sameness. Her most successful song, 'Come back to Erin', is well-constructed and tuneful building to an effective climax. Another amateur composer who indulged in a whimsical pseudonym[16] was Ellen Dickson (1819–1878): her many songs were published under the name of Dolores and several enjoyed popular esteem. Miss M. Lindsay (Mrs J. Worthington Bliss) produced more varied works which included duets, school songs and sacred songs. Much of what Tennyson[17] wrote she rendered into song and her many settings were often favourably commented upon in *Musical Jottings*.

The year 1877 produced two of the most popular of all Victorian ballads, both tinged with a sanctimonious air and which, in their twilight nostalgia, epitomise so much of that which was dear to the Victorian heart. Sullivan's 'The Lost Chord' and Lady Arthur Hill's 'In the Gloaming' (later to become a hymn and a regimental march for the 2nd Middlesex Artillery) eclipsed all other songs in popularity.

In the ballads of Hope Temple, such as 'In Sweet September', 'A Word of Love' and 'Love's Temple' one is closer to the theatre than the drawing room and in this respect they have much in common with the songs of Guy d'Hardelot. Her songs usually begin with an extended piano introduction, the voice beginning in a fairly low register which gradually rises through a variety of keys to a fine vocal climax. Cristabel, a pseudonym for Florence Attenborough, was as much an arranger as a composer, and published her songs in the 1890s and early 1900s. Under the title of 'Sabbath Bells' she included Mendelssohn's 'Oh, for the wings of a dove', preceding it with a verse of her own words and music. It does actually make quite a good introduction to the song. She arranged many songs including 'Darking through the snow' which enjoys popularity today under the better known title of 'Jingle Bells'.

It was, however, in this last decade of the century that the three most outstanding women song-writers came to the fore. Frances Allisten, Maude Valérie White and Liza Lehmann were professionally trained musicians who brought greater harmonic richness and variety to their compositions than had been previously evident. Frances Allitsen, the most productive of the female composers of ballads, made her debut as a singer in 1882, but it was her patriotic song, *There's a Land* by which she really became known. It is powerfully written with forward momentum which, in a jingoistic age, was such that it could be sung wholeheartedly. There is nothing particularly feminine in its full-blooded directness (Example 11) and it calls to mind the early works of Elgar in its nationalistic fervour. Her other patriotic songs, 'England, my England' and 'When the Boys Come Marching Home' are in a similar vein. Some of her songs were republished in 1953 and 1954, namely 'There's a Land' and the sacred cantata for S.A.T.B. 'The Lord is my Light'. Her songs have an emotional intensity often achieved by rich harmonies and full chords and usually have an impressive opening. In 'The Lute Player' the piano has a few bars bravura before the final verse in a song where the colours of both voice and piano are effectively exploited.

Maude Valérie White came to the fore in 1879 with her song 'Absent, yet Present' which was first performed at a 'Monday Pop' by the singer Charles Santley. He identified himself with this and several other of her songs including 'To Althea from Prison' and 'The Devout Lover', both of which also became very popular. It was in the very same year, 1879, when she captured the public's attention, that she won the Mendelssohn Scholarship at the Royal Academy of Music where she was studying under George Macfarren. In doing so she was the first woman to achieve this distinction: and although ill health interfered with her studies she did later take up the scholarship to study orchestration in Vienna. In an article in the *Musical Times* dated 1 February, 1887, an

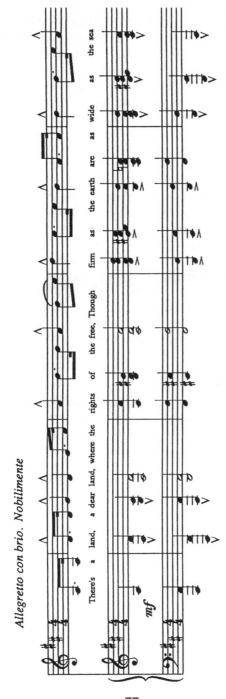

Example 11 *There's a Land (Frances Allitsen)*

anonymous writer held up Maude Valérie White as the best example of a woman song-writer, and there is no doubt that her musical talent coupled with her wide knowledge of languages and appreciation of literature were largely directed towards song-writing. Her attempts at extended orchestral works, which she undertook in Vienna, were not successful whereas the best of her two hundred or more songs can be considered, perhaps not favourably, but nevertheless in the same context as those by Schumann and Fauré. In her two settings of poems by Sully-Prudhomme, 'Ici bas' and 'Au bord de l'eau', a comparison with the settings of these poems by Fauré reveals a composer with a sensitivity to poetry, yet one lacking in the harmonic subtlety of the French master. On the other hand the lightness and melodic freshness of 'Un Facheaux' rivals Offenbach. A comparison with Schumann is also possible in that Maude Valérie White set, to her own translations, a group of poems of Heinrich Heine, several of which Schumann had previously set in his masterpiece, 'Dichterliebe'. These settings by Maude Valérie White were student works and Schumann was the model: as such one can but admire several good imitations. The final song of the set is redolent of Schumann in its broken chord accompaniment, overlapping phrases and extensive piano postlude (Example 12): even so, it does contain elements all of its own. The first of her four settings from Tennyson's 'In Memoriam', 'I Sometimes Hold it half a Sin' is notable for the independence of its accompaniment with a fine 'cello-like melody set against the vocal line, and for its use of dissonance. One is generally aware of the traditions of the art-song in her settings and even her most popular ballad, 'Absent, yet Present', has an attractive flowing arpeggio accompaniment which gives the piece momentum. One of Queen Victoria's favourite songs was Maude Valérie White's 'To Mary' which has a simple, yet direct lyricism. The singer Ben Davies always included it in his repertoire when called to sing before the Queen. The 'Trois Chansons Tziganes' are stylistically and harmonically adventurous. A free-flowing recitative-like statement builds to colourful refrains in these settings where tonal shifts, such as the abrupt change from D major to F major in No. 3, *Come to the Dancing*, add to the excitement. Refreshing also is her avoidance of trite cadences and this is particularly so in her fine setting of Byron's 'So We'll go no more a-roving.'

Whilst her songs are tinged with a Victorian sentimentality at times, many do reflect her fastidious taste in literature, being equally at home in settings of French, German and English poets.

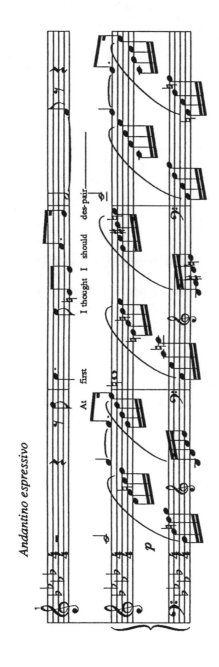

Example 12   Extract from a setting of a group of poems of Henrich Heine (Maude Valérie White)

Like her contemporary, Ethel Smyth, Maude Valérie White travelled extensively and several of her songs are based on folk tunes
heard in Finland, Sweden, Italy and Germany. Like Ethel Smyth
also, she had considerable literary gifts and produced two
interesting volumes of autobiography as well as several book translations. She was a lively, vivacious person capable of producing
craftsmanlike songs of merit, without pandering to the more
debased tastes of Victorian England.

This is even more true of her close friend Liza Lehmann who
disliked intensely the commercial ballads of her age and who pioneered the song-cycle made up of solos and ensembles. In the script
of a broadcast on *Liza Lehmann* by Perceval Graves (No. 1 of
three scripts) it is claimed that 'In a Persian Garden' was ' . . . the
first British song-cycle of any consequence, predating Elgar's 'Sea
Pictures' which were anyway modelled on German lines, being for
solo voice.' (Graves: undated). It was in 1896 that her first cycle
'In a Persian Garden' was published. It met with acclaim both in
England and in America. Writing in the *Sunday Times* (12 July
1896), Hermann Klein, the music critic, described these settings as
' . . . quite a revelation – not of mere talent, but of unsuspected
power and variety of expression, of depth of melodic charm and
technical resource.' Certainly, this and the later song cycles which
she wrote represent the most ambitious song-writing by any women
in nineteenth-century England. The twenty-two settings from the
Rubaiyat of Omar Khayyam (translated by Fitzgerald) for four
solo voices and piano accompaniment achieve a musical unity
through rhythmic and thematic transformations of the opening
theme (Example 13) and is very well written for voices. The tenor
aria, 'Ah, Moon of My Delight' (Example 14) justifiably became
popular on account of its sustained lyricism: the solo quartet
writing is also attractive, particularly in its avoidance of trite harmonies, though the piano accompaniment is perhaps less successful
revealing in its simulated orchestral tremulos some of the limitations of the keyboard. The extension of the solo song-cycle to
that using a quartet of voices widens the expressive scope and
affords the opportunity of greater variety of texture. However, in
so doing, something of the intimacy of chamber music may be lost
and the sense of unity impaired: such a work more closely
resembles a cantata.

Following the success of *In a Persian Garden*, Liza Lehmann
did revert to the more traditional song-cycle in her setting for
baritone, or bass and piano, of poems from Tennyson's *In Memo-*

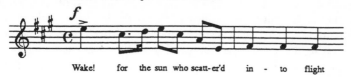

Example 13 *In a Persian Garden (Liza Lehmann)*

Example 14 *Ah, Moon of My Delight (Liza Lehmann)*

riam. In her autobiography she maintains that some of her best work is contained in these twelve settings, which are continuous and loosely linked thematically. An extended Epilogue (optional) with spoken voice and piano, is an original feature, though not one that was successful. Insufficient variety of mood is afforded by her choice of text and this may account for its lack of appeal. Her next song-cycle, 'The Daisy Chain', was a setting of twelve separate poems by different writers and revealed a much lighter vein and sense of humour. No attempt is made at thematic unity, each song being joined by a few modulatory chords. The success of this cycle led to 'More Daisy Chains' and 'Nonsense Songs from Alice in Wonderland', the latter being very popular in America, where Liza Lehmann undertook two extended tours performing her song-cycles. Of her many individual songs one of the most adventurous is 'Magdalen at Michael's Gate': here she juxtaposes at one point keys a semitone apart and ends with an accompaniment of fourths and fifths. The ballad becomes an art-song in her hands.

Liza Lehmann made her debut as a singer at the 'Monday Pops' in 1885. At one time in her career she stayed with Clara Schumann in order to learn how to interpret Schumann's songs. Her repertoire also included songs by Purcell, Arne and Hook which she had copied out from manuscripts in the British Museum. A frequent encore piece was the song 'When love is kind' which had been written by 'A.L.', the initials standing for her mother. She married a musician, Herbert Bedford, who was himself both a composer and painter and it was in the same year, 1894, that she began composing. As a young girl she had met Verdi and Liszt: her father Rudolph Lehmann had taken the family to Italy whilst he painted a portrait of Verdi. Thus her cultural background and professional singing career were influential upon her as a composer: her songs are tasteful and tuneful. As the first President of the Society of Women Musicians (1911) she spoke in her inaugural address about the importance of all composers having singing lessons and a few years later produced a useful textbook on singing.

In the songs of Maude Valérie White and Liza Lehmann English art-song was rescued from the pernicious clutches of the Victorian ballad. Though not part of the folk-song revival, both included folk-song arrangements in their output, the Gaelic settings by Liza Lehmann being particularly attractive. Like her contemporaries, Parry and Stanford, they attempted to restore the art-song to something of its former glory, taking as their models the nineteenth-century *lied* of Schumann and Brahms. The restoration was not complete until the true glory of English song had been revealed in the music of the Elizabethans and Purcell, and it was a later generation of English composers who were able to benefit from the experience of this music. Even so, several of their songs are worthy of performance today.

Both Maude Valérie White and Liza Lehmann came from well-to-do middle-class backgrounds and in this were representative of the many women composers of nineteenth-century England. (For a succinct consideration of the social position of the middle class woman in nineteenth-century England see Scott: 1987, pp. 60–65). It was in a limited field of solo/ensemble song that they both achieved success, distinguished by their freshness of treatment and response to poetry. In *The Life of Liza Lehmann by Herself* there is no word of recrimination against male domination in music. Her songs were readily published and received, particularly in America, critical acclaim and frequent performances. She followed the tradition of a successful female singer who turned to composing having already won an enviable reputation on the concert platform. She was content to write within the more accepted female genres and her songs, both serious and humorous reaped an enthusiastic response from a large audience.[18]

It is interesting to note that her inaugural address as President of the Society of Women Musicians in 1911 was not concerned with women's rights or women musicians but with the need for all

Moderato assai, con molto sentimento

Example 15 *Kashmiri Song (Amy Woodforde-Finden)*

composers to study the human voice. She regarded her compositional activities as of prime importance and in later life regretted her nine years on the concert platform as time wasted. When asked by an American journalist what inspired her to compose she did stress that she did not regard dealing with the abstract as the exclusive property of the male (Lehmann: 1918 p. 160). Whilst her success as a composer owed much to her reputation as a singer and interpreter of her own works it was enhanced by her magnetic and balanced personality: ' . . . she revealed herself not only as a lyrical composer of rare versatility . . . but as that rare thing, a musician with a sense of humour. This latter gift is the more remarkable because she is a woman, and ladies with the artistic temperament are usually deficient therein.' (Lehmann: 1918, p. 156).

The nineteenth century, in social and cultural terms, continued in England until the beginning of the First World War. In the early years of the twentieth century there was no decline in the production of ballads by women composers. The 'Four Indian Love Lyrics' (1902) by Amy Woodforde-Finden (with words by Laurence Hope, a pseudonym for Mrs Nicholson, who as wife of General Nicholson put her Indian colonial experience to good account) are distinguished by their exotic touches of harmony (Example 15) and flowing melodies. The influence of Puccini is detectable in the frequent underlining of the melody at the octave in the accompaniment. 'Sincerity' (1903), words and music by Emilie Clarke, also employs this device in a song which is well-conceived. The world of opera is not far away in Guy d'Hardelot's 'Because' (1902) and 'I know a lovely garden'. After studying at the Paris Conservatoire she toured America in 1896 with the singer Emma Calvé, and after her marriage settled in London. Her songs were very popular in Edwardian England, being sung particularly by Melba.

There were many other women composers whose songs were sung and enjoyed by a large number of people, but to list them all would serve no purpose. A sufficient number of songs by women composers have been discussed for it to be evident that their contribution was distinctive and impressive. There is a danger of judging the taste of one age in terms of another and we should seek to evaluate these songs against the backcloth of the society from which they sprang. Many have endured for their own intrinsic value.

Notes

1   The famous continental Academy, the Leipzig Conservatorium, was established in 1843, with Mendelssohn as Director. During its first year it recruited forty-four students, of whom eleven were female.

2   The first Principal of the Academy, 1823–1832.

3   For a detailed study of this remarkable woman musician see: *Une Musicienne Versailles – Augusta Holmès* by René Pichard du Page. There are also interesting comments on Augusta Holmès in *A Final Burning of Boats Etc.*, pp. 126–136 and *What happened next*, pp. 156–157, by Ethel Smyth.

4   The music of Ethel Smyth will be considered separately and does not therefore come under consideration in this chapter.

5   Mary Moody's dates are not known. Where dates are known they will be given under the first entry of the composer.

6   English edition, Vol. 2, pp. 99–100.

7   He was Director of Music at St Paul's Girls' School, London, from 1905 until 1934, and during that time composed some excellent music for female voices.

8   Burnand and Sullivan's one-act operetta for three characters was first publicly performed in London in 1867.

9   Pearsall: 1969, p. 221.

10   Ethel Smyth's *The Boatswain's Mate* and *Entente Cordiale* are discussed in a later chapter.

11   Harriet Grote (1792–1878), the wife of the distinguished historian, George Grote, was an accomplished musician and friend of both Jenny Lind and Mendelssohn.

12   H.F. Simpson in his *Century of Ballads* relates that when Henry Russell sang *There's a good time coming, boys* at a concert in the Potteries, a member of the audience called out, 'Muster Russell, can you fix the toime?' This song became a hymn at certain revivalist meetings.

13   It is a nice touch of irony that after his second wife left him, Sir

Henry Bishop's licentious habits led him to bankruptcy and a life of anything but domestic bliss.

14 Augusta Holmès, the French composer of Irish parentage and pupil of César Franck, achieved success at the Paris Opera House with *La Montagne Noir* in 1895.

15 A celebrated German violinist and composer who settled in England in 1849.

16 Whilst one can understand why women composers preferred the anonymity of a pseudonym, it is perplexing to come across the lyrics of a certain Benjamin Britten under the female pseudonym of Grace Campbell. Perhaps he anticipated his eclipse by his twentieth-century namesake!

17 Emily, Lady Tennyson, was an amateur pianist and composer and set several of her husband's poems to music, many prior to their publication. The Mss. are preserved in the archives of the Tennyson Research Centre, Lincoln, together with a complete checklist of all Lady Tennyson's compositions, compiled by Dr. Copley. (For further comment on Lady Tennyson's compositions see *Lady Tennyson, Composer* by I.A. Copley, in the Tennyson Research Bulletin, November 1976, Vol. 2, Number 5.)

18 An interesting comparison of the career of Louise Adolpha Le Beau (1825–1927), (see Olson in Bowers and Tick: 1986, pp. 282–303) with that of Liza Lehmann reveals a different climate of responses to the German composer. Certainly the scepticism and obstructionism that Le Beau encountered in the acceptance for performance of her orchestral extended works was not experienced by either Maude Valérie White or Liza Lehmann which suggests that genre was a determining factor.

3 Sarah Glover and the Contribution of Women to Music Education

Sarah Anna Glover (1786–1867) and Sol-fa

> ... it has been repugnant to my taste as a female and private individual to attach my name publicly to a treatise of any kind; but the musical system described in a work originally entitled 'Scheme for Rendering Psalmody Congregational' has been so confounded with a modification of it, that I wish by annexing my name to this edition, to secure speedily, if possible, the identity of the genuine system. (*Glover*: 1850, Preface)

In adding her name to this publication (one of the very rare occasions when she did so), Sarah Glover wished to make it clear beyond all doubt that her *Sol-fa Scheme* was distinct from that of Curwen's *Tonic Sol-fa*, and that she still believed her method to be better than Curwen's. This was the fourth edition of what was substantially the same work, first published in 1835, followed by a second edition in 1839 and a third edition in 1845. Certain modifications and additions are to be found in the subsequent editions and the general tenor becomes, overtly maybe, more disillusioned with the state of music in England generally, and particularly with the condescending attitude of musicians to her *Sol-fa Scheme*. The fourth edition of 1850, and the Preface from which the above quotation was taken, were no doubt a riposte to Curwen's *Grammar of Vocal Music* which had been published in 1848. Although she had agreed, albeit reluctantly, to Curwen's modification of her *Sol-fa Scheme* as the basis of his *Tonic Sol-fa*, she remained ambivalent in her attitude. On the one hand she was genuinely delighted in the growing national success of Curwen's method and, be it noted, Curwen was always at pains to point out his indebtedness to her, yet on the other, she remained curiously impervious to any 'improvements' to her system and obviously believed it to be superior.

That Sarah Glover believed so strongly in her *Sol-fa Scheme* is not surprising, for the greater part of her life had been devoted to finding a simple, rational system of music notation that would be the means whereby congregational singing in churches, and in particular the singing of psalms,[1] sung metrically, in the manner in which hymns are sung today, would be improved. The result of her work was far greater than she envisaged, though to come to fruition it did need the perception, organizing and publicizing ability that the Rev. J. Curwen was able to bring to bear. Without him, her pioneer work, quietly conducted at several schools and in her father's church in Norwich in the first quarter of the nineteenth century, might well have been neglected by the world at large.

The eldest daughter of the Rev. Edward Glover, M.A., rector of St Lawrence Church, Norwich, Sarah Glover grew up in a city which had become, in the latter half of the eighteenth century, a centre for radical philosophers, social reformers and men of letters. Philip Martineau, who founded the Norwich Public Library in 1784, Sir T.E. Smith, the botanist, and Amelia Opie[2] were amongst the group of non-conformists who were particularly active in Colegate, that part of the city known as 'over the water' (the River Wensum), where they used to meet in the fine Presbyterian Octogon Chapel. It was just across from this building that Sarah Glover carried out her musical experiments in the school which she and her two sisters ran at the Black Boy Yard. Her teaching methods and musical experiments were equally non-conformist in approach, engendered by a true spirit of enquiry and scientific research.

Norwich, during Sarah Glover's lifetime, was no provincial backwater. Throughout the Middle Ages it had been one of the largest and most influential cities in Britain and during the eighteenth century, though it had become a provincial centre with its own spirit of independence, it was saved from insularity through its proximity to London and to the Continent by way of Great Yarmouth. The most famous Norwich contemporary of Sarah Glover was Harriet Martineau, the economist, whose fame was such after her publication of *Illustrations of Political Economy* in 1832, that she was consulted by the then Chancellor of the Exchequer, Lord Althorp. Indeed, in their respective spheres, both

Sarah Glover and Harriet Martineau were attempting similar undertakings; both attempted to explain in simple terms, for the understanding of the largely uneducated, the mysteries of music notation on the one hand, and the complexities of financial economy on the other. Both were female pioneers, intruding into predominantly male preserves with dedication and sacrifice, for throughout her life Sarah Glover received no financial reward for any of her work. Of the two, there is no doubt that Harriet Martineau was the more successful. Her economic moral tales, stories of ordinary people in simple situations, revealed a capacity for interesting the masses and for putting across in easy terms complex material. It was an ability that for all her strivings, Sarah Glover lacked, at least, in print.

Sarah Glover lived and worked in a city that produced two of the outstanding philanthropists of the age. In 1817, Elizabeth Fry, a daughter of John Gurney[3] (1749–1809), merchant banker of Norwich, began her work with the underprivileged in Newgate Prison, and from this courageous beginning came the demand for prison reform. Not only in Norwich, where Amelia Opie and others founded the Norwich Ladies' Association for Prison Reform in 1823, can her influence be traced: indeed, the lead she took was followed not only in Europe but in Russia and America. She was related, through marriage, to the other leading philanthropist from Norwich: her sister, Hannah, married Sir T. Fowell-Buxton who, with Wilberforce, led the long and successful campaign for the abolition of slavery. There is no direct evidence to suggest that Sarah Glover actually met Elizabeth Fry, though it is highly probable, since for many years, Sarah Glover was Governess in the family of Sir T. Fowell-Buxton,[4] as was also, at a later stage, her sister Christina. One cannot fail to relate Sarah Glover's deep humanity and social/educative work with the underprivileged with the circumstances of her employment and the humanitarian and radical thought that was part of her environment.

The strong radical and dissenting communities in Norwich may have had something to do with the freedom of thought and activity that women like Amelia Opie, Elizabeth Fry, Harriet Martineau and Sarah Glover[5] shared in Norwich in the early nineteenth century. It is not surprising to find that the subject for debate at the Norwich Mechanics' Institute for 14 and 21 June, 1835 was, 'Is woman naturally inferior to man in mental capacity?' There was certainly evidence on hand to suggest otherwise.

The History of Norwich by P. Browne, published in 1814, gives a fairly comprehensive picture of the musical life of the city during much of Sarah Glover's lifetime. A musical festival lasting three to four days was a regular occurrence: it was first recorded in 1775 when a 'Grand Oratorio of Sacred Music' was performed at St Peter's Mancroft Church. In 1787 it took on what was to become its usual dimension of performances in St Peter's Mancroft Church and in St Andrew's Hall. The festival is recorded for the years 1790, 1802, 1811, 1813 and 1814 when a grand music festival was held to celebrate the end of the Napoleonic wars. The Norwich Music Festival became one of the great provincial music festivals of the nineteenth century, bringing international artists and the performance of new works to Norwich. Recalling his early music experiences in Norwich, Hermann Klein, who later became music critic to the *Sunday Times*, says:

> I was born in the musical city of Norwich. The epithet 'musical' is not undeserved. Search the whole United Kingdom through, and you will scarcely find a place that can boast an older or more intimate connection with the 'divine art' than the ancient capital of East Anglia. Its noble Cathedral, its threescore churches, its chapels without number, are ever helping to create and sustain in the population a love of music. Above all, it is the scene, once in every three years, of a famous musical gathering. The 'Norfolk and Norwich Musical Festival' (to give the full title) not only vies in age with those of the Three Choirs ... but very nearly ranks in importance with the triennial meetings of its richer sisters, Birmingham and Leeds. (*Klein*: 1903, p. 3)

Reference to the long-established civic musicians is contained in an account of 1783 of the Woolcombers Jubilee, which procession was preceded by 'trumpets and other musical instruments'. The entry for 29 February, 1814, recording the recital to mark the opening of the newly-erected organ in St Andrew's Church reminds us that most churches had no organs at this time and it was during Sarah Glover's lifetime that organs were being introduced into the town parish churches. It is with this in mind that we should consider her remarks concerning unaccompanied singing and the deleterious effect that organs can have on congregational singing.[6] Undoubtedly the Cathedral, with its two services a day and the numerous parish churches of Norwich accounted for a large proportion of the music making in Norwich during Sarah Glover's lifetime. She had music lessons from 1792 with Dr J.C. Beckwith[7] and, according to her niece Mrs Langton Brown, became a capable pianist and composer. Her most famous contemporary musician in

Norwich in her early days was the boy prodigy, William Crotch, who gave his first public performance in 1778, aged two years nine months. He became Professor of Music at Oxford University at the age of twenty one, and later, Principal of the Academy of Music: his meteoric rise to fame no doubt encouraged others in the pursuit of music. Evidence of the musical life of Norwich can be assumed from the fact that Sarah Glover's *Scheme* went into four editions, and as a result of her work with the singing in her father's church, St Lawrence Church became celebrated for the standard of its choral music.

Little is known of her parents except that her father, the Rev. Edward Glover, was ordained deacon in the Church of England at Norwich in September, 1785. His parish of St Lawrence was of reasonable size which at the 1801 census contained 248 families, whereas the largest parish in Norwich, St Stephen, contained over twice that number. The church had been founded in 1472: divine service was celebrated once only on Sunday as was the custom. There was a move afoot as a result of Bishop Porteus's *Challenge* to include Evensong at some of the parish churches in Norwich. A plan was put forward in 1813 but it is not recorded whether it was implemented. St Lawrence Church is now closed: the house in which Sarah Glover lived, 91, Pottergate, still stands and is close by the church. Sarah's interest in music was obviously caught from her father who had a love of music and who obviously realized its importance in congregational worship. The non-conformist churches, particularly the Wesleyan, had through their hymns captured the heart of the ordinary man in a way that only Luther previously had equalled. Norwich was a centre of non-conformist activity[8] and it is more than likely that the importance attached to music in Methodist worship encouraged the Anglicans to wake from their slumbers in this respect. Indeed, it was through the Wesleyan movement that a new musical impulse was aroused in people which greatly affected the nature of public worship throughout the country.

Of Sarah's mother, all that is recorded[9] is that she was a strict disciplinarian, influenced by the writings of Mrs Trimmer.[10] From Sarah's writings we can gauge something of her educational background which would appear to be a fairly traditional one for a middle-class girl. Her knowledge of French enabled her to quote from a theoretical treatise, *Encyclopedie de Musique* by M. de Monsigny, and amongst her papers in the Strangers' Hall Museum, Norwich, are pieces from the repertoire of the Galin-Paris-Chevé

School in figure notation, and the *Méthode Elémentaire de Musique Vocale* by Nanine and Emile Chevé (1850). She also refers to Rousseau's numerical system of notation in her *Scheme*, and it was from her acquaintance with Burney's *A General History of Music*, published in 1776, that she got her information concerning Guido's system of notation. Her theoretical and harmony studies were very thorough, as the many manuscript notebooks testify, and were largely based on Pasquali's *Thorough Bass*. Mention is also made in her writings to Morley's *Introduction to Practical Music*. Her interests were not restricted solely to music, for amongst her possessions in the Strangers' Hall Museum are articles on acoustics and architecture. Indeed, there is a strong scientific streak to her nature, as is demonstrated by her preoccupation with theoretical problems in music, the invention and design of the harmonicon, an ingenious instrument which became an integral part of her *Sol-fa* system, and in her attempt in later life to devise a colour notation based upon the analogy of the properties of prismatic colours and those of a vibrated string. It was Newton who first propounded this theory in 1704; it was later discredited by Helmholtz in the 1860s. In 1859, after much correspondence with several scientists, including the Professor of Mathematics at Oxford University, she produced her *Dissertation upon the relationship between colour and music*. No doubt she benefited from the new public library which had been opened in Norwich two years before her birth; in 1814 this library held 6,000 volumes.

Unlike Harriet Martineau who abandoned Norwich for London, the latter offering a better platform for the dissemination of her work, Sarah Glover did not leave Norwich until the latter years of her life. It was in 1851, a year after the final publication of her *Scheme*, that she retired first to Cromer, thence to Reading in 1855, and finally to Hereford in 1864 or thereabouts. She died in 1867 in Malvern, where she is buried, having been taken ill at the house of a friend where she had been staying for a short while. During these closing years of her life she busied herself with the colour notation scheme, with an attempt at teaching part of her method to the blind, and particularly with the redesign and manufacture of the harmonicon with which she tied her *Sol-fa* system more closely, seeking, unsuccessfully, Curwen's patronage of the instrument.[11]

It was from her concern about the poor state of parochial psalmody[12] that Sarah Glover was prompted to find ways to remedy the situation. A *Charge* delivered to the clergy of the

Diocese of London in 1790 by Beilby, Lord Bishop of London (Bishop Porteus) had been reprinted in 1811, and it is in this *Charge* that we can see the starting point of Sarah Glover's work. The improvement in the singing of the psalms remained throughout her life her main object.

The Bishop declared that parochial psalmody had been

> ... rendered almost totally useless: in country parishes it is generally engrossed by a select band of singers, who have been taught by some itinerant master to sing in the worse manner, a most wretched set of psalm-tunes in three or four parts, so complex, so difficult and so totally void of all true harmony that it is altogether impossible for any congregation to take part with them ... (Beilby, *Porteus*: 1790, p. 16)

In London, matters were not much better: ' ... this business is in a great measure confined to the charity children ... [who] yet for want of right instruction to modulate their voices properly, almost constantly strain them [to] so high a pitch as to disgust and offend the ear.' (*Porteus*: 1790, p. 16). His remedy was to select and train voices of the charity children and the Sunday School children in the parishes ' ... and have them taught to sing well in their natural tone.' (*Porteus*: 1790, p. 17). Bishop Porteus concluded by asserting that the singing of psalms ' ... from its known and powerful influence on the minds and morals of the great mass of the people, is of more real and national and practical importance than even those sublime and elaborate compositions of our great masters.' (*Porteus*: 1790, p. 21).

The identification of music with moral probity should be seen as part of a much wider resurgence of a moral conscience awakened by the evangelical movements of the late eighteenth century. Methodism had provoked churchmen to do something about its recumbent, and often absent, clergy who, in 1792, could advertise for ' ... a curacy in a good sporting country where the duty is light and the neighbourhood convivial.' (Jaeger: 1956, p. 10). It was very largely the result of the work of William Wilberforce, who had suffered an evangelical 'conversion', that a *Royal Proclamation Against Vice and Immorality* was made in 1787. It was Bishop Porteus, after his translation from Chester to London, who gave Wilberforce his wholehearted support in his efforts to transform the over-tolerant eighteenth-century aristocratic attitudes to religion, well-epitomized in Lord Melbourne's comment, 'Things are coming to a pretty pass when religion is allowed to invade private life.' (Jaeger: 1956, p. 39).

Several of the 'Blue-Stocking Ladies' were influenced by Wilber-force, and Hannah Moore particularly, along with Mrs Trimmer, put her energies into the campaign for the Observance of the Sabbath. The new Puritanism, substituting bigotry for easy-going tolerance, permeated society in the first decades of the nineteenth century. John Bowdler went to work on Shakespeare and Mrs Sherwood on children's education; Christian virtues and morals were extolled above all else for women especially, because of their family responsibilities: 'Be good, sweet maid and let who can be clever.' (Charles Kingsley). No wonder, as Muriel Jaeger comments in her study of the changing standards and behaviour of the years 1787–1837, ' . . . that the outstanding women of the Victorian Age should be women of ferocious goodness and devastating strength of purpose.' (Jaeger: 1956, p. 130). It was in such a climate that Sarah Glover, daughter of a clergyman, began her life's work in response to Bishop Porteus.

Whilst Bishop Porteus called for the 'teaching of children to sing in their natural tone' he at no point in his *Charge* referred to the problem of reading music, and it was this aspect that Sarah Glover, and later, John Curwen, took up. They put their energies into devising a system of music reading that could be understood by the masses. That both of them achieved an improvement in the technique of singing was a by-product, albeit an important one, of their work. It is then in this *Charge* that one finds the rationale for the life's work of Sarah Glover which she began one year after its republication in 1812.

The most formidable stumbling block to the training of children in music, so as to be able to lead the singing of the psalms in church, was the absence of any simple, teaching method of reading music. Guido's original hexachord, *ut re me fa so la*, had been modified in England to an arrangement of overlapping groups of four notes, *fa sol la mi*, and as such was the basis of pitch reading, a system both illogical in its use of the same syllables for different pitch notes, and complex. Several attempts had been made to simplify it, of which those by Hickson and Turner in the late eighteenth century were the most noticeable.[13] In the Preface to her *Scheme* of 1835[14] Sarah Glover refers both to Guido, on whose concept of the tetrachord she based her system, and to Bishop Porteus. The omissions of the former she claims to amend, and the challenges of the latter form the basis of her response.[15]

In her *Tetrachordal System* Sarah Glover lists what she sees as the four main defects of existing staff notation. Firstly, she points to the lack of distinction between tones and semitones as represented on the staff. Secondly, to the prevailing use of sharps and flats in the key signature which results in some keys being more abstruse than others. Thirdly, the confusion arising from the use of clefs which results in characters alike in appearance representing different names and sounds, and fourthly, to the complications arising from the use of ledger lines. In putting forth her system she says,

> I hope that a new notation may not only provide a remedy for these defects, but add the following advantages, viz., define rhythm more clearly, characterise each interval of the key, mark the scale, express the relationship (generally) existing between keys where modulation occurs, render transposition perfectly easy, and furnish a set of syllables favourable to good intonation. (*Glover*: 1845, pp. 17–18)

As a final recommendation she points out that the notation 'here proposed' can be printed in common type, thus avoiding the complicated and expensive typing press needed for the usual staff notation. Like all good propagandists she forestalls criticism by answering what she considers will be the principal objection to her system, which is, music already published will prove unintelligible to those acquainted only with her system of notation. This she does not deny, but counters with what basically has proved to be the real value of her system and what it later became, *Tonic Sol-fa*:

> The new notation however, may easily be applied as an introduction to the pointed notation, and in such a manner as to divest it of much of its seeming irrationality. I am persuaded that on the whole a more rapid progress would be made by pupils thus instructed, than by those who are obliged to encounter the defects, seeming and real, of the pointed notation at the commencement of their musical studies, while those who require no more knowledge than would qualify them for skill in psalmody, might easily be supplied with a collection of tunes printed in the Sol-fa notation, ample enough for all the purposes of social and congregational worship. (*Glover*: 1845, pp. 18–19)

We know from her writings that Sarah Glover became increasingly depressed by the condescending attitude of musicians to *Sol-fa* and *Tonic Sol-fa* notation. It is an attitude that still persists today, though there are many musicians, most noticeably Kodaly, who have recognized the truth of what she says here. There is, however, a certain ambivalence in Sarah Glover's attitude to *Sol-fa* and traditional notation. She began by trying to discover a simple means of reading music for a very limited purpose – that of the psalm tune. As she progressed she appeared to see her system as a possible replacement for the 'old' notation. Finally, towards the end of her teaching career she recognized that she must relate her system to existing notation and under Curwen's influence accepts, reluctantly, *Sol-fa* and *Tonic Sol-fa* as an introduction to it.

One of the weaknesses in Sarah Glover's system was that it was designed for a limited kind of music and its wider application raised more problems than it solved. This was pointed out by one of her critics, Arthur H. Dyke Acland, in an article *On Musical Notation and the present state of Musical Education* (Acland, January 1841). Of Miss Glover's system he says: ' . . . I do most exceedingly regret her having put it forward', for, he argues, the old system has not been proved unsound, citing existing cathedral and collegiate choirs as evidence. He also mentions the parish church choir of Hurliscombe near Honiton, where a certain Miss Head had produced an excellent choir using the old notation.

> I do not say there are no difficulties to be objected against it [traditional notation], but there are more serious objections to her own [Miss Glover's].
>
> First it proposes an actual return to those principles of ancient notation which proved unequal to the development of all the higher parts of music.
>
> Secondly, the great difficulty of remote modulations, which are scarcely alluded to, and which indeed may not be required in a common psalm-tune, but which constantly occur in services, chants and the higher order of even simple psalmody.
>
> Thirdly, the fact that, in some instances in her own works, modulation takes place in the treble where none takes place in the bass, presenting no difficulty if the various parts are looked on as independent, but being manifestly inconsistent when looked upon (as they really are) connected together. (*Acland*: 1841, p. 43)

In conclusion he says, ' . . . it is a serious thing to have sent through the country a new nomenclature for such a science as music, when the existing one has not for years had a proper trial, and its construction possesses advantages immeasurably above any others.' (Acland: 1841, p. 44).

Curwen's answer to these criticisms, for by this date he had discovered Sarah Glover's *Scheme*,[16] reflected the view which Sarah

Glover reluctantly came to accept, which was that *Sol-fa* or *Tonic Sol-fa* was not meant as a replacement to the traditional notation but as an introduction to it.

Even more fundamental a limitation was her concept of the tonic, DOH, as the centre of the heptachord:

SOLE LAH TE[17] *DOH* RA ME FAH

Whether this tetrachordal grouping arose in her mind as a result of the modifications that had been made to Guido's original hexachord, or whether it arose because it reflected basic melodic construction, that is, the tendency of many melodies to exist equally above and below DOH, is never made clear: however, it remained fundamental to her *Sol-fa* system and was the major point of divergence in Curwen's *Tonic Sol-fa*, where DOH is regarded as the first degree of the heptachord.[18]

In order to modulate to the relative minor key, Sarah Glover introduced two new syllables, BAH and NE, and based her system on two moveable scales or ladders, the DOH scale and the LAH scale:

DOH Scale (for example on C)

FAH	F
ME	E
RA	D
DOH	C
TE	B
LAH	A
SOLE	G

LAH Scale (for example on A)

Ascending			*Descending*	
RA	D		RA	D
DOH	C		DOH	C
TE	B		TE	B
LAH	A		*LAH*	A
NE	G sharp		SOLE	G natural
BAH	F sharp		FAH	F natural
ME	E		Me	E

The dominant seventh to tonic chord progression for each scale was also introduced at the outset:

DOH Scale (for example on C)
```
F
      M
R
      D
T
S     S
```

LAH Scale (for example on A)
```
R
      D
T
      L
N
M     M
```

It should be noted that the tonic chord in each case is taught in its second inversion which is, harmonically, unfortunate.

The gains, thus far, are many. A distinguishing initial letter identifies all seven notes of the major scale whatever their relative pitch may be. Visually, the semitones between T–D and M–F are easily distinguishable by having the initial letters written more closely together. Bothersome clefs, ledger-lines and accidentals of staff notation are done away with. However, the complications of notation arise largely out of the need to be able to change from one scale to one of several others in the course of a short piece of music. Sarah Glover was concerned only with modulation to fairly closely related keys and her Compound Ladder shows the three such keys to the DOH and LAH scale respectively:

DOH Scale	C Major	G Major	F Major
LAH Scale	A Minor	E Minor	D Minor

To make these limited modulations possible Sarah Glover used additional syllables. These were added after the initial letter, dependent upon the degree of sharpening or flattening entailed in the ensuing modulation. For the key adding one sharp the vowel 'u' was substituted: for two sharps 'oo' was substituted and for three sharps 'oze' was substituted. Similarly for flats, 'i', 'awe' and 'aze' were substituted.[19] Transient accidentals were taken care of by the substitution of 'oy' after the initial consonant. Examples of the use of some of these syllables can be seen in the notation of the tune 'Rockingham', where modulation to the dominant key, the sharp side, is seen by the substitution of 'u', and on its return to the tonic, hence to the flat side, the substitution of 'i'.

A study of the notation, as shown in the example, will draw

MISS GLOVER'S NOTATION.

HERE is the tune "Rockingham" printed in Miss Glover's notation. The signs need some explanation. The words "Column W. o" refer to the column in the glass harmonicon which gave the pitch, W being the letter which represented F, the key-note of the tune, and "o" being O, a fifth above. "Foot" explains the measure. "Metronome 60" is obvious; "Pendulum 30" means that a string 30 inches long, with a weight attached, will vibrate at the same rate. The curve) is equivalent to a slur. An acute accent ∕ denoted a higher octave, and a grave accent ∖ a lower, but the octave was reckoned from *sole* to *sole* and not from *doh* to *doh*. There were no bridge-notes in Miss Glover's notation. The dagger † placed in various ways, † ┼ ⊣ ⊢ showed the direction of the transition. The letter U added to a Sol-fa name meant one remove to the right (du): the letter I one remove to the left (di). A comma divided a beat, and a hyphen (-) prolonged a note beyond the time of a beat or part of a beat.

ROCKINGHAM. L.M. *Solemn.*

Columns W. o.   Foot . | .)   Metronome 60.   Pendulum 30.

| W . D | M.F) .R | D. — . M | Ś . — . Ĺ | Ś . — . Ś | D . — . T́ |
| W . D | D.L) .T | D. — . D | M. — . F | M. — . M | M . — . R |

| Ĺ. — . Ś | Ś .F) . M | Ṁ . R) ⊢ .su | d . — . r | m . —† . Śl |
| D. — . T | L.R) . D | D . T) ⊢ .ṁu | ṁ . — . s | d . —† . Fl |

| Ḋ.M┼.tu | d . —†.DI | F.—.M | R . —.Ḋ | D,-R.M).R | D . —) |
| M.—†.s fu | ṁ . —┼.DI | R.—.D | R.T) .D | D . —.T | D . —) |

Sarah Glover's Notation, *Independent Magazine*, 1842

our attention to several other features of Sarah Glover's system. The 'Columns W.o.' at the head refers to the column in the glass harmonicon which gave the exact pitch. Sarah Glover chose to use the letters of the alphabet from H to Z to identify exact pitch, and to avoid any resemblance, and therefore any possible confusion with staff notation. The pitch note A was identified as H and with the omission of the letters I, R, S and T, which could lead to confusion (the latter three are initial letters in *Sol-fa* and the first could presumably be confused with a Roman numeral) the substitution results as follows:

Existing Pitch-Note Designation		New Pitch-Note Designation
A	=	H
A sharp or B flat	=	J
B or C flat	=	K
C	=	O
C sharp	=	P
D	=	Q
D sharp or E flat	=	U
E	=	V
F	=	W
F sharp	=	X
G	=	Y
G sharp	=	Z

Thus the pitch-note, or key of the piece cited, is F and the small 'o' indicates the fifth of the key, the note C.

This innovation appears as an unnecessary complication and one feels that it is one which Sarah Glover might well have modified with later experience. However, it was the means, when incorporated in her 'Table of Tune', of lining up the correct column in the glass harmonicon, and to have modified or scrapped this innovation would have meant finding a completely new system for selecting the correct pitch on the harmonicon. In its favour, it should be stated that it was a foolproof system for finding the exact pitch, and it did have the advantage of bearing no relationship to staff notation in its use of the middle and last letters of the alphabet.

'Foot. 1.' refers to the measure, or rhythm. The scansion of the poem was the guiding factor, accents being shown by bar lines and unaccented syllables by dots. Hence the scansion of the hymn, *When I survey* is .—. An exclamation mark was used to describe subsidiary accents. 'Metronome 60' reminds one of the importance that Sarah Glover attached to its use: 'The imperturbable calmness with which the metronome clicks time to an enthusiastic pupil, who would convert by degrees an andante into an allegro, makes it answer the purpose of a master in an important requisite in acquiring the art of music.' (*Glover*: 1845, p. 65). For those not possessing a metronome a weighted piece of string was advocated: in the example quoted, 'Pendulum 30' means that the weighted string should be thirty inches long for it to oscillate at an identical rate to the clicking of the metronome at 60.

The harmonicon was a portable keyboard instrument which Sarah Glover had designed. It was between two and three feet in length, covered the vocal range (G alto to g″) and kept well in tune. It was not meant to accompany the voices but mainly to serve as a means of locating the exact pitch at the beginning of a piece, and of helping to train the ear: 'Accuracy in tune will be much promoted by the pupils taking alternate feet[20] with the harmonicon: the voice is rested while the ear is cultivated.' (Glover: 1845, footnote p. 79). Its purity of tone was a good example for the voice to imitate and its ingenious system of rollers operated in conjunction with the 'Table of Tune' made it possible for a person with little musical experience to find the correct pitch of any piece of music. Its expense (£1.11s.6d) restricted its use to the teacher or monitor, and one does wonder how extensive its use was where *Norwich Sol-fa* was taught; certainly, very few instruments have survived. There are three in Norwich, one at St Peter's Church, Hunford,[21] which it is thought was made for the Great Exhibition of 1851, and two in Norwich Castle Museum.[22]

In conjunction with the *Scheme* a whole battery of aids were proffered. Sarah Glover lists the following apparatus for instructing a school:

1   A *Scheme for rendering Psalmody Congregational*
2   A Guide to *Sol-fa-ing*
3   A dozen *Sol-fa* tune books
4   A dozen time-beaters
5   A compound ladder in large type
6   Two wands or pointers
7   Three diagrams (Table of Degrees, Table of Keys, Table of Tune)
8   A *Sol-fa* harmonicon
9   A Piano-forte card
10   A pendulum.

A box containing the whole kit could be purchased for £2.10s.

Any system relies upon the skill of the teacher to make it come alive and be successful, and one suspects this to be particularly so in the case of *Sol-fa* and Sarah Glover. It must always be remembered that her aim was the specific one of devising a music reading/performing system that would make 'psalmody congregational': indeed, even when viewing singing as part of a national system of education her mind remained set on this limited target: 'I trust singing is becoming a branch of national education, not only in schools for the children of labourers and mechanics, but in academies for the higher order of society, and thus the main point will be attained towards rendering psalmody truly congregational.' (Glover: 1845, p. 6). Had she been concerned with secular music it is likely that several features of her *Scheme* would have been modified, particularly her notation of rhythm which served adequately for the rhythmically simple psalm-tune, but which would have needed enlargement for the rhythmically more varied secular tunes. It was one of the features which Curwen changed.

There was, though, no doubt in her mind as to the value of music in education:

> For example, let the influence be considered of the cultivation of music *en masse* in a school of children: the precision requisite in this art renders labour and discipline necessary; both these have a good moral tendency, and come practically recommended to the young community by pleasing associations. Health is also promoted by the exercise of the lungs, and the recreation afforded by so refreshing a variety in their occupations: music attracts them to the school, unites them in heart with their leader and with each other, composes whilst it raises the spirits, refines the mind, and, under judicious regulations, is favourable to the growth of piety and religion. (*Glover*: 1845, p. 14)

In ascribing moral virtues to the cultivation of music Sarah Glover reflects the ideas of her age, but she is also perceptive in recognizing in the cultivation of music both its recreative and pleasurable attributes, which can only be achieved through a disciplined approach.

Sarah Glover began her teaching of music in 1812, ' . . . in an effort to train a young man to teach the Sunday School children of her church' (Curwen: December, 1867). She progressed to three girl pupils from the Charity School, and in conjunction with her sisters set up a school in Black Boy Yard where she taught reading, writing, gave religious instruction (for which her niece records a large number of carefully prepared sermonettes), and music. It was here that she carried out the bulk of her experiments in teaching music and it was to this school that several visitors, including the Rev. J. Curwen came. The Rector of Pakefield allowed her to use his school for teaching music and printed the first of her Psalm Tunes for use there. In the 1840s she taught at Lakenham School, the Girls' Central School in Norwich and taught children at the

Norwich Workhouse. Also at Pakefield, Sarah Glover ran an evening class for men and women in part-singing. The choir which she trained in her father's church attracted, by its fine part-singing, many visitors.

Whilst recognizing the variety, scope and demands made upon her in teaching children and adults from a wide social spectrum it must be remembered that, unlike her contemporaries in the Charity Schools of Norwich, Sarah Glover was never confronted with huge numbers to teach. The staffing at these schools in the early nineteenth century was one mistress to teach 106 girls reading, knitting and arithmetic, and three masters to teach 256 boys reading, writing and arithmetic. Whilst it is not recorded how many pupils there were in her school at Black Boy Yard it would certainly not have approached in number those at the Charity Schools, which would therefore have allowed her a much more individual, experimental approach. Her two sisters[23] and a friend, Miss Catherine Hansell,[24] also assisted at the school. In an article in the *Independent Magazine* of 1842 entitled, *A Visit to Miss Glover's School*, we learn that ' . . . as an infant school it does not differ in its general aspect and arrangement from other infant schools' (p. 214) except in its singing: ' . . . those little children conduct their Singing Exercises with so much facility and delight, and at the same time, with such accuracy both of time and tune, as to fill with astonishment all who hear them.' (p. 214). The writer goes on to say that ' . . . this was done from notes, without any instrument to lead them on', and that ' . . . the training that has produced such results does not occupy more than two hours in the week, a length of time not greater than is given to singing exercises in every infant school in the land.' (p. 215). In Miss Glover's method, the writer says, is contained ' . . . more of true science and less of technicality than any other method now taught in England' (p. 215) and it is for this reason that the singing is so successful. The writer then describes how the children were divided into two groups: the younger children seated, singing eagerly from the 'Musical Ladder', were led by a monitor who pointed to the *Sol-fa* syllables with her wand. The children graduate to the higher class after a few months of this instruction. In the higher class, of about twenty children, which is conducted in another part of the room, the children each have a *Sol-fa* Tune book and hold in their right hands a short wand for the purpose of beating time.

The tune books were supported on a small instrument in the shape of a cross, with the longest bar extending beyond the book to the right hand. Upon this projecting part of the 'book-holder' as soon as the tune began, the loud beats of the measure were pretty sharply struck, while the soft beats were indicated by gentle touches of the wand on their left arm. (p. 216)

The writer goes on to describe how the group is divided up to sing canons, each group having its own leader who beats time for the group, whilst the individual members of each group sing and mark the time by touching with their wands the accent marks on their books. The younger children also join in the singing of the canons, the melody being pointed on the 'Musical Ladder' by the monitor. The writer concludes his description with a comment that shows that Sarah Glover's system was certainly regarded, at this time, as an introductory stage to staff notation:

> ... on the following day Miss Glover very kindly exhibited to us, with a select class, her method of teaching the minor scale, and the manner in which the more advanced children were introduced, by easy steps, to the correct use of the old notation. From a very careful inspection we felt quite convinced that, considering this method of teaching music as only *introductory* to the use of common notation, it is the best introduction, the quickest and most efficient... (p. 217)

It is from such a description, and together with Sarah Glover's own writings, that one can get an idea of her methods as a teacher.

The school-room, the upper of a three-storey building, had a gallery, was lofty and well-lit and was suitable for the sort of classroom organization that Sarah Glover's method entailed. All visitors to her school commented upon the evident pleasure that the children got from singing,[25] and one can see from the article quoted, how the feeling of progression, the challenge of part-singing and the responsibility of conducting groups must have provided a great incentive to the children. Much of her success also results from her streaming of the children into groups according to their ability, but above all in providing for all children, as the writer says, '... an accurate pictorial representation of interval', which the children carry with them always in their mind's eye. It was for this same reason that Sarah Glover wrote MI–FAH and TE–DOH closer together than the other intervals on her 'Musical Ladder'.

According to her own writings, all theory is deduced from practice and all theory not immediately relevant to practice is omitted.

How different in concept this was from the traditional instruction afforded in music can be gauged by referring to the theoretical treatises with their question-and-answer methods, relying upon rote-learning, in vogue in the early nineteenth century. It is as much in her philosophy as in the practical details of her *Scheme* that Sarah Glover can be seen as the revolutionary pioneer.

In the section of her *Scheme* entitled 'How to instruct a school' she describes her method. With the minimum of verbal instruction, the names of the seven *Sol-fa* letters of the DOH scale are taught as two tetrachords with DOH in the middle uniting them both, and these are pointed to on the 'Musical Ladder'. The pupils are then launched into the tonic arpeggio of D major, which key she preferred for children. Unlike Curwen later, Sarah Glover preferred to sing with the children rather than, as Curwen did, first patterning the phrase for the children to imitate. In the following exercise one can see how the teacher's voice is used to establish the pupils' note first, and then when established, to add a harmony note against it:

By further subdivision of the group the tonic chord is practised in four parts, the larger group, the least able, singing simply the upper DOH. Those that are unable to sing the correct notes are seated together and made to sing either quietly, or simply to listen to the others. In a similar manner other common chords are practised as well as the dominant seventh to tonic chord progression. It is interesting to note that pitch and harmony are taught before rhythm, and that intervals are taught harmonically from the start. For her purposes, pitch is more important than rhythm and the judging of the intervals and the building up of mental sound-pictures of them, is one of the great advantages of *Sol-fa* and *Tonic Sol-fa*. The subdivision of the class according to ability seems practical: above all, the teacher's singing voice is largely the medium of communication rather than the spoken voice, imitation being a major part in the process of learning.

With regard to rhythm, pupils are encouraged to externalize it by striking their palms together for loud beats, and their fists or arms for soft beats. Rests are physically recorded by striking the forefingers downward for the accented, and sideways for the unaccented beats. Rests of several pulses or more are spoken numerically. By inventing specific physical actions to correspond to the beats Sarah Glover ensured that not only have the pupils an active contribution to make, but that the teacher is able to check the nature of the response.

Once tune and rhythm had been established Sarah Glover then progressed to the German Canons.[26] The first twelve canons she designed so that all the intervals of the DOH scale are included. They are taught by imitation of the teacher and by use of the 'Musical Ladder'. The canons lead on to the two-part singing of the hymn-tunes which contain modulation. The progression is then to the LAH scale which is taught similarly to the DOH scale. Music dictation forms a part of the teaching, and there is insistence on the more able pupils teaching the less able. Variety is the keyword, with different groups having independent roles to play in the singing, thus avoiding the boredom and slackness that often occur when everybody sings everything. With justification Sarah Glover regarded her system as a self-teaching method. The teacher's role is as much one of organiser as instructor. The degree of independence in the singing and conducting entrusted to the pupils is, perhaps, the most noteworthy of her innovations.

In a publication of 1838, *Rewards and Punishments in Week-Day Schools for the Labouring Classes of Society,* Sarah Glover[27] puts forward a sensible and detailed list of rules for running a school, obviously based on her own practice. Long before the advent of Parent Associations, Sarah Glover advocates parental involvement in the school:

> Assemble the mothers in the evening, refresh them with tea etc., and then address them on the objects of the institution, on the ways in which they may co-operate with the patrons of it, on the importance of seeking Divine blessing on their exertions and on the efforts of those who desire to unite them in training up their children in the way they should go. (*Glover* 1838, pp. 7–8)

She believed that schools should be fee-paying: ' . . . parents esteem a school which costs something, above one which costs nothing.' (Glover: 1838 p. 20). Though this may suggest that Sarah Glover only wished to teach those whose parents could afford the fee it is not, in fact, the case: ' . . . A very poor child need not be excluded as the money may be furnished privately; but no child should come without money in its hand.' (Glover: 1838, p. 5). It was her belief that education was something to be valued, and in the payment of a fee the outward expression of this belief would be made visible.

Regular attendance was rewarded financially: indeed she recommended a quite complex system of credits for attendance and good work, which could be converted into tickets with which articles of clothing, made in the school, and books, could be purchased.

With regard to discipline she is guided by practical considerations rather than idealism. She hoped that by the system of credits for good work, good behaviour would be encouraged. However, where necessary she believed in 'judicious discipline conducted in a Christian spirit': 'A child who gets more than two discredits in one morning' [the hours were 10 a.m. to 3 p.m. with five minutes allowed for eating lunch which the children brought with them] 'should receive a stroke on the hand with a leather strap, for every mark beyond the two first.' (Glover: 1838, pp. 11–12). Other controls mentioned:

> Bandages are occasionally used to confine mischievous or lazy hands, a pinafore is pinned over an impudent face, and restless feet are sometimes put on a stool ... In some cases of very refractory conduct, it may be well to send the child home before the usual hour of dismissal, and employ a girl of trusty character to convey a note to the parent most feared by the culprit, stating the time when she was sent home. (*Glover* 1838, p. 12)

One must bear in mind that many of the children she was dealing with were unruly and that corporal punishment was an accepted means of discipline in nineteenth-century schools. The credit system and the parental involvement advocated are most forward looking and the idea of children making articles of clothing for sale can be traced to *The Oeconomy of Charity* (1786), by Mrs Trimmer, in which it was recommended for Sunday School children.

The detailed development of Sarah Glover's work by the Rev. John Curwen and its successful conversion into a national singing method involving, by 1891, an estimated two and a half million children, is recorded elsewhere.[28] It was a conference of non-conformist Sunday School teachers at Hull, in 1841, that commissioned the Rev. Curwen to find some easy way of teaching children to sing the congregational parts of the church service, which led him to contact and visit Sarah Glover at Norwich. He first heard about her through the Rev. and Mrs A. Reed of the Old Meeting House, Norwich; and with the help of one of Sarah Glover's former pupils, Mrs Tapleton, who became the first of Curwen's *Tonic Sol-fa* teachers, he was able to listen to the results of Sarah Glover's work at Norwich.[29] He was very impressed, as his letters testify, and immediately set to work modifying her system in accordance with his own theories. The major change Curwen introduced, amongst several others, was to abandon the tetra-chordal arrangement of the scale with Doh in the middle, and substitute a system with Doh as the first note of the scale; hence the new title, *Tonic Sol-fa*. Within two years, Curwen had published his system, *Singing for Schools and Congregations* which, in an enlarged edition in 1848, was entitled *The Grammar of Vocal Music*.

To what extent did Sarah Glover's system succeed? In her address books she lists about thirty people who had bought har-monicons up till 1849 and she had many converts to her cause both in Great Britain and abroad. For example, in 1841, the mid-Somerset *Sol-fa Tune Book* was printed, based on Sarah Glover's *Scheme*, and there are several letters, mainly from clergy, describing their success with her *Sol-fa* system. On the other hand one is rather surprised to discover no mention of Sarah Glover in the *Norwich Tune Book*, a collection of psalm and hymn tunes made up by a committee of choirmasters in Norwich and published nationally (London, Norwich, Liverpool and Manchester) in 1844. She was unfortunate in that the publication of the *Scheme* in 1835 was so closely followed by Curwen's modification of it in 1842, which prevented it from establishing itself in its own right. She acquiesced in the modifications at first, but when she realized that Curwen's *Tonic Sol-fa* had won the day she obviously regretted the confusion that had resulted. Hence the 1850 publication of her *Scheme* and the manuscript 1859 edition, which was never published. ' . . . I am of the opinion that the system itself had been impaired in Mr. Curwen's hands.' (Glover: 1860, Ms. p. 19). Comparing *Sol-fa* and *Tonic Sol-fa* she concludes: 'Either method is serviceable when applied to music not presenting modulation: but the original system (especially in its present state of maturity)[30] is better calculated to express music embracing modulation.' (Glover: 1860, Ms. p. 19). Yet in defeat she was generous:

That these modifications are improvements may admit of doubt, but only one opinion can be entertained of the consummate skill,

and astonishing energy and perseverance with which Mr. Curwen
has organised and conducted an Association which has with wonderful celerity, diffused a knowledge of the leading principles of
music throughout this country and beyond it. (*Glover* 1860, Ms.
p. 19)

In their dealings with each other, both behaved with reserve and
respect. From a collection of some of the letters exchanged between
them, over the years 1841 to 1867, and printed in the *Memorials
of John Curwen* by J. Spencer Curwen (Chapter V: 1882) one can
trace something of the ambivalent attitude that Sarah Glover had
with regard to her *Scheme* and Curwen's modification of it. To the
end of her life Sarah Glover would not accept the major change
that Curwen had instituted, that is, the concept of Doh as the first
degree of the scale.

In spite of Curwen's generous acknowledgement of his indebtedness to Sarah Glover and his fairness in all his dealings with her,
it was inevitable that she should feel, at times, outmanoeuvered:
' ... for I do think you have not acted quite generously in stating
publicly (in contradiction to my private opinion) that your modification of my notation is an improvement upon the original.'
(Hereford, Oct. 1864). Curwen had come across a letter in the
Nonconformist Newspaper of 26 October, 1864, in which a Mr
Waite, who had recently had an interview with Sarah Glover,
insinuated that Curwen had not acted entirely honourably in his
dealings with her. He wrote to Sarah Glover immediately challenging her on this point, and this occasioned the sharpness of her
reply, quoted above. One can see the issue from both sides. Curwen
denied that he had stated publicly that his modifications were
improvements, although he admitted that he believed they were
such. He stressed that he had always made more of the foundations
(Sarah Glover's) and less of the superstructure (his) than it deserved,
and that he never pretended to the public that she approved of his
modifications.

Curwen had many advantages over Sarah Glover. Being a Congregational Minister and male, he was able to publicize and
organize on a scale that was not acceptable or available for a
woman in mid-nineteenth-century England. He was an oppor-
tunist, projected into a national figure by the growing momentum
of state education, with music as a significant part of such education, and the explosion in adult education which was unequalled
in its fervour until the present decade. In comparison, Sarah Glover

was a provincial figure, out of her depths in such a world. In a letter to Curwen dated March 1864, which she did not send she shows more idealism than common sense in regarding Curwen as the person to promulgate her *Scheme*:

> Fame and money I ask not, but I am going to ask for something which I am aware is no trifle – that is your cordial and effectual co-operation in my efforts to leave to posterity a notation so invulnerable to criticism as to preclude the probabilities that the world will be troubled with future attempts to effect a reformation in an elementary notation of music.

Her common sense and realism is seen more in her practical work in schools, in developing over twenty-five years her *Sol-fa* scheme before attempting to publish it, rather than as a publicist and propagandist. However, what reconciled them both was the almost missionary zeal with which they both viewed their work: 'Do not concern yourself to vindicate my originality' she wrote in a letter dated September, 1867, to Curwen, but, ' . . . let the question be not who was the first to invent it, but is the thing itself good and true and useful to the world.' Describing their last meeting together, in Hereford, in 1867, Curwen said, 'Our interview was not only pleasant, but sacred.' (Brown: 1892, p. 8) and it was in this common bond of regarding singing as a means of moral uplift and glorification of God, that one can account for the dedication and sacrifice that both Sarah Glover and the Rev. John Curwen so generously gave, thereby bringing the possibility of music-making to millions of people. Her niece, writing about their work and relationship, commented in 1892 that: 'One had sowed: the other cultivated and had the joy of reaping. Knowing her as I did, my wonder was that she was able to rejoice so much in the success of a system which, though based upon hers, in effect superseded it.' (Brown: 1892, p. 10).

Curwen, it should be recorded, offered Sarah Glover a share in the profits from his work, which she declined, and in 1864 also offered to reprint, at his own expense, Miss Glover's *Scheme* with an appendix giving her latest views. This offer she debated for a long time, but finally rejected. His offer of a commissioned portrait of her was also rejected: ' . . . I am much too old to be disposed to sanction such an expenditure of money upon the preservation of a resemblance of my withered face.' (Letter dated November 1864). Thus his overtures were not accepted. However, Curwen was able to repay some of his debt to Sarah Glover in 1874 when he himself was presented with a testimonial, portrait and a purse containing £200. He generously gave the money to the establishment of two 'Sarah Glover' scholarships at the newly established Tonic Sol-fa College.

That the pioneer work of Sarah Glover formed the very great basis of Curwen's *Tonic Sol-fa* cannot be disputed, and therefore the influence which she indirectly asserted upon the development of music in Britain in the nineteenth century, and Europe in the twentieth century through the work particularly of Kodaly, cannot be over-stressed. Her preoccupation with the tetrachordal arrangement of the scale with Doh in the middle, lack of clarity concerning whether she regarded her system as a replacement for existing notation or as an introduction to it,[31] and the rather sketchy treatment of rhythm generally in her *Scheme*, are all insignificant details when one considers what Sarah Glover's labours gave rise to. She was great enough as a person to submerge her own sense of failure in the overall success of Curwen's work. She was perfectly entitled to believe in her *Scheme* and to believe it superior to Curwen's *Tonic Sol-fa*, but to her everlasting credit, she did not allow this belief to become a stumbling block to their cooperation.

*   *   *

Women writers on music and their contribution to music education

The influence of literature on nineteenth-century music was all-pervasive, begetting not only the *lied* but the programme symphony. The oratorio, which tells a story in music, as well as the poetic lyricism of Chopin also belongs to a literary-conscious age. In the 'gesamtkunstwerk' of Wagner one recognizes the most deliberate attempt to unify and merge the arts into one indivisible whole. The 'Correspondences' of Baudelaire, the colour-evoking works of Scriabin and the symbolist-inspired music of Debussy are further examples of this attempt to blur the edges of the separate art-forms, a preoccupation of so many poets, painters and musicians in nineteenth-century Europe. The literary work of composers such as Berlioz and Schumann, and particularly their literary-inspired music, belong to an age which had transplanted its music and musicians from the distant, cold brilliance of the court, to the everyday reality of the new concert hall. Instrumental music was no longer an abstraction but was 'about' something more tangible, be it an identifiable emotional state or the seeming reality that literature was able to give to music.

It was through literature that English women, particularly, first came to the fore as artists. The novels of Jane Austen, the Brönte sisters, Elizabeth Gaskell and George Eliot, as well as the poems of Elizabeth Barrett-Browning and Christina Rossetti provide a literary backcloth to any discussion of women artists in nineteenth-century England. Much of their art was based on situations observed from everyday life and it is from their writings that much of our understanding of nineteenth-century middle-class mores is based. It is not surprising therefore to find several English women musicians whose literary work commands more than ordinary respect. The poetry of Caroline Norton, a grand-daughter of the playwright Sheridan, was most highly regarded in her day, and her literary fame quite eclipsed that of the composer of 'Juanita', notwithstanding the immense popularity of the song. In a similar way the autobiographical writings of Ethel Smyth brought her more fame than her compositions, indeed, even served to create an interest in her as a composer. Whilst some women musicians took to writing to further social or political ends, for the majority music was the subject which engaged their interest and about which they wrote.

In 1905, Florence May, a composer and pianist, published her two-volume work, *The Life of Johannes Brahms*, which became a standard work on the composer for much of the present century. Brahms emerges as a kindly person and as an excellent teacher. It was not a romanticized picture but one based on friendship and respect arising from six months of lessons which Florence May received from Brahms. It was on Clara Schumann's recommendation, whose pupil Florence May had been, that these twice-weekly lessons were arranged in 1871. From them she learnt much about Brahms's musical sympathies, having persuaded him to play to her at the conclusion of each lesson, and gained a musical insight into the composer which illuminated her writing about him and made it possible for her to become the foremost exponent of his piano music in England. The biography contains an excellent catalogue of his music, benefits from the authenticity of first-hand knowledge and was a major contribution to the appreciation of his music in England. In 1912, Florence May published *The Girlhood of Clara Schumann*, which is notable for its ability to organize biographical details into a readable and convincing whole. Whilst she makes no claim for originality and lists the German sources for much of her information, she does attempt, successfully, to relate the formative years of Clara Schumann to the musical developments of the period. The inter-relationship of composers such as Chopin, Mendelssohn and, of course, Schumann is engrossingly revealed. Friedrich Wieck, Clara's father, emerges as a much more understandable person, the self-made man whose major achievement had been the soundly thought-out musical education he had given to his devoted daughter. His determined and unreasonable opposition to the marriage of his daughter to Robert Schumann is placed in context: to understand is, however, not to condone his behaviour. The greatness of Clara Schumann was nevertheless of his making.

Two books on Handel, one a popular biography and the other a story based on events of Handel's life in England, are of a less scholarly nature. The first, *Handel: his life, personal and professional, with thoughts on sacred music* (1857) by Mrs Bray, author of several novels, gives expression to the veneration with which Handel was regarded in England, that is to say, the Handel of the oratorios. Unapproached as he was, so she claims, by Mozart, Haydn or even Beethoven (though she does mention in a footnote that since making such a claim, Costa had written 'his splendid oratorio of Eli'!), she proceeds to argue that all great men, and Handel is surely one, are, *ipso facto*, good men. Indeed, when we come to her thoughts on sacred music we get to the very heart of the book; 'the manners and morals of the lower orders' would benefit, so she claims, from an appreciation of the music of Handel. She thus propounds the commonly-held belief that the best way to rectify the viciousness of the 'lower orders' was by the improvement of their morals through music. Music and morals, incidentally the title of a nineteenth-century book by the Rev. Haweis, it was thought went hand in hand: 'A young lady's taste in the fine arts is often a tolerable indication of the character of her mind.' (Bray: 1857, p. 88). It found its most eloquent expression in the writings of Ruskin.

A Story of Handel's Day (1900) by Emma Marshall, is centred on the Foundling Hospital and Handel's very great generosity towards that institution. Whilst the references to Handel, and much of the background, have a basis in fact, many of the other characters are fictitious and much opportunity is made, and taken, for sentimental moralizing, a necessary ingredient in most nineteenth-century tales. Pauline Townsend's *Joseph Haydn* (1884) is a straightforward biography in the 'Great Musician Series', edited by Francis Hueffer. She acknowledges her debt to C.F. Pohl particularly, as well as to several other German sources, and then tells the story simply and clearly.

This is certainly not the case with Georgina Weldon whose *Gounod, and my orphanage in England* (in French) and her *Mémoires* (1902) which, although they tell us much about Gounod's two and a half years in London, living in Tavistock House, the home of Mr and Mrs Weldon, are a mixture of adulation, sheer farce and the hatred which arose when Gounod 'deserted' her. As such, they would be of greater interest to a psychologist than to the music historian. Rosa Newmarch's memoir, *Mary Wakefield* is, on the other hand, a good detailed account of the achievements of this remarkable woman and contains a valuable record of the programmes of the Kendal Festivals.

Fanny Raymond-Ritter's *Woman as a musician – an art historical study* (1877), is one of a group of books and articles that deals with music aesthetics. It was written by 'an English poetess and musician' for the Centennial Congress in Philadelphia of the 'Association for the Advancement of Women' in 1877, and attempted to stimulate the members of that Association into some kind of practical involvement in music. The first part of this short address is rather high-flown in its claims for music: 'It is the most transcendental of all arts ... the most complex ... the most ideal of all arts, for it is the beautiful result of unshaken faith in progress towards perfection, and is itself almost a religion in its purity and sublimity.' (Ritter: 1877, pp. 2–3). Such eulogistic writing fortunately gives way to a down-to-earth assessment of the role of women in music in which the rise of opera is seen as the real beginning for women as public artists. She makes a good point about women's contribution to folk-music: 'I have no doubt but that many of those simple, touching, heartbreaking melodies and poems were of women's creation.' (Ritter: 1877, p. 4), citing lullabies and cradle-songs particularly, and certain places, such as Ireland and the Basque provinces, where women improvised the wakes for the dead. She mentions several women active in folk-song collection, including Fernan Caballero, the nineteenth-century Spanish collector, Countess Dufferin and Miss Brooke as translators of many Irish folk-songs from the original Celtic into English, and records the assistance given by Countess de la Villermarqué to her son in the collection of Breton folk-songs. Coussemaker, she claims, wrote down the larger part of Flemish folk-songs from the lips of the poor lace-makers of Holland and she mentions that

Chopin and Pauline Viardot Garcia spent many hours together noting down French peasant songs. A certain Fraülein von Jackob she credits with the collection and publication of a large number of Servian folk-songs.[32]

Of women performers she dwells particularly on the prima donnas, stating that Vittoria Archilei, a singer at the court in Florence, took part in the first public Italian opera in 1600: unfortunately she does not state which opera this was. 'Eurydice' by Jacopo Peri, performed in Florence in 1600, is usually regarded as the first opera and Francesca Caccini, soprano, appeared in it. The first public opera house is usually associated with the opening of the Teatro San Cassiano in Venice in 1637, and perhaps some confusion exists here in her claim for Vittoria Archilei. She mentions Faustina Bordoni, the wife of Hasse; Caterina Gabrielli, a pupil of Metastatsio, both of whom had medals struck in their honour; Madame Mara, for whom Goethe wrote a birthday poem; and Mrs Billington who, she says, was accused by the superstitious Neopolitans of causing the eruption of Mount Vesuvius in 1794 by her wonderful vocal powers. Turning to nineteenth-century performers she sees in Clara Schumann and Pauline Viardot Garcia the ideal female artist corresponding to that envisaged by George Sand in her novel, *Consuelo*.

In composition she sees the utmost value for women:

> I would suggest the adoption of the science of Composition as an elective, if not obligatory, branch of the higher course of study in Ladies' Colleges ... I do not hesitate to pronounce it equal ... to Mathematics ... and is far more likely to prove of practical benefit to women in after-life, than the study of the other science. (*Ritter*: 1877, p. 10)

In regarding composition as a science of practical value to women, Fanny Ritter shows her limited understanding of music and allows enthusiasm to run away with her. She admits that women have not made their mark as composers because of the 'long and deep scientific study involved', but does cite a few women composers such as Princess Amalie, sister of Frederick the Great, who composed operas and cantatas, and Fanny Hensel, Mendelssohn's sister, whose ability as a composer has already been referred to in Chapter 2. She believes that as patrons women have served composers very well and mentions Marie Antoinette's support of Gluck in Paris and Madame von Breuning's 'intellectual mothering' of Beethoven. She firmly believed that all women should sing for health's sake, since singing animates the face and improves respiration, and that music exercises a 'positive moral force upon her hearers'. She concludes by imploring her listeners to sustain 'the efforts of gifted women-artists compelled by sacred duty or sublime adversity to make a public display of their talents.' (Ritter: 1877, p. 14). Whilst it is a superficial and sometimes erroneous work, it is however an example of a nineteenth-century English woman musician examining the role of women in music, and is certainly an address of hope rather than one of recrimination.

In an article entitled *Music* by Lady Eastlake, reprinted from the *Quarterly Review* in 1852, there are some refreshing thoughts on the nature of music. To her own question 'Can music make us more intelligent, or more prudent, or more practical or more moral?' (Eastlake: 1852, p. 9), she replies quite categorically that it cannot. All that it can do is to kindle our imagination. 'She [music] appeals neither to our reason, our principles nor our honour ... she can as little point a moral as she can paint a picture ... We can only make her a means of harm when we add speech to sound ... Nor is it possible to form any theory of the class of minds most susceptible of her influence – facts stop and contradict us at every stop.' (Eastlake: 1852, p. 9). To a later generation this may all seem very obvious, but hers was very much a lone voice in mid-Victorian England. From Sarah Glover and George Hogarth at the beginning of the Victorian age, through Curwen to Ruskin in the latter part of the century one tenet remained inviolate: music was a morally uplifting agent.

A full discussion of Mary Wakefield's *Ruskin on Music* is reserved for Chapter 4 when Mary Wakefield's total contribution to the dissemination of music in nineteenth-century England is considered. A brief résumé is in place here since Ruskin's views, mostly shared by Mary Wakefield, do reflect the aesthetic of his day in seeing in music a force for moral uplift. Though Ruskin was not a musician, or indeed even very knowledgeable about it in a practical way, it did not prevent him from making several dogmatic assertions as to the purpose and nature of music. Mary Wakefield believed that he understood intuitively the 'deep meaning' of music and edited his various comments into a presentable whole.

There was no place for levity in Ruskin's art-world: everything had to be of the purest and loftiest intent. The commercialization of music and its consequent debasement was everywhere to be seen in nineteenth-century England and to some extent it accounted for a reaction similar to that which some aspects of commercialized 'Pop' music has provoked in the twentieth century.

In her long and disorganized collection of letters and articles called *Musical Reform* (1875) Georgina Weldon exposes many of the abuses of this new commercialization. Whilst not subscribing to the views of Ruskin, she does certainly share some of his and Mary Wakefield's concern for the musical education of the young. Being a practical and highly determined woman she set up her own orphanage which she hoped would develop into a National Training School for Music. There are few of her articles which do not refer to this scheme, and from 1870 it became her abiding mission in life. To get money for this project she sang wherever she could get engagements, organized concerts, and inveigled Gounod to associate himself with the venture. Not having been trained professionally as a musician, she quite naturally felt that she was an 'outsider' in the musical establishment of London. Certainly, she was right to see in much nineteenth-century music in London commercial intrigues at work. In a letter to the editor of the *Cosmopolitan* magazine, dated 8 August, 1873, headed 'Musical Reform', she puts her views in no uncertain terms: 'When an Art becomes a trade, and nothing but a trade, it must become prostituted . . . Publishers, critics, agents and managers are leagued together in a gigantic swindle for the ruin of the Art they persuade the public to believe is being encouraged and improved.' (Weldon: 1875, pp. 5–6). Samuel Sebastian Wesley, organist of Gloucester Cathedral, wrote to her in support and there were no doubt several other musicians who would have agreed with her strictures, in private. She cited the National Music Meetings at the Crystal Palace, which were solo competitions, as a particular example of a commercial enterprise to the detriment of music. All competitors had to prepare ten designated songs though each would be required to sing only one or two from the list. Many competitors, she claimed, were never heard, preference being given to Academy or professionally trained students, and thus many poor girls from country districts particularly, were involved in unnecessary expense to no avail. It was only the publishers of the music, she argued, who benefited from such competitions. Another of her targets was the music copyright laws as a result of which, she claimed, Gounod received no royalties for his music performed in England. It was a complicated issue, and one which she may have aggravated by her flamboyant manner of dealing with it on Gounod's behalf, but nevertheless, there was a case for reform. So often the causes for which she fought were worthwhile, but her manner alienated many who could have helped. There are other aspects of the writings of Georgina Weldon which will be dealt with at a later stage; for the present it is interesting to note how she differs from Ruskin in her reaction against the commercialization of music. Ruskin's idealism is as unpractical as Georgina Weldon's scheme for establishing a National Training School for Music. It is, however, to her theories and ideals, and not the way she set about implementing them, that one is drawn in sympathy.

The practitioners of music, rather than music itself, were a more popular topic for some nineteenth-century writers, particularly if the practitioners happened to be the nineteenth-century equivalent of the twentieth-century's film stars, that is, singers. Working on the assumption that 'love of art creates love of artist' Ellen Clayton presents many well-observed portraits of celebrated female singers in Italy, Germany, France and England, the four main homes of opera, in her *Queens of Song* (1863). She informs us that, from the dawn of opera in England, rivalry between respective prima donnas was usual and gives an amusing account of the first two female singers to attract theatrical audiences in England, Katherine Tofts and the Italian, Margarita de l'Epine. In the opera, *Arsinoe* (1705) by Thomas Clayton, Katherine Tofts sang the title role and Margarita de l'Epine, who spoke no English, sang Italian arias before and after the opera. *The Daily Courant*, 8 February, 1705, carried the following letter from Katherine Tofts:

> Sir – I was very much surprised when I was informed that Ann Barwick, who was lately my servant, had committed a rudeness last night at the playhouse, by throwing oranges and hissing when Mrs. l'Epine, the Italian gentlewoman, sung. I hope no one will think it was with my privity, as I assure you it was not. I abhor such practices: and I hope you will cause her to be prosecuted, that she may be punished as she deserves. I am sir, your humble servant, Katherine Tofts.

One suspects that the poor servant girl had not acted entirely on her own account.[33] Ellen Clayton tells us that Mrs l'Epine married (presumably her second marriage) Dr Pepusch, having acquired £10,000 as a singer, thus enabling him to live in a style to which he had always aspired but had never been able to afford. It was hardly a love-match since he referred to her as Hecate on account of her ugliness. Mrs Tofts, alas, ended her days insane.

Perhaps the most bizarre character described by Ellen Clayton, one more understandable today in the light of Freudian psychology, is that of La Maupin, the French singer and one-time pupil of Lully. Having taken to performing men's parts, she took to dressing as a man in real life. Her 'male' adventures included murder and the 'seduction' of a young nun from a convent. She seems to belong more to the surrealistic world of Edgar Allan Poe's imagination rather than to the dawning 'Age of Reason'. It is interesting to discover from Ellen Clayton that it is not a twentieth-century phenomenon for musicians to dictate fashions of dress, for in 1725, when Cuzzoni sang in Handel's *Rodelinda*, the brown silk dress embroidered with silver which she wore was adopted, almost as a uniform, by fashionable young ladies. As social comment her *Queen of Song* is a fascinating book.

Gossip of the Century by Julia Byrne (1892) is much more superficial, being elevated gossip column writing concerned largely with high society. Only volume two relates to musicians, including as it does anecdotes about Mrs Billington, Catalani, Gounod and Mrs Weldon. The latter comes in for barbed comment in true gossip-column style: 'Mrs Weldon – at that time young and very pretty (though it does not appear she had then begun to use Pears' soap.)' (Byrne: 1892, p. 44), which refers to the fact that in order to raise money for her orphanage, Georgina Weldon consented to advertising Pears' soap, and her photo with the caption, 'I am 50 but my complexion is 17 – thanks to Pears' soap' appeared on London buses. Such vulgarity by one who had been fêted by London society was unpardonable.

Autobiographical reminiscences were expected of most artists and containing, as they often did, incidental descriptions of foreign lands and customs, were of more than purely musical interest. Indeed, some of the later writings of Ethel Smyth were simply travelogues without any musical significance at all. Clara Novello's *Reminiscences* (1910), compiled and edited from her diaries by her daughter, Contessa Valeria Gigliucci, is one of the most interesting of the autobiographical reminiscences, being well-written and edited and marked throughout by a refreshing frankness. Of her marriage to the Italian, Count Gigliucci, she recounts that: 'Seven nuns were amongst my nearest new relatives and naturally to these, a theatrical artist could only be an imp of Satan! "Tridini"[34] were offered by them to prevent our union – in vain.' (Novello: 1910, p. 121). Whilst being a religious person, and it will be remembered that she excelled as an oratorio singer, she was not blinded to the faults of the church: 'Priests ever persecuted the stage . . . The

Gallican Church even denied its sacraments to theatrical artists.' (Novello: 1910, pp. 137–138). Again, commenting on Florence Nightingale, whom she admired, and to whom she sang when she was bedridden, she says, 'As ever with superiority and extra, incomprehensible goodness, she was much criticised, blamed as unfeminine, as hunting for a husband (!) . . . Amongst the most censorious, as usual, were the clergy.' (Novello: 1910, p. 163). Her description of Spontini whose ' . . . house was a gallery of portraits of himself, alternating with sonnets in his praise, busts of himself, etc., all the way to his own sort of throne room, where he sat on a raised dais in an armchair with his portraits, busts, medals and sonnets all around him.' (Novello: 1910, p. 70) is as vivid as her more earthy description of Queen Isabella of Spain, 'Such animal eyes I never beheld, and I blushed only to look at her – a very pig's countenance.' (Novello: 1910, p. 149). Of Liszt and his women followers she leaves us in no uncertainty as to her opinion:

> At Venice, as elsewhere, when he broke the strings of the piano during concerts, the women rushed onto the platform to seize them and have bracelets made of them; and when he left Vienna, fifteen or twenty carriagefuls of these cracked creatures pursued him as far as the first station where change of post-horses took place. (*Novello*: 1910, p. 102)

She informs us that Liszt encouraged this behaviour, there being several spare pianos ready in the wings for when the strings were deliberately broken!

In one so open-minded it comes as a surprise to discover that for several years she refused to sing in Verdi's *Rigoletto* because of the male attire required in the last act. Victorian prudery at what she describes as 'exposure of person' was eventually overcome when a special costume was designed for her. Another surprise is to discover from her that it was normal for women singers to take snuff. It was, apparently, Clara Novello who began the practice of using 'Madame' after she had married, since she objected to the confusion arising from married women retaining 'Miss' for professional purposes. The idea was indiscriminately followed and confusion was as rife as before.

In Mary Cowden-Clarke's (née Novello) *The Life and Labours of Vincent Novello* (1864) the Novello family background is sketched in and tribute paid to the energy and enterprise of both parents. Vincent Novello, celebrated organist and teacher, became increasingly interested in antiquarian research[35] and his large amount of editing included five volumes of Purcell's Sacred Music, some of which would have been lost for ever had he not made his copies before a fire at York Minster which destroyed many original manuscripts. His musical evenings for his family and friends, which often included Charles and Mary Lamb, Leigh Hunt and sometimes Keats and Shelley were imitated by other families and thus set the pattern for many Victorian households. His seven surviving children were all musical and the *Thanksgiving after Enjoyment* which he wrote for one such evening indicates the musical standard of these evenings (Example 16). Mary Cowden-Clarke became a noted Shakespearean scholar, editing the complete Concordance to Shakespeare as well as making studies of Shakespeare's female characters. In 1858 she published her *World-Noted Female Characters* thus showing that her interest in the female character was not only literary but historical. Her very active life is well-documented in her book, *My Long Life* (1896).

The contents of Emily Soldene's *My Theatrical and Musical Recollections* (1897) have already been discussed in Chapter 1. The book is an entertaining account of her singing career, of the early Music Halls and of the setting up and travels of her opera company which she took to America on several occasions. She is very much the female impresario, a person of outstanding vitality and resilience. The two autobiographical books by Maude Valérie White, *Friends and Memories* (1914) and *My Indian Summer* (1932) complement one another, the latter book taking up the story of her life after World War One. Her mastery of several European languages is accounted for by her cosmopolitan upbringing, having been born in Normandy of English parents into a family where all the elder children spoke only Spanish, the family having but recently returned to Europe from Chile where her father had been in business. Her governess was German and it was to Germany that she went for her early schooling, which was continued in England from the age of eight at a boys' preparatory school and finished in Paris. She was taught music by Oliver May, Florence May's uncle, and his excellent tuition led to her gaining a piano scholarship at the Royal Academy of Music. Her foreign travels, which she delighted in, were numerous and adventurous, including visits to the Caucasus, America and to Italy particularly. Liza Lehmann's *The Life of Liza Lehmann* (1919) is well written and is perhaps more musically interesting than the books of Maude Valérie White. It is very much a factual account of her early musical influences, of her singing career and of the genesis of her major

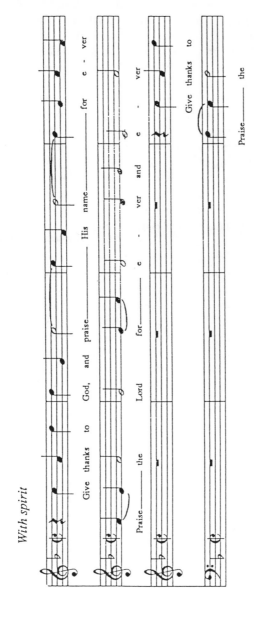

Example 16 *A Thanksgiving After Enjoyment (Vincent Novello)*

121

compositions. A warm, sensitive person emerges, almost by accident, so lacking is the book in egotistical trumpetings. The contrast is the more marked when compared with the autobiographical writing of her contemporary, Ethel Smyth (see Chapter 5).

My Musical Experiences (1890) by Bettina Walker provides first-hand insight into the teaching of Sterndale Bennett, Tausig, Sgambati, Henselt, and other continental masters, as well as containing some interesting impressions of Liszt, to whom she played, and of his afternoon 'soirées' which he held thrice weekly. *Charles Auchester* (1853) by Elizabeth Sheppard was a popular novel which contained thinly-disguised portraits of Sterndale Bennett ('Starwood Burney') and of Mendelssohn ('Seraphael') that so captured Walker's imagination that after much persistence she was able to persuade her parents to arrange lessons for her with Sterndale Bennett. He appears as a most painstaking teacher of limited musical tastes, having no sympathy for Chopin, or at first, for Schumann. The book is particularly informative on Liszt and his circle of fawning pupils (of which she was one) at Weimar. She studied piano at the Berlin Academy and eventually under Henselt at St Petersburg. As a study of certain nineteenth-century piano teachers in England, Germany and Russia it is an interesting book, particularly if considered in conjunction with Florence May's writings on Brahms as a piano teacher. Another book, *Music-Study in Germany* (1855) by Amy Fay is mentioned in passing, since, though written by an American, it does cover similar ground to that of Bettina Walker. It became a very popular book, being reprinted on seven separate occasions, as well as being translated into German. The authoress describes music study in Berlin in 1869 under Tausig and Elhert, based on letters sent home. As a result the descriptions have an immediacy and contain many interesting observations on German culture at that time. Certainly her fellow students were international, many of them being women.

It was in 1859 that Sarah Glover produced her *Dissertation upon the relationship between colour and music*. She was not alone in this preoccupation for two other women published books on the subject. *Rainbow Music, or the Philosophy of Harmony in Colour-Grouping* (1886) by Lady Campbell lacks the scientific mind that Sarah Glover was able to bring to the subject, and in its attempt to describe the 'harmony' of the colours of a room in musical terms exposes the poverty of her thought. *Harmonies of Tones and Colours developed by Evolution* (1883) by Mrs F.J. Hughes is much more lavishly produced and of even more dubious value. On the slender basis of being related to Charles Darwin, the authoress, it would seem, attempts to trace some evolutionary colour-sound pattern in the build-up of scales. This is also linked with copious quotations from the Bible such as, 'As silver tried in a furnace of earth, purified seven times.' (Psalm xii, v. 6) with which the reader is to be persuaded that there is some mystical relationship between colour and the major scale. Both books deserve their long rest in oblivion.

A much more profitable and lasting labour was that carried out by Lucy Broadwood (1858–1929). Following in the footsteps of her uncle, John Broadwood, who in 1843 published the first genuine collection of English folk-songs noted down from folk-singers. Lucy Broadwood, in collaboration with J.A. Fuller-Maitland published in 1893 *English Country Songs*. This collection, in which all the songs had been noted down from singers, with words and melodies unaltered by editorial quirks, set an example to all subsequent collectors in its scholarly presentation and attention to detail.[36] An attempt was made to include at least one folk-song from each English county, and the date, place and singers were noted with each song that was included. Whilst many women singers[37] and collectors are acknowledged in the text, including Mary Wakefield who contributed two Cumberland songs, *Sally Gray* and *A North Country Maid*, special reference is made in the Preface to the *Nursery Rhymes and County Songs* collected by Miss Mason (1877) and the Shropshire folk-songs collected by Miss Charlotte Burn. The collection also includes the Suffolk song, *Oliver Cromwell* which had been collected by Lucy Broadwood herself. In the Preface it was noted that in country districts where the *Tonic Sol-fa* choral movement had penetrated, folk-singing had tended to disappear: 'It is perhaps natural, after all, that young people brought up on the Tonic Sol-fa system, with all that it involves in the way of fatuous part-songs and non-alcoholic revelries, should turn up their noses at the long-winded ballads or roystering ale-house songs beloved of their grandparents.' (Broadwood & Fuller-Maitland: 1893, Preface, p. iv). *Tonic Sol-fa* arose originally out of the need for a simple system of notation which would facilitate the singing of psalms and church music generally: as such it tended to have strong moral overtones which brought in its wake much banal music. A lot of education was needed to enable the newly-awakened musical conscience of the nation to learn to distinguish between music of enduring worth, such as folk-songs, and the trivialities of the age.

Lucy Broadwood devoted many years of her life to rescuing English folk-song from total oblivion. Reference has already been made to John Broadwood's collection, published in 1843, which Lucy Broadwood reissued in 1889 with additional songs which she had collected under the title of *Sussex Songs*. Her main areas of activity were Surrey, Sussex, the Scottish Highlands and Ireland. In an appendix (B) to Walter Jekyll's *Jamaican Song and Story* (1907) Lucy Broadwood shows something of the wealth of her knowledge of folk-music when she attempts to trace English folk influences in the music of Jamaica. That the English Folk-Song Society was founded was largely due to her efforts, and for several years she was the very active secretary. In 1908 she published *English Traditional Songs and Carols* and her many contributions to the journal of the Folk-Song Society are testaments to her indefatigable industry and expertise.

Whilst Lucy Broadwood was pre-eminent amongst women folk-song collectors in England, there were others who also contributed to the very late harvest of English folk-song. Alice Gomme published *Children's Singing Games* in 1894 and extended her work, in collaboration with Cecil Sharp, in the series of publications of the same title in the years 1909–1912. Alice Gillington published several collections which included *Eight Hampshire Folk-Songs*, *Breton Singing Games* and *Old Christmas Carols of the Southern Counties*, and Anne Gilchrist jointly edited with Lucy Broadwood a collection of songs from Skye. In 1906, Anne Gilchrist joined the editorial board of the Folk-Song Society and made a significant contribution to its work, becoming an authority on the history of folk-tunes and hymn-tunes. Her work has been carried on by Maud Karpeles, who worked with Cecil Sharp from 1911–1924, the consideration of whose contribution is outside the scope of this study, as is that of Marjory Kennedy-Fraser.[38]

Many and varied were the avenues of music explored by English women in the nineteenth century. Ability to speak a foreign language, usually French, German or Italian was usual for educated English girls, and was a practical necessity for singers. It is not surprising that translating texts into English became a popular occupation for some women musicians. Lady Clara Natalia Macfarren translated many opera texts into English as did Constance Bache: the text of Bach's *St Matthew Passion* was translated into English by Helen Johnston for the first English performance in 1853. Lady Wallace, whom we have already mentioned in connection with her translation of Elise Polko's *Reminiscences of*

Mendelssohn, translated letters by Mendelssohn, Mozart, Beethoven, Gluck and Haydn. Liszt's letters were made available to English readers by Constance Bache along with the texts of many of his songs. She also translated Wagner's *Descriptive Sketch of Beethoven's Ninth Symphony,* the libretto of Humperdinck's *Hänsel and Gretel* and other writings by Schumann and Wagner. Like Schumann, Constance Bache had aimed at a career as a concert pianist, but a damaged hand had prevented this.

Two Mozart biographies were translated by women: Otto John's *Mozart* was translated into English by Pauline Townsend and an exhaustive index added by her, and Lady Wallace translated Nohl's *Mozart.* Ehlert's *Letters on Music to a lady* and Schumann's *Music and Musicians* were translated into English by Mrs Raymond-Ritter, and Mary Grant Carmichael translated Ehrlich's *Celebrated Pianists of the past and present.* Of a more technical nature were the thorough-bass methods, piano method and singing-school method translated from the German by Sabilla Novello, the exact details of which can be found in the bibliography. Her sister, Mary Cowden-Clarke, translated Berlioz's *Modern Instrumentation and Orchestration* in 1856 as well as a treatise on harmony by Catel. Maude Valérie White's command of languages can be judged from her translation of books in Swedish, German and French, though none include works related to music. (See bibliography for details.)

Agnes Zimmermann was pre-eminent as an editor of piano music which included the piano sonatas of Mozart and Beethoven and the complete piano music of Schumann. In addition to her folk-song editing Lucy Broadwood found time to edit some Purcell songs in 1896, whilst a Mrs J.D. Bate compiled the *North India Tune-Book* in 1886, the tunes having been taken down from native singers. The introduction attempts to explain something of the nature of Indian music, and the book is an example of interest being shown in music of a non-European origin.

Increasingly throughout the nineteenth century women contributed to the many musical journals. Indeed, for the years 1853 to 1856 the *Musical Times* was edited by a woman, Mary Novello.[39] She also wrote several articles which included *Music in Dresden* and the *Festival of the Salzburg Mozart Institution.* The latter arose out of her visit, with her sister Sabilla, to Salzburg exactly fifty years after that of her father and mother, who had presented a sum of money on behalf of English Mozartians to Mozart's sister. Mary and Sabilla were accordingly treated with great respect in Salzburg. The Novello sisters Clara, Mary and Sabilla made a most distinctive contribution to English musical life, following the example of their father. Articles of an antiquarian nature by Mary Armitt appeared in the *Musical Times* and the *Quarterly Musical Review* on subjects such as 'Old English Viol Music' and 'Old English Fingering'. She devoted much of her life to musicology and was for a period of time music critic to the *Manchester City News*. Other contributors to music journals included Mary Wakefield,[40] Anne Gilchrist, who contributed particularly to the journal *The Choir*, Lucy Broadwood and Georgina Weldon, a prolific letter writer.

Whilst the presence of women was certainly felt in a whole variety of musical spheres, it was perhaps as teachers and in music education generally that they brought the greatest influence to bear. The work of Sarah Glover is perhaps the single most important of these contributions, though the work of Maria Hackett in improving educational facilities in Choir Schools, of Mary Wakefield and her competitive choral festivals and a host of other female educationists need to be examined and evaluated. Collectively, their impact was considerable and was a significant offering to the development of music education in England.

Music was afforded an honoured place in the curriculum of the emerging state elementary schools, being regarded as important as reading and writing because of its 'civilizing' influence. It was on account of the latter that the Committee of the Council in 1840–1841 argued its place in the curriculum, and Hullah's edition of Wilhelm's *Method of Teaching Singing* was issued as the official method of instruction in schools by the aforesaid Committee. It was not supplanted by Curwen's *Tonic Sol-fa* until 1872 when the deficiencies of the former method had been fully realized: the moveable 'doh' of *Tonic Sol-fa* having already been proved, through its adoption by adult classes, a much more useful concept when dealing with key-changes. Music in the state elementary schools meant class-singing and several collections of school songs were published by women. Helen Heale had been a pupil of Hullah and it is therefore to be expected that she would involve herself with the classroom music. Her *Class-Singing School* (1887) is in four progressive books beginning with the rudiments and moving through the major and minor scales to songs in two, three and four parts. Solfeggio exercises taken from actual music, and canons, are included. In addition to *Tonic Sol-fa* names she uses figures for the degrees of the scale, which is slightly confusing, as is her use of the continental 'Si' for the seventh degree of the scale. Her

Short Voice-Training Exercises in Two and Three Parts for Singing Classes (1898) are systematic and foreshadow the early two-part intervallic exercises of the much later Kodaly. *The Day School Hymn Book*, edited by Emma Mundella, contains a good selection of hymns at a suitable pitch for children's voices. *Voice and Vocal Art* (1856) by Sabilla Novello is a short treatise written for teachers and students of singing, which is a straightforward, largely non-technical account of voice production, a treatise which was very much needed in an age which made such a mystique of the art of singing.

The opinions of Georgina Weldon on the matter of singing instruction anticipate twentieth-century developments in Hungary. In a letter to the *Cosmopolitan* in 1873 entitled 'The National Training School of Music', she called for a uniform system in which all future teachers would be trained, for vocal training to begin at three years of age concentrating on naturalness and simplicity of style, and claimed that all children, whatever their background, could be taught to sing. She regarded sight-singing as a most important element in any form of musical education and contrary to accepted thought at that time she encouraged boys to sing whilst their voices were changing. Above all she emphasized the value of good diction and was strongly opposed to all unnecessary ornamentation. Certainly she did achieve some remarkable results with the children in her orphanage as Julius Benedict implies in his letter to her of 1871: 'I heard three of your pupils – poor boys from eight to fifteen years of age, who after a few months' instruction only, without any previous knowledge of music, sang the inner parts of a grand and difficult composition with faultless intonation, distinct enunciation of the words, and in excellent style.'

The Schools' Inquiry Commission of 1864 was very critical of girls' education in its 'want of thoroughness and foundation' and led to the inauguration of many girls' high schools. There were several older schools which served as examples and these included the North London Collegiate School, where Miss Buss was Headmistress, Cheltenham Ladies College under Miss Beale, the Ladies' Educational Institute at Leeds, the Godolphin School in Salisbury and the Quaker boarding school, 'The Mount', which began at York in 1821. Until the later decades of the nineteenth century, education for the majority of girls was restricted to elementary education; the more wealthy were able to afford to send their daughters to private boarding schools and the fee-paying endowed schools where they usually stayed until the age of eighteen.

Music, as one of the 'accomplishments', played a large part in the private schools as this extract from *The Life of Francis Power Cobbe as told by herself* indicates:

> Everything was taught in the inverse ratio of its true importance. At the bottom of the scale were Morals and Religion, and at the top were Music and Dancing: miserably poor music, too, of the Italian School then in vogue . . . It mattered nothing whether we had any 'music in our souls' or any voices in our throats, equally we were driven through the dreary course of practising daily for a couple of hours under a German teacher . . . The waste of money involved in all this, the piles of useless music, and songs never to be sung, for which our parents had to pay, and the loss of priceless time for ourselves, were truly deplorable . . . and the result of course in many cases (as in my own) complete failure. (*Godsen*: 1969, p. 146)

One of the great problems in getting musical education onto a realistic basis in the girls' schools was the lack of opportunities for women to train as music teachers.[41] Indeed, the concept of teacher training as opposed to pupil-teacher training in the schools, was still a relatively new one in the middle years of the century, and for women the opportunities to train as teachers were limited. Unless they attended full-time one of the Colleges of Music – and until the 1870s there was only one, the Royal Academy of Music – women were not able to acquire worthwhile musical qualifications. Universities would not allow women to graduate and thus it was in order to provide a system of graded musical qualifications open to anyone, that Trinity College of Music began local examinations in 1876 in both theory and practice of music, and also inaugurated a Special Higher Examination for Women at the College: ' . . . in response to an increasing demand for a system of Certificates guaranteeing the musical proficiency of Governesses and other Female Teachers and practitioners . . .' (Rutland: 1972, p. 15). In 1877 there were over one thousand entries for the first examinations in Elementary Musical Knowledge and a five pound prize was offered to the candidate with the highest marks. It was won by Emilie Grant who eventually became a Doctor of Music of Dublin University. That Trinity College of Music had discovered a large market for its certificates there was no doubt, and shortly afterwards other London Colleges of Music set up their own local examination systems.

The need for training music teachers was acute: class music teaching required different skills and attitudes from individual private tuition and no one recognized this more than Walter Carroll who, in 1907, founded the first training course for music teachers in Manchester. One hundred and twenty-seven teachers enrolled. He recruited two very able women to help him, namely Hilda Collens, who had proved a capable music teacher at Sale High School for Girls, and Annie Curwen, the daughter-in-law of John Curwen. Hilda Collens later began her own Academy with nine female students, an Academy which developed into the Northern School of Music.[42] Annie Curwen set forth some of her views on music education in two stimulating articles in *Child Life*, April 1899 and October 1899. The first is entitled 'Music in Concrete' and the second 'Should all children be taught music, or only the gifted?' both of which appear as Appendix 1 and Appendix 2 in Mrs J. Spencer-Curwen's book, *Psychology Applied to Music Teaching*. Her first article deserves wider circulation, so soundly argued is it in every detail. Ideas such as 'one should teach theory through practice, not before' and 'nothing but music can teach music' were fairly novel in the nineteenth century. When she says that 'the less apparatus we use in music teaching the better [since] musical thinking has to be done with songs, not things' she speaks with a relevance to the late twentieth century. The question posed by her second article, as relevant in the state-supported schools of today as in hers, she answers as follows:

> The aims of musical education, bien conçue, I take to be these:
> a) To aid in the general development of the human being, so that every sense may contribute to the whole soul-content.
> b) To create intelligent listeners, for whom the artist, the gifted one, may work.
> c) To find the talent which shall be worth cultivating to a higher degree: the material from which to make the fine executant: and – more precious still – the wise teacher, who will help to create and hand on a better tradition.
> Admit these principles, and not only must we recognise the claim of *every* child to be musically educated up to a certain stage, but we shall see the advisability of a process of selection after that stage has been reached; seeing that music is only part of general culture, and that natural ability may be making loud calls in quite another direction. (*Curwen*: u.d., p. 295)

Walter Carroll was most fortunate in his two assistants!

Little has been recorded of the musical activities of the nineteenth-century girls' high schools even though the Schools' Commission of 1864–1867 estimated that on average a girl spent one quarter of her time on music and only one third on arithmetic. This may not have been the case in the more academically conscious schools such as the North London Collegiate School, where curriculum time for music would be less generous than in elementary schools. As it has already been noted, 'music' in girls' schools usually implied private tuition and not class music. However, certain girls' high schools attracted some very able women music teachers, for example, Angela Macirone was in charge of music at Ashe's School for Girls, Hatcham, from 1872 to 1878, and then at the Church of England School for Girls, Baker Street, London where, it is claimed, 'She systematised the music teaching with the best results.' (Brown & Stratton: 1897, p. 262). The Baker Street school appears to have had a strong music bias offering both Junior and Senior School scholarships in music. Oliveria Prescott also taught at the school from 1879 to 1893 and both she and Angela Macirone contributed many articles on music education to various magazines. 'A Plea for Music' by Angela Macirone appeared in the *Girls' Own* as part of a series of essays on music and was well reviewed in the *Musical Times* of 1 November, 1884. In it, Angela Macirone argues that the idea of music as an 'accomplishment' in girls' schools should be abolished and calls for a much more 'professional' approach to school and amateur music generally. She was herself a respected composer and Professor of piano at the Royal Academy of Music. Oliveria Prescott presented six lectures, *About music and what it is made of*,[43] in 1893 which arose out of her work as harmony teacher at the Baker Street school. Amongst her many activities was that of correspondence tutor in harmony and composition for the correspondence course organized by Newnham College, Cambridge. Manchester High School for Girls attracted the first woman B. Mus. of Manchester University (1894) in Marian Miller; Edith Swepstone taught at the City of London School and Emma Mundella was music mistress at St Elphin's Clergy Daughters' School for Girls. In most cases the teachers named had established a professional reputation in one branch or other of music and adapted their music skills to teaching. The 'Girls' School Music Union', founded in 1904 with Lady Mary Lygon as President, heard at its first meeting of the poor state of music generally in the Girls' High Schools. With regard to singing, they were not as competent as the elementary schools – at least, that was the opinion of Dr Arthur Somervell who was the guest speaker. The boys' Public Schools had made great strides with music, largely influenced by the work of Thring of Uppingham, showing what could be achieved with pupils of the secondary age range. The Board of Education Memorandum, *Music in Secondary Schools* (1906), was timely, arguing for the recognition of music as an integral part of the curriculum, and its recommendations were welcomed by the 'Girls' School Music Union' which went from strength to strength in the early years of the century. Schools like the Baker Street High School for Girls and Roedean were exceptional in the range and standard of music achieved.

When considering Sarah Glover's contribution as a teacher it was said that in her many attempts to engage the pupils in music rather than instruct them in theory she was ahead of her time. Annie Gunn, a contemporary of Sarah Glover, who was also a teacher of young ladies, faced the same problems as Glover, namely, the extreme complication of existing notation. In her *Introduction to Music*, published in Edinburgh in 1803, Annie Gunn discusses, as she saw them, the two methods of instruction available to a teacher, either 'by a steady and rigorous discipline' or ' . . . by employing some means which may engage the fancy, and rendering the subjects of instruction, in some degree, amusing and interesting. This last is certainly to be preferred, whenever it is practicable.' (Gunn: 1803 Preface, i). She found that what she taught of 'musical science' in one lesson was soon forgotten, even if it had been understood at the time. Whilst Sarah Glover took a much more revolutionary step and formulated a new notation, Annie Gunn put her energies into making existing notation comprehensible through the use of games, the aim of which: ' . . . is to facilitate the acquisition of musical science. Subordinate to this it has been the wish of the inventor to render them amusing and interesting.' (Gunn: 1803, p. ix). These games had been first published in 1801; the 1803 *Introduction to Music* was the means of explaining them and their purpose. A second edition was published in 1820. A 'dumb clavier' was provided so that the pupil had to 'rationalize' the games, although the writer stresses that the harmony 'games' should be attempted on a piano first.

Whilst in theory her method had a great deal to commend it, a perusal of the games on key-signatures, intervals, harmony and modulation contradicts this view. One of the points made in Annie Curwen's article *Music in the Concrete* that 'The tendency of musical apparatus is not so much to over-condense as to over-elaborate.' (Curwen: u.d., p. 208) comes very much to mind when confronted with 'musical games' involving double sharps and double flats. It was a pity that such a forward-looking attitude to teaching was not matched by a more revolutionary approach to the teaching of the language of music.

Many indeed were the theoretical treatises produced throughout the nineteenth century which were simply catechisms. *A Catechism of Music for the use of Young Children* (1856) by Gertrude Place consists entirely of questions and answers on musical theory, devoid of any explanation. Kate Paige's *Exercises on General Elementary Music* (1881) took the process one stage further, and omits the answers. It did become a popular 'primer' for the new local examinations instituted by the London Colleges of Music and as such went into five editions. Oliveria Prescott's *Form, or Design in Music, Instrumental and Vocal* (1882, revised 1894, with assistance from George Macfarren) appeared originally as articles in *Musical World* and the book bears witness to the fact. Whilst various chapters contain much information they hardly relate to each other and do not contribute to any kind of overall unity. Part analytical, part historical it is a disjointed affair with the 'ballad' claiming disproportionate space in relation to its significance as a musical form.

Treatises for private tuition abounded, particularly on singing and playing the piano, and many of these were by women. Two particularly good vocal tutors by Helen Sainton Dolby (1872) and Liza Lehmann (1913) claim our attention first. *Madam Sainton Dolby's Tutor for English Singers (Ladies voices)* is an attempt to provide an English method of voice production suitable for oratorio and ballad singing. All the exercises are drawn from existing music, principally that of Handel, and build to songs chosen from oratorios and ballads, with helpful comments on technical and interpretative matters. In *Practical Hints for Students of Singing*, Liza Lehmann draws on some of the help and advice she received as a student from Jenny Lind, encouraging, for example, the student to develop the use of the head voice throughout the whole range of the voice. Many exercises are included and an excellent selection of songs drawn from Handel, Schubert, Stanford and Scottish folk-songs are chosen for the practice of various techniques. Georgina Weldon's *Hints on Pronounciation in Singing* (1872, revised 1882) contains some good advice and exercises in diction. Agility exercises are to be found in Sabilla Novello's *Exercises for a Contralto Voice* (1860); musically they are rather dull.

Of the pianoforte tutors by women, the most commercial and therefore most empty is *A Piano Instructor for the Million*, subtitled *The Railway Music Book* by Mrs Joseph Kirkman.

Supposedly a self-tutor for railway passengers, it being on sale at all railway stations from 1854 onwards, it consists of a dummy keyboard with a cut-away keyboard dial, which by rotating shows all the possible major and minor key-signatures. It is an attempt to relate theory of music to the keyboard and concerns itself solely with the reading of music. Adelaida Thomas, on the other hand, provides some quite attractive two-part exercises in her *Forty Short Artistic Studies on an Original System of Pianoforte Touch in Connection with Emotional Expression* (1908). It was published for the Scientific Training School of Pianoforte Playing, Brighton, and whilst appearing somewhat over-particular about hand positions, it does explore quite successfully different styles of touch. *A Few Words on Pianoforte Playing with Rules for Fingering Passages of Frequent Occurrence* (1855) by Caroline Reinagle tends to be rather dogmatic over relatively unimportant matters. No fundamental rules for fingering seem to emerge. The *Daily Exercises for the Pianoforte* by Kate Paige (1883) is basically a scale book with cadences in each key.

Outstanding in every respect, that is in its notes, exercises, and choice of examples is Annie Glen's *How to Accompany* (1894). The early exercises require the pianist to sing against simple chordal accompaniment and these develop so that particular skills are isolated and practised. The music chosen ranges from Carissimi and Purcell to Verdi. It certainly satisfied a need and soon went into a second edition.

Music magazines of late Victorian and Edwardian England contain many advertisements by women offering tuition in various aspects of music. Their Vocal and Piano Academies, their teaching roles at the Academy and Colleges of Music, as well as in schools, and the examples of musical philanthropy such as those of Georgina Weldon with her orphanage and Helen Kenway's orphan school for girls, a music school which first began in Bath and then moved to Notting Hill, all suggest that by the end of the nineteenth century English women had infiltrated quite appreciably into a wide range of music teaching. They also took up important educative roles in music in the community at large. Nineteenth-century philanthropism was not restricted to the abolition of the Slave Trade and the various Factory Acts: the dissemination of music particularly amongst those who lived in 'the other England', described by Disraeli in his novel *Sybil*, was seen by many as a most important agent in the humanizing of those made brutish by the industrial revolution: 'The humanitarian novels of Dickens coincide with the efforts to transform society through temperance and music.' (Nettel: 1952, p. 117). Singing classes were a frequent occurrence in the Mechanics' Institutes and Guilds,[44] and a Guild for working men and women in Nottingham provided musical groups for entertaining at various institutions in the area. This guild which, in 1886, had four hundred members, was run by Mrs Mary Bowman-Hart and certainly afforded an example to other amateur musicians and groups in the area. As Mackerness says in his *A Social History of English Music*, 'The Nottingham Bowman-Hart Musical Guild did excellent work in showing uneducated people how to entertain themselves.' (Mackerness: 1964, p. 203). He states also that it was a woman who encouraged the brass band competitions, by being patron to the first large-scale contest at Burton Constable, near Hull in 1845, which, as he says ' . . . enjoyed the patronage of Lady Chichester, who was familiar with the brass band festivals in France and believed that something of the same kind might be attempted in Yorkshire.' (Mackerness: 1964, p. 168).

Even in so male-dominated a sphere as the Cathedral Choir School the female influence made its mark in a long battle with a Cathedral Chapter over the lack of provision of adequate education for the choristers. Maria Hackett (1783–1873) began, very politely, her campaign with the Dean and Chapter of St Paul's Cathedral in January, 1811. The grounds of complaint were that the choristers were provided with no education, being required to attend daily for the Cathedral services and left to their own devices in-between whiles. Further, that to pay the fees of the 'Singing-Master' the boys were often required to sing at functions such as tavern dinners, midnight clubs and theatres, and were left to find their own way home. The Cathedral Chapter paid the parents a small annual sum for their services and as soon as the boys were of no further use they were dismissed and, being uneducated, were unable to find employment. The ancient statutes, which Maria Hackett translated from the original Latin, required the Cathedral Chapter to provide 'Board and Education, both musical and classical', at least, this was how she interpreted them. Her documentation on so compli-cated an issue was most scrupulous, and only when she could get no response from the cathedral authorities concerned, did she make public her grievances.[45] It is interesting to note how the tone of her letters gradually changed from the obsequious, 'I have the honour to be with profound respect, Your Lordship's most obedient and most humble servant' of the first letter to the 'In the meditated arrangements your part is entirely wanting; but I still indulge a hope that you will no longer suffer yourself to continue the subject of a reproach, so general and so severe. I am etc. Maria Hackett' of her letter to the Chancellor of St Paul's Cathedral, of 25 January, 1813.

Faced with intransigence she was in no way deflected, and presented a petition on behalf of the choristers to the Master of the Rolls, which was heard in 1814. Though it was found to be outside his jurisdiction, it was directed that an Enquiry be held to determine exactly of what the Trust consisted. To further her case, Maria Hackett contacted every Anglican Cathedral Chapter, and made a detailed summary of its choral establishment, its present numbers and educational provision. This she published in 1824 under the title of *Brief Account of Cathedral and Collegiate Schools*, and from it emerged the fact that the 'Ancient School attached to St. Paul's Cathedral' was the exception in its lack of educational provision.[46] In her *Correspondences and Evidence* of 1832 the remainder of the letters are published, and in this publication she is able to record that the choristers at St Paul's are now provided with tuition in Latin, Algebra, Mathematics and the Theory of Music, that there is a good school library, and that the boys are retained as monitors for up to eighteen months after their voices change and receive in return a gratuity of £30. Several other small benefits are also recorded. It had been a twenty-year struggle against monumental lethargy and prejudice: her resolution had been unshakeable. Characteristically, she does not dwell on her successes, indeed, one of the final letters concerns one of her original grievances which had still not been answered, and she drives her point home, yet again, in a letter to the Bishop of London in 1830: ' . . . no temptation of unholy profit to the Master should induce the patrons of these schools to hazard the principles of their youthful charge among such associates as they are likely to meet behind the scenes of a theatre.' (Hackett: 1832, p. 83). Her single-minded devotion to the choristers' welfare became a lifelong preoccupation, which involved visits to most cathedral choir schools in the country at her own considerable expense. Her cause was taken up by G.A. Macfarren in an article entitled 'The Music of the English Church' in the *Musical Times* of March, 1867. Having paid tribute to what Maria Hackett had achieved he took up the cause of the choristers at Westminster Abbey whose educational opportunities were also sadly deficient.

Whilst it took many years of remonstrance and litigation to get the Dean and Chapter of St Paul's Cathedral to provide adequate schooling for its choristers, the erection of a tablet to her memory in the Crypt of St Paul's Cathedral in the year of her death, 1874, was speedily agreed to, as is recorded in the obituary that appeared in December, 1874 in the *Musical Times:*

> By the death of Miss Maria Hackett the choristers of England, past and present, have lost a friend and patron ... For more than fifty years she made an annual visit to the several cities to look after her 'dear children' ... The Dean and Chapter of St. Paul's, pleased to mark their high estimate of her many noble qualities of heart and head, have consented to allow a tablet to her memory to be placed in a conspicuous part of the crypt of the Cathedral, which is to be erected by the choristers of England.

Would that they had shown such generous response previously.

Women thus played a substantial part in the process of music education in nineteenth-century England. Its fruition can be seen, in part, in the English Musical Renaissance of the 1880s and particularly in the field of amateur choral singing. Nowhere is this more apparent than in the Choral Competitive Movement which was largely the outcome of the work of yet another woman. It is to the achievements of Mary Wakefield that we must now turn.

Notes

1   In the *Scheme* of 1835 Sarah Glover quotes from *The Life of Bishop Porteus*, a biography which influenced her thinking about church music considerably: 'Of all the services of our church none appear to me to have sunk to so low an ebb, or so evidently to need reform as our parochial psalmody.' (p. 109).

2   Amelia Opie (b. 1769), a minor English novelist who enjoyed quite a vogue at the beginning of the nineteenth century, specializing in love stories with a moral. She married the artist John Opie. (See Smith College Studies in Modern Languages, Vol. XIV, Nos 1–2, Oct. 1932, Jan. 1933.)

3   His son, Joseph John Gurney (1788–1847) became a most influential Quaker and close friend of Sir T. Fowell-Buxton. (The Gurneys are immortalized by the Judge in Gilbert and Sullivan's *Trial by Jury* when he tells us, 'At length I became as rich as the Gurneys'.)

4   He was born in the same year as Sarah Glover (1786) of an Anglican father and Quaker mother. He experienced an evangelical conversion which set him on the road to prison reform, the propagation of the Bible and the abolition of slavery, the latter achieved in 1838 by

Act of Parliament. (See Buxton C. 1848: *Memoirs of Sir T. Fowell-Buxton.*)

5 She taught in several schools in and around Norwich, including Norwich Workhouse, cared for the poor and taught music to the blind. (See Mollowitz, K., 1933: *Ueber die Musikerziehung bei Ann Glover Und John Curwen*, p. 11.)

6 ' . . . does it [the organ's] power not encourage indolence with respect to the cultivation of the human voice?' (Glover: 1845, p. 9) and again, in a letter to Rev. J. Curwen, quoted in the *Tonic Sol-fa Reporter*, April, 1855, she says: 'It is a great satisfaction to me that you have proved in practice two favourite positions of mine in theory; viz. that no instrument constructed by man can compare in beauty with the human voice, and that the aid of instruments is not indispensable to the preservation of tune in vocal performance.'

7 Dr. J.C. Beckwith (1750–1809) was appointed organist of St Peter's Mancroft Church, Norwich in 1794; he succeeded Thomas Garland as Cathedral Organist in 1808. Thomas Garland, a pupil of Maurice Greene and teacher of the Norwich composer, James Hook (1746–1827), had been a most influential musician in Norwich. It was Dr. Beckwith who gave Sarah Glover the idea of the 'family of keys', i.e. C as the father of the family, G as the elder son, and F the younger son, and in this is suggested a teacher capable of presenting ideas in a way suitable for a child's understanding.

8 The most outspoken preacher and writer of religious tracts in Norwich in the late eighteenth century was another Rev. Glover, the Rev. John Glover, a Methodist Minister, who died in 1774. No relationship between him and Sarah Glover's father has been established.

9 In the *Tonic Sol-fa Jubilee Magazine* of 1892: the article by Mrs Langton Brown, Sarah's niece, on Sarah Glover.

10 A prodigious campaigner for moral education and the first woman in England to promote Sunday Schools. Her major work was *The Oeconomy of Charity* (1786).

11 Curwen objected to the harmonicon on the grounds that it was constructed on the principle of temperament and was as inaccurate a guide for the voice as the piano.

12 It is known that, at least until 1790, no hymns were sung as part of any service of the church.

13 There were several regional attempts to provide a simple method of music reading. In 1760, *The Leicestershire Harmony* was published, as was, in 1772, William Sewell's *Book of Psalmody (Cumberland) as taught by Arthur Smith*. Granville Sharp published in 1767 *A Short Introduction to Vocal Music . . . a little treatise intended for the use of children*, and in the late eighteenth-century also Samuel Webbe published his *Forty Two Vocal Exercises in Two Parts*. Norwich Sol-fa of Sarah Glover should be seen as one of several attempts at remedying the situation.

14 Published locally by Jarrold & Son, Booksellers, Printers, Bookbinders, Stationers, Music Sellers, Patent Medicine Vendors Etc. . . . . (!)

15   See *The Life and Work of John Curwen* by Dr John Rush (1971), a thesis in the University of Reading School of Education, for a detailed discussion of the development of *Sol-fa* notation.

16   Curwen was at first critical also. In the introduction to his *Grammar of Vocal Music* (1848) he recounts his first impression to Sarah Glover's *Scheme*: 'Well', said I, after a cursory glance, 'if the old notation is puzzling, I am sure this is more puzzling far.' However, after trying various other methods without success he then saw 'that Miss Glover's plan was to teach, first the simple and beautiful thing, *MUSIC*, and to delay the introduction to the ordinary antiquated mode of writing it, until the pupil had obtained a mastery of the thing itself.' (Curwen: 1848, p. xii).

17   SE in Continental Solmization, which she appropriated, changing SE to TE to avoid duplication of the initial letter with that of SOLE.

18   There is no evidence to suggest that Sarah Glover was aware of the treatise *The Pestalozzian Method of Teaching Music as contrived by Pfeiffer*, published in 1809 by Naegeli, in which the tonic is placed as the centre of two tetrachords in the same manner as Sarah Glover, viz.,

Scale of C:

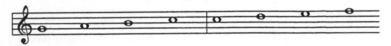

19   In her 1835 treatise, Sarah Glover gives additional syllables to cover modulation to keys further afield.

20   One assumes that she means here alternate phrases.

21   See *The Glass Harmonicon Rediscovered* by Bernarr Rainbow. (*Music in Education*, January, 1974).

22   See *The Life and Work of John Curwen* by Dr John Rush, in which he suggests that these two instruments were exhibited at the 1891 Crystal Palace Exhibition in conjunction with the Jubilee Celebrations of the Tonic Sol-fa Movement.

23   Christina and Margaret Glover.

24   See Appendix 2 *A Valentine*, a poem by Miss Catherine Hansell concerning Sarah Glover and *Sol-fa*.

25   Rev. J. Curwen and Dr Zachariah Buck, Organist, Norwich Cathedral. The latter visited her school in 1851.

26   Why German? There is nothing particularly Germanic about them, consisting as they do of canons based on the tonic triad.

27   Though, in accordance with her usual practice, the work is published anonymously, it is advertised as being by the same author of the *Scheme* in the 1839 edition.

28   See *The Land without Music* by Bernarr Rainbow.

29   They first met in 1841 when Sarah Glover was 55 and John Curwen, 24.

30   She had just undertaken the 5th revision (1859), which was unpub-

lished, and in which the *Scheme* is more closely linked with the re-designed harmonicon.

31   The later editions of her *Scheme* and her work in the 1840s point strongly to the latter.

32   It will be noted later how many women folk-song collectors were active in England in the later nineteenth century.

33   It was not many years later that Francesca Cuzzoni (1700–1770) and Faustina Bordoni (1700–1781) actually fought on the stage at the King's Theatre, London, which led to the abandonment of Italian opera in London for several months. In 1728 Gay satirized the fighting prima donnas in *The Beggar's Opera*.

34   Three days of prayer.

35   Charles Lamb liked to tease Vincent Novello about his antiquarianism and jocularly 'sent' him a 'nail that came out of Jomelli's coffin' saying that 'any memorial of a great musical genius, I know, is acceptable.' (See *Musical Times*, December 1896, the review of Mary Cowden-Clarke's book, *My Long Life*.)

36   See *Musical Times*, April, 1905 for a summary of Lucy Broadwood's lecture to the Musical Association on *Collecting of English Folk-Songs*.

37   The most frequently mentioned is Mrs. Wilson of Northamptonshire.

38   *Songs of the Hebrides* (3 volumes), 1908.

39   Mary Cowden-Clarke.

40   Discussed in Chapter 4.

41   A report of the address entitled 'The desirability of special training in the teaching of music' prepared by Mrs Woodhouse of Clapham High School and Miss Elsa Froebel – the main item at the third meeting of the Girls' School Music Union – is carried in the *Musical Times*, April, 1905.

42   See *Northern Accent* by John Robert Blunn.

43   Published as a book in 1903.

44   Miss S. Ashworth's 'Ancoats Choir' drawn from the Manchester and Salford Girls' Institute became quite celebrated at festivals for its part-singing.

45   See *Letters and Evidences respecting the ancient Collegiate School attached to St. Paul's Cathedral* (1813).

46   Llandaff Cathedral was also an exception in that it had no choir, the Trust having been appropriated for the Fabric.

4 Mary Wakefield (1853–1910) and the Competition Festival Movement

> It is not too much to say that no other of her sex in this country has done so much as Miss Wakefield to stimulate and foster popular musical study. (*McNaught*: 1900, p. 529)

It is a large claim, made by one of her co-workers, but nevertheless, apart from Sarah Glover with whose attitudes Mary Wakefield has much in common, there is no other woman in the nineteenth century who by her example and influence brought so many people to an active participation in music-making of such a worthwhile nature. During the years 1885–1900, when she was actively engaged in establishing and organizing the successive competitive festivals at Kendal in Westmorland, she developed a formula for success wherein competition was seen as but a stimulus to the practice and study of music, leading to the fuller enrichment to be gained through combined singing of a large-scale work. The formula was taken up nationally, involving thousands upon thousands of people hitherto untouched by music. When to this is added the recognition due to her for the illustrated music lectures which she gave up and down the country, introducing to a largely lay public the glories of England's musical heritage, her writings, her many song recitals, distinguished by the quality of the programmes as much as by her rich mezzo-soprano voice, something of her immense contribution can be ascertained, fully justifying W.G. McNaught's claim for her. It was as a composer of songs that she first became known nationally, and although these were slight and of no real consequence, they do possess a freshness that owes something to her study of and familiarity with folk-song. As her article on 'National Melodies' (see 'Foundation Stones of English Music') reveals, it was an area in which she was knowledgeable from her assimilation of 'Border' tunes in childhood: her later collecting and editing of north country tunes was a natural extension of her musical awareness.

The achievements of any individual depend upon several factors, not the least important being the ability to recognize what is needed and what is possible. She saw in the new-found appetite for choral singing a great potential: the seeds had been sown by Sarah Glover and John Curwen but the harvest had yet to be. Fundamentally her approach was that of an enlightened teacher realizing that music education of any value derives ultimately from immersion in music, and in music broad in its variety, challenging in its scope. She did not originate the competitive festivals but she saw in them the possibility of harnessing the competitive spirit to a far greater end: and who can deny that for rural communities to take part in performances of large-scale works accompanied by a professional orchestra directed by the leading conductor of the day was an end worth achieving? She was a hard realist, motivated by high idealism.

Mary Wakefield came from an old Westmorland Quaker family, and whilst neither she nor her parents were Quakers, the spirit of George Fox of nearby Ulverston, and his followers, can be detected in many of her attitudes. It was the Quaker movement that first recognized the equality of women, having women preachers and encouraging the freedom of thought and expression so long denied to them. The movement has long been identified with a down-to-earth approach to social problems, going about its work in an unostentatious but strictly practical way. One of Mary's relatives, Priscilla Wakefield, who died in 1832 and who was herself an aunt of the great reformer, Elizabeth Fry, started the Savings Bank movement for poor people, which proved of inestimable value to them. She was also concerned with the position of the female in society and wrote her 'Reflections on the present condition of the Female Sex with suggestions for its improvement'. One senses that Mary Wakefield identified closely at times with her Quaker forbears; in her book *Cartmel Priory and sketches of North Lonsdale* there is a very evocative description of 'Height Chapel', an old Quaker Meeting Place. She describes persecution that

Friends suffered for their faith in the area, and conjures up the atmosphere of the many past Meetings held at Height Chapel. She was so attracted to the place and its setting that she enquired of the caretaker whether it was possible to be buried there. It was a passing thought, but in it one catches her spiritual identification with her family's past. Her social mission of bringing music to the greatest possible number of people, whilst reflecting Benthamite thought, owes its origin to the same reforming spirit that infused the work of both her distant relatives, Priscilla Wakefield and Elizabeth Fry.

Mary Wakefield was born in Kendal, Westmorland, in 1853, where her father was a director of the family banking business. Her mother, of American-Irish descent, had a lively sense of humour, which characteristic Mary seems to have inherited from her. In 1858 the family moved to a country house outside Kendal, and in 1868 to a large house which the family inherited at Sedgwick. The first festival was held there. Mary's musical leanings were catered for by a music teacher in Kendal and she began also to teach herself to play the violin. Perhaps her skill as a horsewoman was the more remarked upon: indeed she remained steadfastly a countrywoman throughout her life. Her knowledge of local customs, love of flowers, observation of birds, are all pointers in this direction. In an unpublished and undated essay by her cousin, a Miss M.B. Cropper, which is to be found in the Cumbria Records Office at Kendal (WDX/318), we learn something of the boisterous nature of the Wakefield family: 'There were seven of them. Mary, the eldest was the contemporary cousin and a very great friend of my father. It was a roistering sort of household. My mother, who had been brought up rather primly in the south found it disconcerting in its very outspoken jollity.' (*Cropper*: u.d., p. 2).

When Mary was sixteen she was sent to a finishing school in Brighton where she stayed for two years. Although she underwent singing and piano lessons of the kind associated with such institutions, it cannot be said that her abilities were developed. Musically, she got most out of going to concerts in Brighton where she heard, amongst others, Adelina Patti, who made a lasting impression on her. Of her educational background little else has been recorded. Miss Cropper hints at an unsuitable romance as the cause for her despatch to Brighton: certainly there are suggestions that she was developing a headstrong personality. An amusing drawing made by her uncle on her departure for Brighton carries the revealing caption: 'Come back, and in future you shall have your own way in everything.'

During the years 1871 to 1880 she gained increasing experience as a singer, giving her first local concert in 1873. Although her father was strongly opposed to any thought of a professional career he did approve of her having singing lessons in London from Randegger, and it was from this time onwards that she developed rapidly as a musician, taking lessons not only in singing but in piano, harmony, violin and Italian. Her circle of friends included Maude Valérie White with whom she did several concert tours for charity, and who frequently stayed at Sedgwick. She composed, whilst staying there, her most famous song, 'Absent, yet present'. Another acquaintance was J.A. Fuller-Maitland, who later became the *Times* music critic and who was a leading collector of folk-songs. However, the two most important of her new friends were Ruskin, whom she met at Oxford in 1875 and who for the next twenty-five years helped direct her idealism into positive channels, and Henry Leslie, who directed the Amateur Musical Guild. He was renowned for the excellence of his choral training and particularly for his knowledge and interpretation of Elizabethan madrigals. She joined his choir and he became, in practical terms, the most formative influence upon her future work. During a prolonged visit to Italy she met and sang to Clara Novello and also spent many hours singing Grieg's songs, to the accompaniment of the composer, who was staying close by. The foundation of her future work was laid during these years and her growing achievements as a singer brought her to her first major crisis in the year 1880. As a result of her success as a soloist at the Three Choirs Festival in Gloucester in 1880, she was invited to sing at both the Norwich and Leeds Festivals. A career as a professional singer with all its many attractions now presented itself. In deference to her father's wish she renounced this possibility, though no doubt after a great inner struggle. She thus remained an amateur singer: little did she realize then that it was to the cause of the amateur musician that she was going to devote most of her future energies.

It was during this period of uncertainty about her future that she composed most of her songs. She achieved immediate popularity with 'No Sir', a simple, yet attractive song, which brought her national fame. The text bears a close relationship to the folk-song, 'O No John', whilst the melody is unpretentious and tuneful. The title page does describe the song as being arranged by Mary Wakefield and thus strongly suggests that it was based on a song

Example 17   *Sally Gray (Arr. A.M. Wakefield)*

that she had 'picked up' rather than composed. No song recital by
Mary Wakefield was deemed complete unless she sang the folk-
song, 'Sally Gray', and her arrangement of this Cumberland
folk-song is tasteful. The slightly varied repetition of the final
phrase is particularly successful (Example 17). The remainder of
her songs, whilst achieving a certain popularity, particularly 'A
Bunch of Cowslips', are not memorable and need not detain us
here. The chorus, 'Queen of Sixty Years', which she wrote for the
Queen's Jubilee and which was performed at the 1897 Festival was
a fairly innocuous unison song with two-part refrain that served
its purpose as an occasional piece. Whilst most of her compositions
show a degree of competence, they achieve little more. Her future
path was not destined to be that of a composer.

The next five years were largely occupied in organizing and
performing at numerous charity concerts, some being given at
Grosvenor House, London, which the Duke of Westminster made
available to her for these events. Much of her activity was centred
in London and she obviously enjoyed high society life and meeting
artists like Alma-Tadema, the poet Matthew Arnold and the
amateur musician, Lady Folkestone, who conducted a women's
orchestra. A visit to Herefordshire to see and hear what Henry
Leslie had achieved with amateur forces, both vocal and instrumental in that county, was the turning point for her. Her article in
the *Musical Times* for March 1884 is therefore prophetic and in it
she describes the Herefordshire Philharmonic Society, which Henry
Leslie began in 1863, and its activities which included twice yearly
concerts in surrounding counties, the enthusiasm which it engen-
ders and the excellent quality of its unaccompanied singing. She
continues,

> Should this short account . . . encourage any musical amateur to go
> on with the great work of musical education in himself and those
> around him, its object will have been reached: for if music as a
> serious art is ever to be appreciated here, as it is in Germany, the

formation of an educated, enlightened public is the first requisite; and in order to produce this valuable result most surely will the root of the matter prove to be the cultivation and encouragement of the musical amateur. (*Wakefield*: 1884, p. 144)

She had found her life's work.

During this visit to Herefordshire she had long discussions with Henry Leslie on the purpose and organization of competitive festivals and drew upon his vast experience of work with amateurs. Whilst she had several models on which to build her own festival, they tended to point to what she wanted to avoid rather than imitate. Any form of commercialization or denigration of music through the baser instincts of competitiveness were alien to her nature. The Welsh Eisteddfod, of great antiquity, had certain valuable features, particularly the love of music that it was both an expression of, and stimulus for, but it also at times engendered a too keenly competitive spirit, as vouched for by this account by an adjudicator in 1903:

> At the conclusion of the Eisteddfod at Pontypridd – where I learned much regarding the inner workings of these meetings – the constable who had attended me all that day cheerily informed me that it was 'Quite safe sir' when I rose to leave. The utterance might have been made with less confidence at Newport in the following year, when a splendid body of well-groomed stalwarts were received with prolonged howls of disapproval on appearing on the platform to compete with another male choir. An ugly interference with the wooden benches began, a cordon of police was drawn around the hall, and sufficient order restored to allow us to listen to an admirable rendering of an unaccompanied Psalm by Mendelssohn. (*Mackenzie*: 1927, pp. 238–239)

He goes on to describe how he was detained by the committee with offers of refreshment which aroused his suspicion: he was eventually told, 'They are waiting for you.' He 'escaped' by a side door and spent the evening shut away in his hotel.

There had been several competitive festivals held at the Crystal Palace in the 1860s and again in the years 1872–1875. Piano competitions known as 'Bees' were also common and various choral festivals outside London are also recorded, [1] in Manchester in 1855 and Bradford in 1864. In 1881 there was an Anglo-French Choral Festival at Brighton which concluded with combined performance, both vocal and instrumental. However, by far the largest competitive music festival held, prior to those at Kendal, was the Stratford Festival of 1883, organized by John Spencer Curwen, with the object of stimulating music-making in London's East End. In Germany competitive festivals had been long established and the four-day male voice competitive festival at Düsseldorf in 1852, described by Lowell Mason in his *Letters from Abroad* may be taken as fairly typical.

It will be realized, therefore, that in starting competitive choral festivals at Kendal Mary Wakefield was not introducing a new idea, though she was the first to establish them in a truly rural community. As the festivals developed they became more distinctive and original in the emphasis placed upon the combined performance. The principles on which Mary Wakefield based her festivals were that competition is a necessary stimulus, that there should be no money prizes[2] and that all choirs should combine in the performance of a large-scale work. The adjudicators were to concentrate on giving valuable critical help as much as on choosing winners; 'test pieces', distinguished by their technicalities rather than by their musical qualities were to be avoided, and overall should be the educative aim of introducing as many people as possible to the study of worthwhile music and participation in its enjoyment. Great attention was paid to the selection of the music and from its early days children were encouraged to participate, eventually having a day of the festival to themselves, sanctioned by the Board of Education, thus allowing the music to be learnt at school and attendance at the festival being counted as school attendance. The community aspect of the festival, bringing people of different class and educational background together in the common bond of music-making was an important off shoot of the movement. So self-evident to anyone who visited Kendal during the festival were the numerous benefits of community music-making that similar festivals were instituted throughout the country. These had grown so numerous by 1904 that an Association of Competitive Festivals was formed, under the chairmanship of Lady Mary Lygon,[3] to ensure that the principles underlying the festivals were not overlooked and to co-ordinate what had become a national movement.

It is from a perusal of the programmes of the respective festivals at Kendal that the idealism is so apparent. They reflect a most discerning musical taste, remarkable for nineteenth-century England, let alone rural England. Madrigals, both English and Italian, music by Purcell, folk-songs, medieval music as well as contemporary music all feature in these programmes. The 'combined' works include Bach cantatas, Dvořàk's *Stabat Mater*, Mendelssohn's *Elijah* and Brahms's *Requiem* with Elgar, Coleridge-Taylor and Parry all represented by large choral works. The performances were accompanied by a professional orchestra: from 1904 the Queen's Hall Orchestra, conducted by Henry Wood, not only accompanied but performed orchestral works which included a Beethoven symphony and Mendelssohn's violin concerto, with Lady Speyer as soloist. It is in these details that the true nature of the Westmorland (as it had become known) Musical Festival is revealed. The classes were added to and included female voice choirs, village orchestras and a special folk-song class, this latter being the only event to attract a small money prize. Solo competitions were discouraged, there being seen to be greater educative value in concerted music-making. The size of the festival grew till it became a four-day event in 1908 and biennial thereafter. So that due attention would be paid to the preparation of the music for the combined event, it was included in the competition and adjudicators could choose sections from it to test the choirs. The afternoons of the festival in 1908 were given up to rehearsal of this music: such was its importance in the overall scheme of the festival.

The festival was originally called the 'Sedgwick Choral Competition' and then became known as the 'Wakefield Choral Competition' in memory of its first patron, Mary's father, who died in 1891. In 1900 it changed its name to the 'Westmorland Musical Festival' and in 1911, after the death of its founder, the 'Mary Wakefield Westmorland Festival'. From the very humble beginning in 1885 with three quartets competing on the tennis court of the Wakefield house at Sedgwick, it grew rapidly and could claim that within ten years more than 10,000 singers had been involved in the festivals at Kendal.[4]

Until 1900 Mary Wakefield directed the festival. This involved the selection of the music in the early autumn, the selection or coercion of village choirmasters and mistresses, the sectional rehearsals throughout the winter months in outlying villages[5] and the rehearsal and conducting of the combined work at the festival. It involved much else which had to do with her management of people, her galvanizing spirit and boundless energy: but these vital aspects to the success of the venture are not so susceptible to bland description. They are nevertheless integral in any assessment of her achievement. From the outset she relied upon the support of her well-to-do friends and family: 'The scheme is indebted for much of its success to the fact that many residents, chiefly ladies, possessing great social influence, supported the enterprise from the first.' (*McNaught*: 1900, p. 530). The conflicting elements of her personality made her ideally suited to bridge the gaps between idealism and practicality, educated society and rural naivety, professional music standards and amateur aspirations. She had to discover for herself how best to teach the uninitiated: being herself so ready to learn she instinctively infected others, and imparted confidence in their discovery of music. She could rely on one ready-made tool, *Tonic Sol-fa*: 'We would most unhesitatingly recommend its adoption by conductors wherever they have to begin at the very beginning in forming a choral body.' (*Wakefield*: 1888, p. 499). Armed with that and her own invincible spirit she overcame all obstacles.

Although some of the early performances at the festivals were unpolished and her skill as a conductor limited, several eminent musicians later testified to the very high standard of performance achieved. Parry, Elgar and Hadow were all outspoken in their praise. Elgar spoke of it as ' . . . rather a shock to find Brahms's part-songs appreciated and among the daily fare of a district apparently unknown to the sleepy London press.' (*Young*: 1968, p. 155) and Havergal Brian, in a foreword for the Bantock Memorial Concert in 1946 claimed that ' . . . the most remarkable movement in English music for several centuries was that of the a cappella choral singing at the Northern Musical Competitive Festivals.'

Mary Wakefield's illustrated music lectures which she undertook from 1890 to 1900 have already been referred to. It is fortunate that the contents of these lectures have been preserved since they reveal a wealth of knowledge, particularly in relation to Elizabethan, national and folk music. The basis of her lectures is published in *Murray's Magazine*, July to December, 1888 (not 1889 as stated in Rosa Newmarch's Memoir) under the title 'Foundation Stones of English Music'. The subjects she tackled included madrigals, Elizabethan music, Henry Purcell, National Melodies and Carols, subjects that would not have been out of place at a gathering of a learned society in 1890. By a judicious selection of music she was able to bring these antiquarian researches alive and interest her largely untutored audience. She was an active folk-song collector and included two, which she had cited, in the article on 'National Melodies.'[6] She also quotes from Lucy Broadwood's *Sussex Songs*, which had just been published, and in the article on 'Carols' quotes the whole of Byrd's *Carol for Christmas Day*. Her aim was to infect her audience with the same enthusiasm that she felt for this music and by her singing, self-accompanied, she was able to bring her researches alive. The practical side of her nature is again apparent, for the impact of an illustrated lecture is so much greater than the written word. It was a parallel activity to her sectional rehearsals for the festival in the outlying villages, for both depended upon expertise skilfully and enthusiastically presented. The festival programmes benefited immeasurably from her studies in English music.

It was in 1875 that Mary Wakefield first met Ruskin, the doyen of late Victorian art critics and a man of immense influence on the aesthetic views of his age. His knowledge of music and ability in it were limited, though this in no way discouraged him from writing about it. His thoughts were scattered throughout his large collection of writings and Mary took upon herself the Herculean task of collecting and organizing these random thoughts into a presentable entity. That much of Ruskin's attitude to music she identified with is conceded by the very nature of her work in editing *Ruskin on Music*, which she did in 1894. She shared with Ruskin the conviction that art, and particularly music, have a moral purpose and when properly directed could improve society. Here is the source of the idealism that motivated her work in the Competition Festival Movement. Thus, united in this philosophy with Ruskin, the book is more a testament to shared beliefs and close friendship than a critical appraisal of his viewpoint.

Throughout the book two types of print are used to distinguish between editorial comment and the views of Ruskin, a very practical device which leads to a clear exposition of Ruskin's various statements, the heart of which are contained in the chapters on 'Music and Painting', 'Music and Education' and 'Music and Morals'. Pervasive throughout the book is the assumption that music has a 'deeper meaning' – one which Mary Wakefield stressed ' . . . must underlie all true art, and especially the art of Music.' (Wakefield: 1894, p. 8). She quotes Ruskin's dictum, 'The great purpose of Music, which is to say a thing you mean deeply, in the strongest and clearest possible way.' (Wakefield: 1894, p. 4) and claims that great changes in music teaching would follow if this purpose of music was understood by all who taught it. She does not question whether music can be said to have any purpose but accepts this assumption as if it were indisputable fact. Whilst she admits that Ruskin was never a musician, she does claim that he understood it and valued it deeply: 'What is to be admired in what he has said of the art (music) is the beautiful way in which its potential meaning and teaching has been expressed by him.' (Wakefield: 1894, p. 34). From Rosa Newmarch we learn that Ruskin's tastes in music were idiosyncratic appreciating equally the music of 'Cristabel, Corelli and the Christy Minstrels'. (Newmarch: 1912, p. 58).

In the chapter 'Music and Painting', Ruskin draws many parallels between the two arts which are mostly specious, though high-sounding in the manner reserved for those who speak of music from a theoretical point of view. It is disappointing to find Mary Wakefield agreeing with so much of what he had to say in this context, owing perhaps to the high regard in which he was held as an art critic. His views on 'Music and Education' are based largely on a mixture of Plato and his own very narrow concept of music. Mary Wakefield is obviously less happy with some of his dogmatic statements and warns the reader to take the spirit rather than the letter to heart. His ideal music education would consist of vocal music, with nothing but beautiful and 'true' words, with accompaniments subordinated to the voice and with no repetition of syllables – indeed a fairly close parallel with the rules laid down by the Council of Trent in 1562 for catholic composers. His various choirs of youths and young maidens would sing of eternal truths and of that which is uplifting and noble. To which, alas, Mary Wakefield comments that 'No man has more fully realised the spiritual essence of art, or given such true expression to its possibilities.' (Wakefield: 1894, p. 110). She admits, however, that on technical matters he is out of his depth and that technicalities are best left to others more capable.

When Ruskin speaks of 'Music and Morals' there is no doubt that he speaks for Mary Wakefield as well, for she says ' . . . for him, the full importance of all true art exists, principally, in its moral teaching.' (Wakefield: 1894, p. 112). It was a pity that he could not recognize the obvious moral teaching in Mozart's *Don Giovanni* which called forth from him such vehement censure: 'No such spectacle of unconscious moral degradation of the highest faculty to the lowest purpose can be found in history.' (Wakefield: 1894, p. 124). One wonders whether he ever saw the work or whether he was restating, though more forcibly, Beethoven's avowed distaste for it.

Whilst Ruskin's views on music are of historical interest only, Mary Wakefield's identification with them does at times seem contrary to her down-to-earth nature. She, more than anyone else, could surely see how impracticable and divorced from reality many of his views were. Two factors should be borne in mind in this respect; one of these is her very close friendship with him, particularly after he moved to Coniston and she was able to visit him quite often. Ruskin valued her company as the dedication of *Sesame and Lilies* shows: 'Mary Wakefield, to whose bright and gifted nature – good in the kindest sense, the author is thankful for some of the happiest hours of his old age.' Where so close an affinity existed, the critical faculty could well be blinded to what otherwise might appear as arrogant nonsense. The other aspect is perhaps the more understandable. Mary Wakefield, along with many of her generation, regarded music as a force for moral good in the community. It was the great belief of her age. It is only when this view is taken to its extreme, as Ruskin did, that it is shown to be untenable, for whilst music can be a morally uplifting force, it is not necessarily so, or any the worse as music for not being so. Once theoretical dogmatism takes hold of a general intuition all sorts of indefensible standpoints are reached. Mary Wakefield was, at times, embarrassed by Ruskin's more extreme utterances, but being in sympathy with the general sentiment she was unable to challenge the conclusions at which he arrived.

Most of her other writings are not concerned with music. Before we move on to these mention should be made of the article 'A Medieval Singer and his Songs' which appeared in the *Commonwealth Magazine* in August, 1896. Once again it shows her interest in the music and musicians of the distant past and is concerned with the twelfth-century musician and poet, Walther von der Vogelweide. Commenting on the article, Rosa Newmarch says it ' . . . expresses most keenly what she feels about music. One can readily understand that this knight-errant of song, who added to his chivalry patriotism, and to his patriotism an almost religious devotion to his art, would appeal in a peculiar way to her admiration and love.' (Newmarch: 1912, p. 78).

An observant writer with an eye and ear attuned to local scenery and dialect is revealed in many of her other articles. She is capable at times of evoking country scenes with a vividness and at the same time a statuesque quality that impinge with the authenticity of a photograph. In 'Grange-over-sands', from *Cartmel Priory and Sketches of North Lonsdale*, she used her folk-song collecting technique and simply recorded the comments and dialect of the older residents. The musician had become the social historian. Whether it be descriptions of cockling at Morecambe Bay, of local churches and their history, of birdwatching at Walney Island or of the enclosed pew on castors that could be moved around Grange-over-sands church and which belonged to the Brigland family, her absorbing interest in everything around her captivates the casual reader.

Upon the death of her mother in 1894 and the marriage of her sister, the family home was broken up and Mary Wakefield bought a house, 'Nutwood', set above Grange-over-sands, overlooking Morecambe Bay. Here she had many visitors and she was never short of company. Although she had always worked well with men 'her deepest affections were given to women. Perhaps it was the result of the suppression of that early love affair.' (Cropper: u.d., p. 11). The assumption of a role traditionally perceived as masculine was often the price that many successful women in the nineteenth century had to pay; sometimes it was by inclination, but often induced by circumstances. Wakefield was an enthusiastic supporter of the Women's Suffrage Movement and although not active in the movement herself, her achievements alone were sufficient vindication of the claims for women's recognition in the affairs of the country.

Notes

1 *The Mirror of Music* Vol. 2 by P.A. Scholes.
2 In actual fact until 1899 approximately one-third of the £300 income of the Festival was spent on prizes, many of which were money prizes. These were, however, gradually eliminated.
3 As Lady Mary Forbes-Trefusis she will be remembered as the dedicatée of the thirteenth variation of Elgar's *Enigma Variations*. She had started a competitive festival in Malvern in 1903.
4 St George's Hall, Kendal, served as the venue for the Festival until 1899 when the larger Drill Hall was used. The latter could hold a choir of three hundred on a specially erected stage and an audience of two thousand. In 1910, the Festival reverted to St George's Hall where the seating capacity had been enlarged. In present times Kendal Parish Church, which is the largest church in the diocese of Carlisle, plus various smaller halls, are used for the Festival.
5 But a decade or so later, Ralph Vaughan Williams, that great champion of the amateur musician, was engaged upon a similar venture in the outlying villages of Surrey.
6 In 1902 the Folk Song Competition Class elicited several hitherto unpublished folk songs of the district, the first prize being awarded to the most interesting and as yet, unpublished, folk song.

5   Ethel Smyth
(1858–1944)

In Ethel Smyth we encounter the first 'professional' woman composer in England whose main aim was that her music and its
performance be received on equal terms with that of male composers. To this end she dedicated her life, using whatever means
were available to get her music recognized, usually the time-hon-
oured ones of wealth (other people's), influence (Queen Victoria's
for example) and sheer hard work. Through the circumstances of
her birth she was able to study music privately in Leipzig where
she soon infiltrated musical society and thereby came to know
Brahms and to meet Tchaikovsky and Grieg, amongst other
notable musicians. It can be argued that because she was a woman
her music did arouse more initial interest than if she had been a
man, and as Carl Johnson remarks: 'she was always objective
enough to admit that the element of curiosity had probably brought
people to hear her music who might otherwise not have come, and
that she came into the public eye as a composer much quicker
because of it.' (Johnson 1982 p. 14). However, no one who has
read the many books that she wrote, which are nearly all autobiographical, can fail to be amazed at her tenacious fighting spirit and
vitality, which more than any other factors, made it possible for
her to become a musician against great opposition from her father,
and achieve the success that she did. Indeed, both in her music and
her lifestyle many of the characteristics traditionally associated
with masculinity predominate: she was a born fighter, quite fearless
both physically and morally, and a keen sportswoman, with riding,
tennis and golf her major preoccupations. Perhaps she felt it necessary to adopt certain masculine characteristics so that her music
would be viewed more seriously.[1] The champions of female edu-

153

cation in the late nineteenth century had to adopt similar tactics
to prove that the female mind was as capable of intellectual development as the male and hence the adoption of certain male modes
of conduct in the developing girls' schools. Undoubtedly, Ethel
Smyth did believe that the neglect of her music owed much to the
fact that she was a woman. A letter from Bernard Shaw to her in
1924 in connection with a performance of her *Mass in D* contradicts this view:

Dear Dame Ethel,

Thank you for bullying me into going to hear that Mass.

The originality and beauty of the voice parts are as striking today
as they were 30 years ago, and the rest will stand up in the biggest
company.

Magnificent!

You are totally and diametrically wrong in imagining that you
have suffered from a prejudice against feminine music. On the contrary you have been almost extinguished by the dread of masculine
music. It was your music that cured me for ever of the old delusion
that women could not do men's work in art and other things. (That
was years ago, when I knew nothing about you, and heard an
overture – 'The Wreckers', or something – in which you kicked a
big orchestra all round the platform). But for you I might not
have been able to tackle St. Joan, who has floored every previous
playwright. Your music is more masculine than Handel's.

When have the critics and the public ever objected to feminine
music? Did they object to Arthur Sullivan, whose music was music
in petticoats from the first bar to the last? Can you name a more
ladylike composer than the beloved and much imitated Mendelssohn? Does the very jolly sugarstick called The German Requiem
take you in because Brahms dabbed a little black on it, and wrapped
it in crape? You scorned sugar and sentimentality; and you were
exuberantly ferocious. You booted Elgar contemptuously out of
your way as an old woman. And now you say we shrink from you
because you are 'only a woman'. Good God!

Your dear big brother,

G. *Bernard Shaw*

9 March 1924

(St. John: 1959, p. 185)

Shaw had supported her music from the beginning and when
writing as a music critic in 1893 saw in the *Mass in D* ' ... the
beginning of what I have so often prophesied – the conquest of
popular music by women.' (Shaw: 1932, p. 234).

One should quibble at the use of the world 'popular' in relation to Ethel Smyth's *Mass in D* and disagree with Shaw's prophecy, but with the evidence of nineteenth-century women writers before him, his assumption that women could succeed equally as musicians was certainly a reasonable one. Emerging at a time when the Women's Suffrage Movement was coming to the fore, and for two years actively partaking in it, the career of Ethel Smyth is very germane to the consideration of the role of women in music in nineteenth-and early twentieth-century England.

On the subject of recognition she was touchy and towards the end of her life, more bitter, believing that a combination of male prejudice and the 'establishment' (or the 'machine' as she called it), had been largely responsible for the neglect of her work.[2] It is not easy to be categorical about this because so many different factors enter into it, such as her abandonment of a promising career in 1910 in order to devote two years to the Women's Suffrage Movement, the 1914–18 war and the severing of good musical connections she had built up in Germany prior to it, and above all her deeply-felt conviction that her originality as a woman composer was not understood. She believed that 'There is a bottomless cleft between man's way of feeling and woman's.' (Smyth: 1936, p. 298) and felt that the male-dominated public of her day was not ready to accept feminine modes of expression in music. Shaw's amusing answer to this, in the letter already quoted, does but skate on the surface of the argument. It may well be that there is no argument to sustain at all, in that music of lasting quality exhibits so wide a range of emotional expression that it transcends gender differences. Certainly it is a naïve proposition to regard masculine music as powerful and feminine music as tender: surely Beethoven is at his most eloquent in his more tender, reflective passages? Yet, if one had to select one composer to represent in his music the attributes commonly associated with masculinity, it would surely be Beethoven. The double irony is that Ethel Smyth's music, certainly her *Mass in D* at least, was appreciated for its strength and 'masculine' qualities.

During her lifetime Ethel Smyth became as well known for her writings as for her music. Her lively, rather unconventional style, her honesty and witty observations on human behaviour brought her to a wider public than her music did.[3] Her extensive travels, her lifelong friendship with the exiled Empress Eugénie, through whom she was introduced to Queen Victoria, her lively intellect which engaged men on equal terms (no less a person, for example, than the Kaiser with whom she had long, frank political discussions) and her undoubted ability to portray character in her writings provide for a varied and lively interest in her material.

At a time when English music was largely disregarded in Germany, Ethel Smyth succeeded in getting her operas performed there.[4] Like her contemporary, Elgar, success in Germany[5] became the means by which she could get a hearing in her own country. It might well be argued that the medium she chose to write in, opera, is perhaps the most elusive and costly of all, and that had she concentrated more on chamber music, for which her talents were considerable, she might have succeeded in getting some of her music into the standard repertoire. Whilst she showed an uncompromising militancy with regard to getting her works performed, she undoubtedly indulged in too many distractions, sporting, social and literary, to allow her to devote herself fully to composition. Her output is therefore limited, and in this respect she lacked the singleness of purpose found in the male composers with whom she wished to be equated.

That she was a strong-willed person, prepared to overcome any obstacles in her path, there is no possible doubt. From an early age she proved to be the rebellious one in a large family of six girls and two boys. As the third eldest of the sisters she took a fair amount of responsibility for the younger children, particularly after the marriage of her two elder sisters. Her father, Major-General J.H. Smyth, C.B. was, during Ethel's childhood, Commander of the Artillery Depot at Woolwich and later of the Royal Artillery at Aldershot, and most of Ethel's childhood was spent at the country house at Frimley, near Aldershot. General Smyth was a man of rigid and uncompromising views, ruling his household very much in accordance with Victorian codes of conduct. He came from Irish stock and had followed his forbears in his choice of profession.[6] His marriage to Nina Struth does suggest the attraction of opposites for she brought to the marriage wit, elegance and an artistic temperament. Nina's mother, 'Madame de Stracey', had been well-known in musical circles in Paris where Chopin, Rossini and Auber had been frequent visitors to her salon. One can see in Madame de Stracey's independent artistic life in a foreign city the anticipation of Ethel's life and one wonders to what extent she was influenced by her grandmother's example. Certainly she warmed to her grandmother when reading her letters[7] and came to the conclusion that ' . . . Bonnemaman, gifted, warmhearted, impulsive and thoroughly "injudicious", would have been my favourite relation.' (Smyth: 1919, p. 33). The early days of her parents' marriage, spent in India, were the happiest for her mother where she shone in the social life of Anglo-Indian society. It was not so on return to England where child-bearing, a smaller income and the limited social life of a military environment led to an increasing sense of frustration.

At the age of twelve Ethel decided that she would devote her life to music, and study at the Leipzig Conservatorium. Having shown no particular talent for music until then it is not surprising that her announced intention was not taken seriously. It was prompted by hearing her governess, who had studied at the Leipzig Conservatorium, play a Beethoven sonata. At boarding school, which Ethel attended from 1872 to 1875, music was part of the curriculum, but her first serious study of music began in 1875 with lessons from a Mr Ewing, who was an officer in the Royal Artillery. He was known largely for the composition of the hymn-tune, 'Jerusalem the Golden',[8] and proved a good teacher, introducing his highly motivated student to opera and orchestration by way of the score of *The Flying Dutchman* and Berlioz's *Treatise on Orchestration*. Mrs Ewing was a writer of children's stories and encouraged Ethel in her first literary efforts. The lessons were stopped by her father when he suspected – quite wrongly – Mr Ewing's motives, but the lessons had served to convince Ethel of her undoubted musical ability, thus strengthening her resolve to follow a musical career. For the next two years she resolutely wore down her parents' resistance to her plans, although it would seem that her mother was secretly on her side. Initially her father was violently opposed to her plans and declared that he would ' . . .sooner see you under the sod' than agree to her becoming a musician. Such was her determination, however, that by the age of nineteen she eventually got her father to agree to providing her with a small allowance for her to study music at the Leipzig Conservatorium. She began her studies under Reinecke in the city made famous by Bach and Mendelssohn. Of more value than the lessons was the opportunity to see opera and to go to concerts of a high standard of performance at the Gewandhaus.

The years 1877 to 1885 were years of great assimilation and growth, both intellectually and emotionally. They were dominated by her friendship with Elizabeth von Herzogenberg who exercised a very great hold over her. At this household she met leading musicians of the day and particularly Brahms, who was a frequent visitor and admirer of Elizabeth. Brahms valued Elizabeth's criticism of his compositions, for she was a most able musician, and he regarded her judgement as being as good as that of any man, whereas Ethel felt Brahms disregarded her works because she was a woman. Certainly Grieg, who was also a visitor to the Herzogenbergs, learnt to respect Ethel's comments on music, and at a later stage, so did Tchaikovsky. Being dissatisfied with the tuition she was receiving at the Conservatorium she withdrew and took lessons from Heinrich Herzogenberg, who taught both Elizabeth, his wife, and Ethel counterpoint. It proved a narrow discipline, but the discovery of the music of Bach was invaluable. They were years of great excitement in which many of her student compositions were performed: they were marred by the rupturing of the very deep friendship with Elizabeth Herzogenberg in 1885, causing Ethel many years of distress.

The cause of the break in friendship was the developing relationship between Elizabeth's brother-in-law, Henry Brewster, and Ethel. This relationship, lasting until Brewster's death in 1908, was far from satisfactory in that it was carried on clandestinely at first until the death of his wife, and through correspondence for its greater part. Though he did ask her to marry him when he was free to do so, Ethel declined, fearing a loss of her independence. Yet the relationship was deeply felt by both: he was a writer of a philosophical nature and provided Ethel with the text for her major opera, *The Wreckers*, and her large-scale choral and orchestral work, *The Prison*. Apart from an early engagement to William Wilde, Oscar Wilde's brother, which only lasted a few weeks and was of little consequence, the relationship with Henry Brewster was her only one of any significance with a man.

Throughout her life Ethel was continuously having passionate friendships with women; in a letter she wrote to Henry Brewster in 1892 she says, 'I wonder why it is so much easier for me to love my own sex passionately than yours. I can't make it out for I am a very healthy-minded person.' Recent studies (see Collis 1984 and Wood 1995) have focused on Ethel Smyth's numerous lesbian relationships. Though drawn to imposing women for whom she was overwhelmed by intense and passionate feelings, her real love, though not overtly sexual, was for Henry Brewster who exercised the greatest influence on her life.

One of her later 'passions', for Virginia Woolf, resulted in some amusing, and at times, unkind observations: 'What I like is the indomitable old crag: and a certain smile, very wide and benignant. But dear me I am not in love with Ethel;' (Bell: 1980, p. 314); and again, 'Ethel yesterday in a state of wonderment at her own genius. "Can't think how I happened." ' (Bell: 1980, p. 334).

There is, as Louise Collis says, a certain 'figure of fun' aspect to Ethel Smyth: the uncompromising behaviour at times contrasting so pointedly with that of a Dame Commander of the Order of the British Empire conducting orchestras in full Doctor of Music robes with the triangular headgear sometimes flying to the ground. Perhaps the most trenchant comment, however, by Virginia Woolf relates to Ethel Smyth's sexual ambiguity and instability: ' . . . undoubtedly sex and egotism have brewed some bitter insanity.' (Collis: 1984, p. 88).

The years immediately following her break of friendship with Elizabeth Herzogenberg were very difficult ones indeed: being now no longer based in Leipzig she travelled more widely in Europe and spent longer summers in England. She found it difficult to get public performances of her works, and the few that she did get, of her chamber music in Germany, were not well received.

It was as a result of her meeting and friendship with Pauline Trevelyan, who was a devout catholic, that Ethel turned to religion: it was out of the intensity of this new-found experience that the *Mass in D* was created during the years 1889–1890. Though she had made a successful debut in England with the *Serenade for Orchestra*, which was performed at a Crystal Palace concert in 1890, it was not until 1893 that she was able to get the *Mass* performed: even then it was only possible through the pressure brought to bear upon Barnby, the conductor of the Royal Choral Society, by royalty. Throughout most of her life Ethel Smyth was dependent upon financial support from several people, particularly Mary, her eldest sister who had married well, and the Empress Eugénie who had taken up residence near to the Smyth home in Surrey. Equally important were the contacts with influential members of society that both Mary and the Empress Eugénie were instrumental in making for Ethel. Amongst Mary's circle of friends was the painter, Sargent (who later did a fine portrait of Ethel), and Henry James, the novelist. It was through the Empress Eugénie[9] that Ethel was invited to Balmoral and during her stay there sang to Queen Victoria. She had a fine singing voice and used it effectively throughout her life to further her career as a composer by singing excerpts from her compositions to patrons and conductors. The excerpts that she sang to the Queen from the *Mass in D* so impressed her that Barnby was contacted. The Empress Eugénie paid for the publishing of the work and added to the importance of the occasion by her presence at the performance. It was a landmark in Ethel Smyth's career. J.A. Fuller-Maitland, who was for many years the *Times* critic wrote that 'This work definitely placed the composer among the most eminent composers of her time ... throughout it was virile, masterly in construction and workmanship, and particularly remarkable for the excellence and rich colouring of the orchestration.' (Grove: 1908, p. 490 2nd ed.). There were others who were equally critical of the work, but nearly all praised its orchestration. What was remarkable was the fact that it had to wait thirty-one years for its second performance.

From 1894 onwards most of her energy went into writing her six operas and in getting them performed. One should not under-estimate the sheer cost in time, energy and mental frustration that she experienced in Germany, and later in England and America in getting performances of the operas. That they were performed is a tribute to her indefatigable energy and persuasive personality, which is best summed up in a comment by Francis Neilson,[10] who was stage manager of Covent Garden at the turn of the century: 'No woman I have ever met in my life seems to get so much out of her friends.' (St John: 1959, p. 107). To survive at all she had to be quite ruthless, contending not only with male prejudice, but also with anti-British feeling in Germany at the time of the Boer War. Certainly it was sensible to look to Germany with its fourteen opera houses for performances of her operas. In England there was only the short summer season at Covent Garden for opera. Ethel Smyth's first opera, an opera-buffa, *Fantasio* (1892–4), first performed in 1898 at Weimar, was followed by the more successful work, *Der Wald* (1899–1901), which was performed in Berlin, at Covent Garden in 1902 and in America, at the Metropolitan Opera House, New York, in 1903.[11] In collaboration with Henry Brewster she wrote her most successful opera, *The Wreckers* (1902–4), which was performed in Leipzig and Prague in 1906, and at Covent Garden in 1909, when Beecham made his operatic debut with it. The most popular work during her lifetime was however the comic opera, *The Boatswain's Mate* (1914): it had some notable performances at the Old Vic when Lilian Baylis was director. There followed two more operas, *Fête Galante* (1923) and *Entente Cordiale* (1925), the latter a lighthearted work, which contains a chorus part for women's voices only.[12]

Several smaller works achieved some success during her lifetime. In connection with her work for the Women's Suffrage Movement she wrote the *March of the Women*: it was this piece which she conducted with a toothbrush from her window in Holloway Prison where she was imprisoned for several weeks for militant action. She had opposed the Women's Movement for many years, but no doubt as a result of her experiences as a musician, became a strong supporter of it, devoting two years of her life to the cause itself, from 1910–1912. The *Chamber Music Songs*, settings of four French poems for voice, flute, harp, strings and percussion were very well received in Paris in 1908 and a choral work, with orchestral accompaniment, *Hey Nonny No*, received critical acclaim when performed in Vienna in 1911. Orchestrally, the Overture to *The Wreckers* became her most frequently performed piece and the work by which she was best known.

It was during the 1914–18 war, when she was a supplementary radiographer at a military hospital in France, that she began her career as a writer. The success of her autobiographical *Impressions that Remained* led to her devoting considerable time to her literary work. In addition to the nine books that she wrote, Ethel Smyth wrote many articles for magazines on a wide variety of subjects. One issue that she championed was that of women in British orchestras. In 1920 Hamilton Harty sacked all the women players from the Hallé Orchestra who had been admitted during the war when there had been a shortage of men players. 'This was always a man's show and we mean to keep it for men if we can.' (Smyth: 1921, p. 245). This was the basic argument, let slip by one of the Hallé backers. Ethel Smyth entered the controversy fully, with a vehemence that was powerfully felt. Although the Hallé did not change its ways, it was the Queen's Hall Orchestra under Sir Henry Wood that openly welcomed women orchestral players who, in Ethel Smyth's inimitable description ' ... first started mixed bathing in the sea of music.' (Crichton: 1987, p. 340). Her description of the female harpist in the London Symphony Orchestra certainly packs a punch: ' ... this solitary, daintily-clad, white-armed sample of womanhood among the black coats, as it might be a flower on a coal dump.' (Crichton: 1987, p. 340). Beecham's riposte, in his inimitable manner, about the employment of women in orchestras in the 1920s shows again something of the difficulties that women were up against in this respect: 'If they are pretty, they upset the men; if they are ugly, they upset me.'

Certainly, the 1920s saw many performances of her music in England. This was due partly to the Henry Wood Promenade Concerts which featured new English works, and compared with her contemporaries, who included Vaughan Williams, Holst and

Ireland, the number of performances of her works was favourable. Her final work of stature, *The Prison* (1930), a choral symphony, was first performed in Edinburgh. From this time onwards, increasing deafness led her to eventually abandon writing music, but as a speaker and writer she was active until the end of her very long life. She died in 1944 at the age of 86.

In so many-sided a personality as Ethel Smyth's it is easy to find contradictions. On the one hand she had the fine gift of witty observation of character and a remarkable ability to see herself in an uncompromisingly honest way, and yet, on the other hand, she often showed great insensitivity to other people and their points of view. Brought up in a social climate of respectability she became down-to-earth, unstuffy and often an outrageous person, yet, throughout her life she courted the titled and the wealthy and spent much of her life in those circles. Her enthusiasm for sport was exceptional for a woman of the period during which she lived, and led to her being caricatured in a novel by E.F. Benson, *Dodo*, in which she figures as the contradictory Edith Staines, the sporting woman composer. The conflicting claims of composer, writer, traveller and travel-writer, as in *A Three-Legged Tour in Greece*, dissipated much of her energy which, if canalized, might have produced more durable achievements in any one field. In her sexual relationships there is a similar ambiguity and conflict, seen in the overwhelming passions for other women, too many to list, and the enduring relationship with Henry Brewster.

> Her failing, if such it should be called, was not lack of power or sincerity, but rather of purpose . . . Yet, at her best she could produce an impression of grandeur on the one hand, and on the other, effects of surpassing tenderness and beauty. She has been unjustly neglected these past forty years. (Collis: 1984, pp. 206–207).

There is evidence that this neglect is over and one may look forward to her music taking its rightful place amongst British music of the late nineteenth and early twentieth centuries.

In spite of these conflicts in her own personality, she had an engaging manner allied to a lively and original mind. Indeed, any study of Ethel Smyth reveals that her music represents but one facet of this highly enigmatic latter-day George Sand. Her active music career stretches across forty years (1890–1930) which saw, with the advent of radio and in the greatly improved social position of women, radical changes that only towards the end of her career were of benefit to her. She claimed, with some justification, that she began life with two gross blunders – that of being born fifty years too soon and of being of the wrong sex. It is all the more remarkable that an unknown English woman was able to penetrate the very male-dominated preserve of German music at the end of the nineteenth and early twentieth centuries and one must examine to what extent this was achieved by the originality of what she had to say.

The only reliable source for assessment is the music itself, and to this we must now turn.

A Consideration of the Music of Ethel Smyth

The works chosen for detailed comment are representative of her total output and are spread over her musically creative years, 1890–1930.[13] They are also works which have been generally regarded, either in her lifetime or since, as being amongst the best that she wrote. They are:

Mass in D for soloists, chorus and orchestra	1890
The Wreckers: Opera in three acts	1904
The Chamber Music Songs	1908
Hey Nonny No: A cantata for voices and orchestra	1911
The Boatswain's Mate: A Comic Opera in two parts	1914
The Prison: A Symphony for soloists, chorus and orchestra	1930

Mass in D

The Mass was written between 1889 and 1890, largely at Cap Martin when Ethel Smyth was a guest of the Empress Eugénie. The work is dedicated to Pauline Trevelyan who, as a devout catholic and close friend, rekindled Ethel Smyth's religious convictions. *The Mass* was shown to the conductors of various English Choral Societies who showed no interest in the work, and to Levi, conductor of the Court Theatre Orchestra at Munich, who spoke enthusiastically of it, though unable to perform it himself. It was through the influence of royalty that Barnby, conductor of the Royal Choral Society, was persuaded to perform it in January 1893 at the Albert Hall. The performance aroused considerable interest because it was known that royalty would be present at this first performance of a major work by an English woman composer. It received a mixed reception from the press and was not performed again until 1924. The score was revised and published by Novello in that year and though the work received subsequent performances, it is not often performed.

Considered within the context of its time the *Mass in D* is a remarkable achievement. In its powerful sense of structure and assured handling of the orchestra it stands well above the general level of choral works produced in England in the latter part of the nineteenth century. Unfortunately, this is not to say much, since the early choral works of Elgar, and many of those of Parry, Stanford, Elvey, Barnby and Dykes, are best forgotten. There is also much in the *Mass in D* that is best forgotten: even so, movements such as the Kyrie, the Sanctus and parts of the Gloria are memorable. This is not to suggest that the *Mass* offers anything original, as for example one can see in Vaughan Williams's first large-scale choral work in 1907, *Towards the Unknown Region*. One must disagree totally with Tovey when he claims for the *Mass* that, 'No choral work within modern times is more independent of all classical or modern antecedents except those of artistic common sense.' (Tovey: 1937 p. 231). The antecedents are all too obviously the many counterpoint exercises based on the choral music of J.S. Bach which Ethel Smyth worked at for several years at Leipzig. Bach, Beethoven and Brahms are the progenitors: the harmonic vocabulary is a very limited one, impervious to any influences other than that of German music of the diatonic period. It has all the faults of German music – prolixity, dullness and lack of melodic inspiration, but also some of its strengths seen in its impressive solemnity and an ability to shape phrases into satisfying structures. Shaw saw in the work an 'underlying profanity' whilst Tovey described it as 'God-intoxicated', which suggests that one finds in a work that which is unconsciously being sought. It was her first major work and as such proclaimed a composer of undoubted skill and promise in one of the three most important of nineteenth-century forms, the Mass, Opera and Symphony.

It is a demanding work to perform, requiring a large orchestra and a competent, well-rehearsed chorus. These factors have often been cited as the reason for the neglect of this work by choral societies: it is more likely to result from the very unequal nature of the piece and its lack of genuine musical inspiration, seen in its over-reliance on contrapuntal technique and often forced, dramatic quality. Whilst not going so far as Percy Young in *A History of British Music* when he says of the *Mass* that it is ' . . . a pretentious piece of writing: an exercise rather than an invention.' (Young:

1967, p. 540), one must agree that there is much that is pretentious and trite in the work.[14]

The Wreckers

In any account of Ethel Smyth's works, the opera *The Wreckers* or *Les Naufrageurs* as it was originally called, being written to a libretto in French verse by Henry Brewster, figures very highly.

> The vigour and rhythmical force of portions of *The Wreckers* and *Hey Nonny No* equal anything of the kind written in my time . . . Undoubtedly her masterpiece is *The Wreckers*, which remains one of the three or four English operas of real musical merit and vitality written during the past forty years. (*Beecham*: 1944, pp. 122–123)

Whilst one might consider Beecham's regard for the work as one of his many foibles one must take into account the fact that Bruno Walter, a conductor far-removed in temperament from Beecham, held the work in very high regard also, as did Mahler. Certainly the forty years which Beecham refers to, 1904–1944, were not a very productive period for English opera. No doubt Beecham would have included *A Village Romeo and Juliet* by Delius in the three or four English operas which he considered to be of real musical merit, but for the others, no particular work readily presents itself. Had Beecham been writing one year later his whole perspective would unquestionably have been altered with the emergence in that year of what is generally held to be one of the greatest of English operas, Britten's *Peter Grimes*.

Indeed, *Peter Grimes* is brought vividly to mind in much of the drama of *The Wreckers* to the extent that one cannot believe similarities to be entirely coincidental. Both operas are set in remote fishing villages and are concerned with the growing alienation of individuals – Peter Grimes and his lover, Ellen Orford, in Britten's opera, and Thirza and her lover, Mark, in *The Wreckers* – from the community in which they live. Both communities are dominated by the sea and strongly influenced by evangelical religion, and in both operas the chorus, representing the community, has a vital and powerful role to play. The dramatic impact of Act 2, scene 1, of *Peter Grimes* where Ellen Orford and the Apprentice interpolate their phrases between extracts of Morning Service sung by the congregation in the nearby church, is clearly anticipated in Act 1 of *The Wreckers*, where Pascoe and Thirza do likewise. Both scenes imply a certain criticism of organized religion as a hypocritical ritual which does not concern itself with the real evils in the community. The memorable climax to Britten's opera with the fog-horns sounding out at sea whilst the inhabitants of Aldeburgh search for Grimes has a parallel in *The Wreckers* too, where the villagers search for those who are lighting beacons on the shore to warn ships away, and hunting horns are used here to convey the progress of the search. Unless Britten had studied *The Wreckers* the only explanation that can be hazarded for some of these paral-lels is that both operas are based on historical fact.[15]

The plot of *The Wreckers* is powerfully built and was the result of a visit to Cornwall and the Scilly Isles by Ethel Smyth as a young woman. The stories of the barbarous custom by inhabitants of the Cornish coast of luring ships onto the rocks by false, or absence of signals, and the consequent plundering of the ships and murdering of the crew, dwelt in her imagination for many years. She had read too of Wesley's attempts to convert the people from this practice and of his failure to do so. He had, however, in other respects imparted a strong religious fervour to the community which manifested itself in a closed, puritanical attitude of mind. In Pascoe, the fervent Minister of the community is this conflict seen in that he is also the leader of the wreckers. Thirza, his young wife, is projected as the enlightened, courageous heroine who defies conventional morality in taking Mark, a young fisherman, as her lover: the antagonism of the community towards her intensifies until, defying the community, they suffer an ecstatic death at the hands of the community, who feels itself betrayed by their action in lighting warning beacons to the ships.

The plot, thus conceived by Ethel Smyth, was worked into a libretto by Brewster, and to achieve performance had to be trans-lated into German for performances in Leipzig and Prague in 1906, and into English for performances in 1909 and 1910 at Covent Garden. The work has never been performed in its original language.[16]

The strong dramatic situations which this convincing plot afforded were ideally suited to the musical temperament of its author. *The Mass*, her previous large-scale work, suffered from a certain over-dramatisation, and in *The Wreckers* she was able to give vent to this trait. Indeed, the score abounds in dramatic cli-maxes of one kind or another and had much robust, direct writing in it. Perhaps unconsciously, her servant, a Mrs Falkner, hinted at this tendency to over-dramatize when Ethel Smyth asked her opinion of the work. The conversation, recorded by Ethel Smyth in *What Happened Next* went: 'Mrs Falkner, I've done *The Wreckers*.' Pause. 'I should think you must know it by heart by this time.' Mrs Falkner replied, 'Yes, Miss, some of the soft parts are very pretty, I'm sure.' (Smyth: 1940, p. 257).

The Overture begins in fine style, reminiscent perhaps in its rising 4ths and 5ths of Wagner's *Flying Dutchman* Overture (Examples 18 and 19). This theme underpins much of the first act and appears in the other two rather in the way that Bizet uses the fate theme in *Carmen*. No thorough-going Wagnerian *leitmotiv* procedures are used, though the influence can be seen in the transformations that the theme undergoes (Example 20). A less rewarding influence can be traced in Mrs Falkner's 'soft parts', that of English ballad opera. The first part of Act I progresses effectively with chorus writing until the declaration of Ava's love for Mark and her rejection by him. Here the banal strophic songs in the minor key seem utterly out of place and have little to

Example 18   *The Wreckers (Ethel Smyth)*

Example 19   *The Flying Dutchman (Wagner)*

Example 20   *The Wreckers (Ethel Smyth)*

recommend them either dramatically or musically (Example 21). Matters are not improved by some rather freakish writing for the soprano involving awkward leaps in the high register (Example 22).

Act II begins with an extended orchestral Prologue 'On the Cliffs of Cornwall', which includes some of the melodic material for this act (Example 23). The long and sustained love duet of Thirza and Mark which this act contains reveals a fine lyrical gift, though one that makes great demands upon the singers. Act III moves quickly to the climax: the few attempts at real ensemble are not very successful, the writing for the chorus being the more spontaneous.

Musically, the score highlights both Ethel Smyth's strengths and weaknesses. It is a well-structured work, direct, and containing much good theatre. The characters are well portrayed, apart from Avis, whose expression of love for Mark seems forced. Her use of orchestral motives to suggest character, for example that of Pascoe in Act III, is effective and foreshadows Britten's skill in this respect (Example 24). However, Britten's ability in *Peter Grimes* of

Example 21   *The Wreckers (Ethel Smyth)*

Example 22   *The Wreckers (Ethel Smyth)*

Example 23   *The Wreckers (Ethel Smyth)*

Example 24 *The Wreckers (Ethel Smyth)*

drawing out the psychological undercurrents in imaginative, succinct musical phrases is not to be found in *The Wreckers*. The
work is too heavily scored and suffers from too narrow a field of
influences. At a time when Debussy's *Pelléas and Mélisande*, first
performed in 1902, was pointing the way to new and subtle ways
of drama in music, Ethel Smyth seems unable to escape from the
teutonic grip of her academic studies at Leipzig. Harmonically
the work is restricted and anachronistic, the diminished chords,
particularly the overused 7th, serving for the more intense
moments. The fluidity of tonality that Wagner had used to such
effect in *Tristan and Isolde* is in no way reflected in *The Wreckers*:
harmonically it is closer to Beethoven's *Fidelio* than to anything
Wagner wrote.

Its first performance at Leipzig in 1906 was a great success: this
was after two years in which she had unsuccessfully attempted to
get a performance of the work in its original language, at Covent
Garden under Messager. Something of Ethel Smyth's uncompromising nature can be seen from her action at Leipzig after the
first successful performance. The conductor, Hagel, had broken a
promise he had made to her that he would not allow the work to
be cut in any way. When he refused to restore the cuts, she removed
all the music and departed to Prague and thus in her hasty action
antagonized many who may have otherwise helped her.
Throughout her life she would not compromise over any issue and
one cannot help surmising that so inflexible an approach must
have cost her the possibility of many performances of her works.

Even Beethoven, at the end of his career, was persuaded that a complete movement, the finale of op. 130, was out of place. The very last composition he completed was a substitute finale. *The Wreckers* fared badly in Prague where it was poorly performed and, according to Beecham, the work has never had a satisfactory performance on the English professional stage due to the failure to find a dramatic soprano capable of interpreting effectively the part of Thirza. The work was performed in 1909,1910 and 1931 at Covent Garden and in 1939 at Sadlers Wells.

The Chamber Music Songs

The four songs which make up the *Chamber Music Songs* are set to words by the French poets H. De Régnier and Leconte de Lisle and were, appropriately, first performed, and very successfully, in Paris in 1908. The accompaniment is scored for a chamber group of six players: violin, viola, 'cello, flute, harp and percussion (triangle, tambourine, cymbals and side-drum). Alternatively, the work has been arranged for small orchestra of strings, flute, harp and percussion and for piano and voice. The songs are: *Odelette, The Dance, Chrysilla* and *Anacreontic Ode*, the English translations being by Alma Strettell and Ethel Smyth.

One of the characteristics of the nineteenth-century song was the growing tendency which can be observed in the songs of Schumann, Brahms and Wolf to incorporate the voice in a rich instrumental texture. In the music dramas of Wagner and certain symphonies by Mahler, particularly the ninth symphony, *The Song of the Earth* (1908, first performed 1911), the voice is treated as an instrument in a web of symphonically organized sound. In some of the settings of Schöenberg (*Pierrot lunaire*, 1912) and Vaughan Williams (*On Wenlock Edge*, 1911) chamber music textures provide a more satisfactory balance for the voice. This combination of a small group of instruments and voice has been more recently exploited by Benjamin Britten in works like the *Serenade for Tenor, Horn and Strings* (1943). Thus whilst these *Chamber Music Songs* of Ethel Smyth can be related to a particular development in song writing, they do represent a more experimental and forward-looking approach. In these works she was more free of tradition than in most others she wrote, and several critics who heard the songs performed in Paris wrote highly of them, praising their originality and claiming that they represented a 'new direction' for English music.

Seventy years later one can find little evidence to support the contentions of these writers: the 'new direction' in English music came from a more indigenous source, that of folk music and English music of Tudor times, and neither of these influences are to be found to any marked degree in the music of Ethel Smyth.[17] It is interesting to note in passing that it was French poetry, that of Rimbaud, that fired the imagination of Britten as a song writer in *Les Illuminations* (1942) and that in both the *Chamber Music Songs* and *Les Illuminations* French poetry seems to have called forth vocal lines in which declamation plays a large part.

In none of the four songs under consideration can the instruments be said to accompany the voice: their freshness owes much to the variety of instrumental colour which the voice and various instruments achieve. The textures are varied and the writing for the instruments at times is virtuosic: in fact there is a tendency to over-write for the instruments at the expense of the voice, which in 'The Dance' and 'Chrysilla' has a rather low tessitura. The opening of 'The Dance' (Example 25) is imaginative and delicate in its scoring, whereas the opening of the 'Anacreontic Ode' is perhaps more characteristic of the composer in its vigorous Allegro energico style (Example 26).[18] This last song is the more extended of the four and is through-composed. All four songs are well characterized, and though at times are unnecessarily difficult, represent the composer's more imaginative style of writing.[19]

Hey Nonny No

The short choral work *Hey Nonny No* was very well received when performed in Vienna in 1911 and praised in the *Neue Freie Presse* for its overwhelming strength. Holst, when sent a copy in 1921, thought it 'good fun', though he found it too difficult for his choir at Morley College to give it an adequate performance. There is no doubt that it is beyond the grasp of good amateur performance in that the range and tessitura are demanding and the vocal lines angular.

The text, from a sixteenth-century manuscript extols the virtues of wine and dance and is set imaginatively. Ethel Smyth's fondness for intervals of the tritone and resultant diminished and augmented chords infuses the whole work and tonally makes for good contrasts with the more deliberately diatonic sections (Example 27). Indeed, harmonically, it is one of her most experimental works with

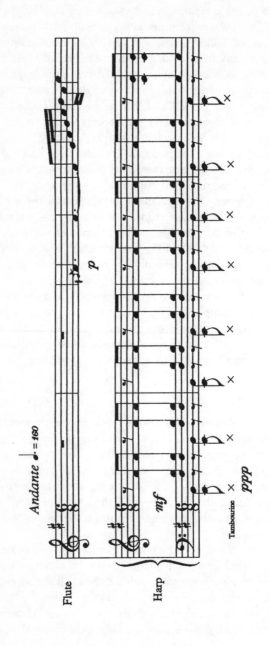

Example 25   *The Dance (Ethel Smyth)*

Example 26   *Anacreontic Ode (Ethel Smyth)*

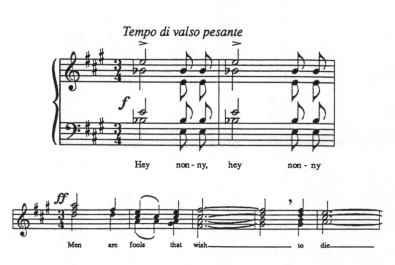

Example 27   *Hey Nonny No (Ethel Smyth)*

atonal sections (Example 28) providing a welcome astringency. The vocal textures are most skilfully varied and the climaxes, particularly the final one, well-built.

To what extent the text demands such powerful treatment is, however, debatable. Both music and text are rather repetitive and a more simple treatment might not only have been more appropriate to the text but might have won more performances of the work. Holst's question, 'Why, oh why, is *Hey Nonny No* so hard?' points to the reason why much of Ethel Smyth's music has been neglected. It was the kind of mistake which both Holst and Vaughan Williams soon rectified in their own works out of their practical experience. Indeed, the examples that Gustav Holst set, of combining a teaching and a composing career, and of Vaughan Williams who, like Ethel Smyth, had an annuity which made it unnecessary for him to have to earn a living but who nevertheless

Example 28   Hey Nonny No (Ethel Smyth)

immersed himself in amateur music-making, are ones that regrettably Ethel Smyth did not follow. Unfortunately for her career as a composer, her energies were dissipated, and whilst she often bemoaned the fact that women were debarred from the musical experience that men were able to gain, she rarely seemed to consider anything but the professional world of music, where her claim was regrettably true. Thus her compositions seem to be almost entirely conceived for professional performance: in aiming so high she missed so much. Even her popular piece, *The March of the Women*, which was written for the suffragettes, suffers from a difficult middle section where the placing of the high E flat often caused problems for untrained voices (Example 29)[20]; whereas with Holst and Vaughan Williams the very challenge of having to write music that was performable by amateurs became a creative stimulant.[21]

The Boatswains's Mate

After devoting two years of her life to the Suffragette Movement, Ethel Smyth began to pick up the threads of her music career again in 1913; she had abandoned it at a time when, as evidenced in the *Chamber Music Songs* and *Hey Nonny No*, she was beginning to break new ground and find critical support, at least, abroad, for her compositions. Musically, she had made a big sacrifice: however, her experience of being caught up in a movement of some magnitude, which sharpened her social and political awareness, afforded some return. Above all, her close contact with Emmeline Pankhurst, for whom she had a great admiration, strengthened her own resolve in her chosen field of women's liberation, music.

Her first thoughts were towards an opera based on Synge's play, *Riders to the Sea*, and for a while she went to Ireland to immerse herself in the sounds and customs of Ireland. What she eventually did was to abandon this idea in favour of a comic opera based upon a story by W.H. Jacobs, *The Boatswain's Mate*, which she began and completed within a year. Both the choice of story and the place she chose in which to write it, Egypt, can be seen as a reaction against the ardours of her two years' work for the Women's Social and Political Union. Its influence can be seen in the dominant role of the seemingly self-sufficient Mrs Waters, landlady of The Beehive, and in the Overture, where the two main themes are taken from *Songs of Sunrise* (1913), nos 2 and 3 (Example 30). This group of songs written to her own verse is

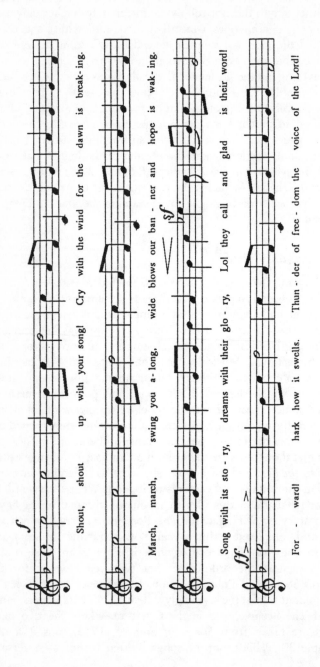

Example 29 *March of the Women (Ethel Smyth)*

Example 30 *The Boatswain's Mate (Ethel Smyth)*

musically weak, the first one, a part-song for female voices being the best of the group: the third one is *The March of the Women*.[22]

The Boatswain's Mate has a simple plot concerning the successful wooing of Mrs Waters by Ned Travers, a former soldier. Harry Benn, who for many years has been pressing his suit, hits upon the plan of engaging Ned Travers as a burglar so that by appearing to fearlessly chase him away Harry Benn could prove to Mrs Waters how essential it is for her to have a man at The Beehive. The plan fails since Mrs Waters surprises Ned Travers with a gun and in no time both have fallen for each other. The story was adapted as a libretto by Ethel Smyth and is set in two parts. The first part has spoken dialogue and belongs to the same genre as Sullivan's *Cox and Box*, whereas the second part is set to continuous music in the operatic tradition.[23] This change of style within a work is certainly unusual and one which Beecham thought regrettable: 'But in the second [act] this happy scheme is thrown overboard for an uninterrupted stream of music involving the setting of portions of the text that one feels would have been more effective and congruous had they been kept in speech as in the earlier section of the work.' (Beecham: 1944, p. 122).

The music throughout has a light touch: the folk-song, 'The keeper did a-shooting go' makes its appearance as a tune that is whistled with flute accompaniment, and there is more than a veiled reference to 'Oh dear, what can the matter be?' in Part Two in a song by Mrs Waters (Example 31). A sentimental ballad is very well guyed with dominant harmonies where tonic harmony is called for (Example 32), and the arrival of the Policeman is to the motto theme from Beethoven's Fifth Symphony. His song is a good example of musical characterization (Example 33) where close attention has been paid to speech rhythms and inflections. The

Example 31 *The Boatswain's Mate (Ethel Smyth)*

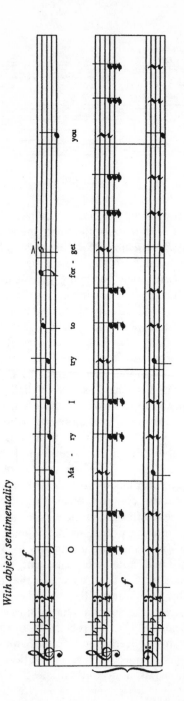

Example 32 *The Boatswain's Mate (Ethel Smyth)*

178

Out - side your house I met this man 'ere, all white and tremb - ling and his 'air as you see it

Example 33 *The Boatswain's Mate (Ethel Smyth)*

opera was to have been premiered at Frankfurt-am-Main, fourteen days after the revival of *The Wreckers* at Munich under Bruno Walter. Neither performance took place owing to the outbreak of war. *The Boatswain's Mate* proved to be the most popular of Ethel Smyth's operas, not without justification.

The Prison

The Prison was the last large-scale work that Ethel Smyth wrote. It was well received at its first performance in Edinburgh with the seventy-two year old composer conducting. The text was selected by Ethel Smyth from a philosophical work of the same title by Henry Brewster and it is one which the composer had long-considered and had closely identified herself with. The prison is the prison of self and the work records the thoughts of an individual approaching death. The work is in two parts: Close on Freedom and The Deliverance. There are three personages: the prisoner, bass-baritone, his soul, soprano, and voices, represented by a mixed chorus.

The text immediately calls to mind that of Cardinal Newman's in Elgar's *Dream of Gerontius*, though not in a specifically religious sense. In both works the individual wins through to an acceptance of death after being assailed by many doubts. When the prisoner sings of immortality there is effective use of the interval of the seventh and the music is concise and expressive (Example 34). Harmonically, the style is rather a mixture: the terseness of Walton is recalled occasionally (Example 35) and yet tonality is in no way jettisoned and there is much that would not be out of place in the music of nineteenth-century composers. The vocal lines lack spontaneity, and emphasis and reiteration often do service for the really telling musical phrase (Example 36).

Generally, the quality of musical inventiveness was not equal to the large-scale forms which Ethel Smyth so often chose to work in. The result is often a bombastic style of writing, full of rhetorical gestures and imitative beginnings that come to nothing. Much of

Example 34   *The Prison (Ethel Smyth)*

Example 35   *The Prison (Ethel Smyth)*

Example 36   *The Prison (Ethel Smyth)*

The Prison falls into this category. Virginia Woolf who was present at a private rehearsal of the soloists in preparation for a perform-ance of *The Prison* wrote:

> I suspect the music is too literary – too stressed – too didactic for my taste. But I am always impressed by the fact that she has spun these coherent chords, harmonies, melodies out of her so practical vigorous student mind. What if she should be a great composer? This fantastic idea is to her the merest commonplace: it is the fabric of her being. (*Woolf*: 1959, p. 168)

It is in the chamber works that a more original voice is often heard, one that attempts to escape from the academism of nineteenth-century Leipzig. Her training certainly equipped her with a good technique and a powerful sense of construction, but because it was not mixed with other influences it became a crippling and limiting straight-jacket to her musical inventiveness.

> Tell them that no man lives in vain
> That some small part of our work
> For reasons unknown to us, has been tossed aloft
> And gathered in for ever. (Brewster: *The Prison*)

This was a hope that Ethel Smyth held before her through the many years of neglect and the many false dawns to the realization of her most ardent desire.

The Literary Works of Ethel Smyth

> Dodo was turning over the leaves of Edith's scorebook. 'I give up', she said at last, 'you are such a jumble of opposites. You sit down and write a Sanctus, which makes one feel as if one wants to be a Roman Catholic Archbishop, and all the time you are smoking cigarettes and eating grilled bone.'
> 'Oh, everyone's a jumble of opposites', said Edith, 'when you come to look at them. It's only because my opposites are superficial that you notice them!' (*Benson*: 1890, p. 76)

A personality so vital, so uncompromisingly honest and so uncon-ventional was bound to attract admiration and hostility, and Ethel Smyth certainly did this during her lifetime. The caricature of Ethel Smyth in the novel *Dodo* by E.F. Benson, as Edith Staines, the sporting woman composer, highlights her unconventionality and the conflicting facets of her personality. No consideration of

Ethel Smyth would be complete without reference to her strong literary inclinations, and her writings are superimposed, like a chord, on to her career as a composer. Indeed, her writing at first complemented her music career but eventually, with the onset of deafness, supplanted it. She was active as a composer for over forty years, approximately 1890 to 1930, whilst her career as a writer, from 1919 to 1940, covered the latter part of her creative life. The two volumes of autobiography, *Impressions that Remained*, which began the series of nine books which she wrote, did much to stimulate interest in her music and to a large extent accounted for the more frequent performances of her music during the period 1920 to 1940.

The success of these two volumes encouraged her to write several more autobiographical books: indeed, although the subjects dealt with in the later books are very varied, there is in all of them a strong element of autobiography. The richness of her life, which of course stemmed from her amazing vitality, provided a varied storehouse of material. Her numerous travels, often quite arduous, her involvement with so great a variety of people and above all her sense of humour and down-to-earth attitude to most things, make for a writer who can hold one's attention from beginning to end. In fact, it is something more positive than that: so often she writes with the same intention as the orator, to arouse one, to change one's attitude, to influence. The writer often becomes the pamphleteer, the propagandist. The main cause that she espoused, often with a vehemence born out of personal experience, was that of equality of opportunity for women composers and women musicians in general compared with that afforded to men. There is a chapter, An Open Secret, in her second book, *Streaks of Life*, which is the opening salvo on this topic: it becomes the main substance of *A Final Burning of Boats, Etc.* and is taken up again in *Female Pipings in Eden* and in the Epilogue of *As Time Went On*. These sections tend to be the least satisfactory of her writings, not because of what she has to say, but because the propagandist, relying on anecdote and sweeping generalizations, tends to take over from the writer with a steady and clear vision. For a comparison, one should remember Virginia Woolf's *A Room of One's Own* where a similar subject, the freedom of the woman novelist, is much more rationally and effectively discussed.

Her greatest strength, as a writer, is to be found in her astutely observed portraits of people with whom she had a close relationship. Here, her ability to see the person as a whole, to pick on revealing detail, and her warmth of spirit come to the fore, and the writing is in a different class altogether. Her portrait of Emmeline Pankhurst in *Female Pipings in Eden* is the most richly drawn, and in some ways, the most generously so, being written after a certain coolness had come between them. Notable also are the portraits of her father in *Impressions that Remained*, Vol. I, of Lady Ponsonby in *As Time Went On*, of the Empress Eugénie in *Streaks of Life* and of Brahms in *Female Pipings in Eden*. Less satisfactory, though interesting, is her portrait of Sir Thomas Beecham in *Beecham and Pharaoh* where one feels that the writing is a little forced at times.

A recurrent theme is the unsatisfactory state of music and musical performance in England compared with that of Germany. Her proposals for the revitalization of opera in England, first hinted at in a chapter headed 'The Opera Fiasco' in *Streaks of Life*, and presented as proposals in the chapter headed 'An Iron Thesis on Opera' in *A Final Burning of Boats*, Etc., are sound and were ones that, to some extent, have been adopted since. As a person, she was acutely observant of people and places: her description of her excursion into the Apennines in Vol. II of *Impressions that Remained*, of Egypt in *Beecham and Pharaoh* and of Greece in *A Three-legged Tour in Greece* amounts in each case to an excellent travelogue, where the real flavour of the countries and their customs are entertainingly recorded. She allows herself to be sidetracked by whatever attracts her attention and we share her enthusiasm and the uniqueness of the occasion which she conveys.

Her books also provide a wealth of anecdote as well as detailed, yet incidental, description of the social conventions prevailing in late nineteenth-century bourgeois England and Germany. In the chapter headed 'A Winter of Storm' in *Streaks of Life* she discusses politics, the politics of the Boer War as seen from the German point of view. She had long and frank discussions with Count von Bülow, Chancellor of Germany, who was responsible for foreign policy, as well as with the Kaiser. Throughout both this chapter and the one headed 'Germany after the War' in *A Final Burning of Boats, Etc.* her sympathies for the country of her adoption, Germany, are apparent.

Rather lofty claims have been made for Ethel Smyth's style as a writer: ' . . . as a writer of English prose she possessed indisputable genius.' (Grove: 1966, p. 862, 5th edn) which cannot be substantiated. As V. Sackville-West states, in her article *Ethel Smyth, the Writer* (St John 1959, pp. 245–250), one cannot separate the personality from the writer: the impetuosity, the passion and the vitality pour into her writings, and in the headlong rush scant attention is paid to syntax. Yet it is because there appears to be no artificial barrier between the person and the writer that her books are so readable and arresting. What she has to say she does say directly, in the simplest terms, although her fondness for quoting in French, a fashion of the age in which she wrote, might today be seen as affectation. At times, colloquialisms blemish the text and her imagery can be rather crude. On the other hand, she has the wonderful ability to pinpoint character in but a few words. Of Webern, whose music, one gathers, she was not drawn to, she writes: 'I never saw an angrier man; he is about thirty-five, dry and thin as though pickled in perennial fury, and erect as a ramrod.' (Smyth: 1928, p. 120). Images from the world of horse-riding, of sport and the great outdoor world add spontaneity. In a chapter on the woman composer Augusta Holmès in *A Final Burning of Boats, Etc.*, she writes: 'In 1902 H.B. was still a very good-looking man, and the sight of him had the effect on Augusta of the classical bugle-call on the demobilised warhorse.' (Smyth: 1928, p. 85). It may not be good literature, but is invigoratingly fresh. When describing Henry Wood she speaks of his dislike of unpleasantness as what ' . . . in a horseman you would call perfect hands, (in a human being it is tact, I suppose)' (Smyth: 1928, p. 85) and it is this incongruity, this non-literary image, which adds a certain swash-buckling element to her prose.

In addition to her books Ethel Smyth wrote the libretti to several of her operas, for example, *Entente Cordiale*, and was a voluminous letter writer, some of which extended to over four thousand words. Articles for magazines, obituary notices, papers read to various learned societies, speech days – all these multifarious literary activities were somehow accomplished in a very full and active life. The sense of structure, so noticeable in her music, is lacking in her literary works: her books were produced as chips from the block of her musically creative life and written at white heat. What they gain in immediacy they lose in structure and form. Even so, that she could use language with great beauty there is no doubt. As an example of her more exalted style, and as a very characteristic epilogue, both in its imagery and content, let Ethel Smyth have the final word:

It is the chase, not the quarry, that makes the splendour of our days – also their anguish; and as the hound that belongs to no pack will hunt a line all by himself for love of hunting, so my life has been a solitary pursuit of the dream that every artist pursues, though seldom, I think, in solitude so utter as mine; the elusive vision that Henri de Régnier's dancing maiden danced after, with outstretched arms, through the autumn-stricken wood, 'Cherchant sa bouche amère ou douce en fuite dans le vent.'

And our only moments of perfect happiness are when we seem to touch a fold of that intangible garment. (*Smyth*: 1928, p. 54)

Notes

1 When discussing the *Mass in D*, J.A. Fuller-Maitland said ' . . . but there was plenty of original thought in the work, and if it may be said with deference, Miss Smyth's work suffers, if at all, from a lack of those qualities usually associated with her sex, namely, grace, charm and tenderness.' (Fuller-Maitland 1902 p. 267).

2 See Appendix 4 for a consideration of this assertion.

3 A similar viewpoint is expressed in a record review of her chamber music and songs suggesting that Ethel Smyth's music is 'more written about than listened to' and that 'maybe her life and personality *are* more interesting than her music.' (Hold: 1993, p. 43). The production of three CDs, interestingly by a German company rather than by a British company, was an attempt to rectify this perceived attitude.

4 Other British composers who were successful in getting their operas performed abroad during the late nineteenth and early twentieth centuries were Balfe, Pierson, Stanford, Thomas and Wallace.

5 Elgar's *Dream of Gerontius* was first recognized in Germany in 1902.

6 In the *Memoirs of Ethel Smyth* there is a perceptive study of her father in which it is surprising to discover that he actually supported female suffrage for propertied females on the grounds of fair play. (Crichton: 1987, pp. 29–33).

7 In the late 1880s Ethel Smyth traced her family tree back to 1630 and it was in connection with this research that she came across her grandmother's letters to her mother.

8 Something of Ethel Smyth's lively style of writing comes over in her description of this tune which she says has 'a sort of groping ecstasy confined in *Ancient and Modern* fetters'.

9 The Empress Eugénie was an ardent feminist: it had been through her efforts that women were first employed in the French post office.

10 In his autobiography, *My Life in Two Worlds*, Neilson gives an interesting account of his dealings with Ethel Smyth.

11 In an article entitled *Ethel Smyth: the only woman composer ever to be heard at the Met* Carl Johnson describes the background and reactions to the performance of *Der Wald* at the Met in 1903. (Johnson: 1982, pp. 14–17).

12 The last two operas, *Fête Galante* and *Entente Cordiale* formed a double bill at the Royal College of Music in 1925. A revival of *Fête*

Galante at the Royal College of Music in 1989 was well received. (Goodwin: 1989, pp. 1139–1140).

13 For a comprehensive listing of works, which incorporates the newly discovered 'cello sonata in C minor referred to in an article in the Strad (Franca: 1981, pp. 718–719) see the compilation by Jory Bennett in Crichton (1987, pp. 373–381).

14 *The Mass in D* along with Ethel Smyth's choral works is the subject of a thesis (Copley, 1990). The Mass has also been recorded on CD.

15 It is a strange coincidence that the last work performed at Sadlers Wells before its closure in 1939 was a revival of *The Wreckers* and that, on its reopening in 1945 the first work performed was *Peter Grimes*.

16 Sir Thomas Beecham thought highly of *The Wreckers* (Abromeit: 1989, pp. 196–211). In the last two decades there have been several amateur revivals at Glasgow in 1972, Bristol 1975, Bradford 1982 and a production by Graham Vick at Warwick in 1983. In reviewing this performance the writer claims it to be ' . . . an unjustly neglected work' (Osborne: 1983, pp. 566–567). A strong plea for a professional revival of *The Wreckers* is made by Banfield (1986, pp. 205–207). An opportunity to assess its musical worth was provided by a concert version performance at the BBC Promenade Concerts in 1994 and subsequent recording.

17 'She thus stands to one side of the [English Musical] renaissance, or was perhaps one of its heralds, a portent of the more strenuous attitude to the art than the Victorians were willing to accord it.' (Howes: 1966, p. 67).

18 Allegro energico seems to be as characteristic an indication of tempo and mood for Ethel Smyth as was nobilamente for Elgar.

19 These have been recorded along with other chamber music by Ethel Smyth on three CDs. In a review (Hold: 1993, p. 43) they are described as ' . . . quite novel for its period.' Apparently, Debussy liked them.

20 Other women composers were active writing suffragette music. Alicia Needham produced *Four Songs for Women Suffragettes* with the militant titles: *Marching On, Daughters of England, Fighting On* and *Clipped Wings*. Indeed, *Marching On* is in many ways a much more rousing and effective song than Ethel Smyth's *March of the Women*. It has the tread of many feet which *March of the Women* lacks (Example 37).

21 For a detailed commentary upon the suffragette period works which include the *March of the Women, Hey Nonny No*, the *Songs of Sunrise*, the *Three Songs for Female Voice* and the opera, *The Boatswain's Mate*, see Wood (1995, pp. 606–643).

22 The *March of the Women* is quoted in full in Scholes (1947, p. 886) in the most impracticable key of A flat major.

23 Writing about a performance of *The Boatswain's Mate* at the Cambridge Festival in 1982 the reviewer, (Smith: 1982, p. 59) commented

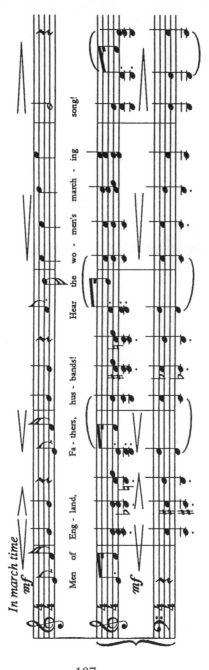

Example 37 *Marching On (Alicia Needham)*

favourably on this transition which in performance did ' ... not seem unnatural or forced' and found the characters well defined and the orchestration clear and supportive. See also Bowers and Tick (1986, p. 316).

Principal Women Singers Appearing in England During the Nineteenth Century

In the following tables please note that:

1   The first entry marks the London debut.
2   A broken line (– – – – –) indicates absence during that period.
3   Names in italic are of women with nationalities other than English.
4   Asterisked names indicate contraltos.

A   Principal women singers appearing in England, 1770–1830

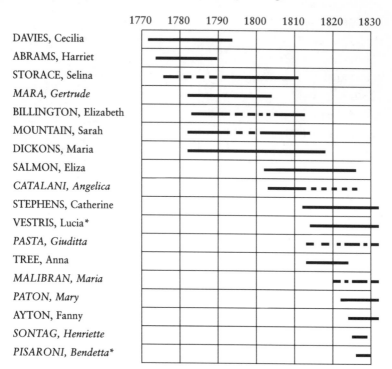

	1770	1780	1790	1800	1810	1820	1830
DAVIES, Cecilia							
ABRAMS, Harriet							
STORACE, Selina							
MARA, Gertrude							
BILLINGTON, Elizabeth							
MOUNTAIN, Sarah							
DICKONS, Maria							
SALMON, Eliza							
CATALANI, Angelica							
STEPHENS, Catherine							
VESTRIS, Lucia*							
PASTA, Giuditta							
TREE, Anna							
MALIBRAN, Maria							
PATON, Mary							
AYTON, Fanny							
SONTAG, Henriette							
*PISARONI, Bendetta**							

B   Principal Women Singers Appearing in England, 1830–1870

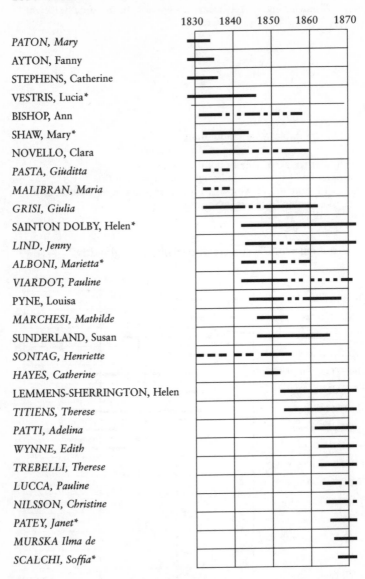

C   Principal Women Singers Appearing in England, 1870–1900

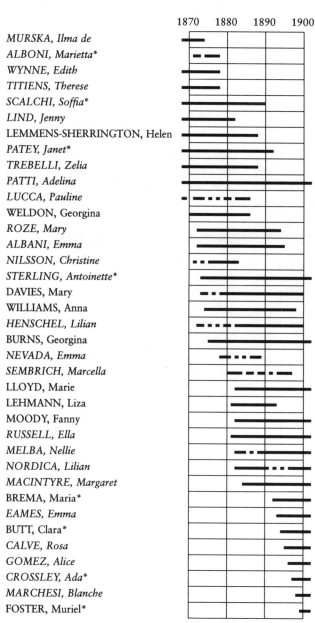

'A Valentine' by Miss Catherine Hansell

(Written in the back of the British Library copy of Sarah Glover's *Scheme* of 1839. It was sent to her in February, 1841.)

The good people who live afar off in the moon
Are wont of some '*scheme*' which their voices may tune.
They have set round to Saturn and Jupiter, Mars,
To Mercury, Venus and e'en the fixed stars;
But through comets and suns in their search they've
    combined
The Spirit of Harmony ne'er could they find.
In Saturn indeed they attempted to sing,
But the tenors and Bass being placed in the ring
The harmony seemed as if to and fro toss'd
And the voices between in the chatter were lost.
The fair maids of Venus too, they raised some strains,
But more on their looks than their sounds bestow'd pains.
The thunders in Jupiter awful rise,
And Mercury's wings beat the air as he flies.
Whilst in Mars nought is heard of harmonious sounds
But what from the clashing of armour resounds.
Yet still from the *Earth* when they listen at eve
Such sweet strains are wafted as Seraphs might give.
And they hear too ('tis this that inflames most their hearts)
A 'Magician' lives there who this knowledge imparts.
That all that she needs is to flourish her wand
Straightway Men, Women, Children obey her command,
That all animal nature is taught to Sol-fa
The cows to low '*Moo*', and the sheep to bleat '*Bah*'
That *Birds, Bats* and *Reptiles* in unison chime
That Babes cry 'in parts' and insects click time.
With as great a respect then as ever was paid
To the Emperor of China when the 'Kowton' is made,
They petition the Author of Sol-fa to send
Some teacher of Music instruction to lend.
And they trust that in time as she roves by moonlight
Soft sounds may thence come through the stillness of night;
Which may show that their teaching has not been in vain
But how anxious they've been due improvement to gain
And further they beg she will deign to partake

Of the offering they send, a *lunar plum* cake,
They hope that their packet may reach Mother Earth
At the season that gave good St. Valentine birth;
Because they have heard and believe it is true,
That free and full leave is then granted to do
What at some other time might a liberty seem
But would not (as it is) no presumption they deem.
And many a hearty and kind wish they send
That all good may the 'Mighty Enchantress' attend,
And trusting she'll send them an answer right soon,
Subscribe themselves humbly, *her friends in the Moon.*

Volcanic Valley, The Moon.

P.S. Passengers may be conveyed, or parcels and letters
forwarded by the Atmospheric Railroad.

By Miss Catherine Hansell,
Lower Close,
Norwich.

Sarah Glover's Works

1834 *The Sol-fa Tune Book*, Jarrold & Sons, Norwich.
1835 *A Scheme for Rendering Psalmody Congregational*, Hamilton, Adams & Co, London, Jarrold & Sons, Norwich. (To be found at the British Library and Norwich Central Library.)
1837 *The Sol-fa Tune Book* (2nd edn).
1838 *The Norwich Guide to Sol-fa-ing*, Hamilton, Adams & Co, London, Jarrold & Sons, Norwich.
1838 *Rewards and Punishments in Weekday Schools for the Labouring Classes of Society*, Hamilton, Adams & Co., London, Jarrold & Sons, Norwich.
       (To be found at the Strangers' Hall Museum, Norwich.)
1839 *A Scheme for Rendering Psalmody Congregational*, (2nd edn), Hamilton, Adams & Co., London, Jarrold & Sons, Norwich. (To be found at the British Library. The copy carries a dedication to her niece, Christiana Rachel Bird, 3 June, 1839. Written in the back of this copy is the poem quoted in Appendix 2 by Miss Catherine Hansell.)
1839 *The Sol-fa Tune Book* (3rd edn).
1841 *The Sol-fa Tune Book* (4th edn).
1844 *A History of the Norwich Sol-fa System for teaching music in schools*, Hamilton, Adams & Co, London, Jarrold & Sons, Norwich. (To be found in Ms. at the Strangers' Hall Museum, Norwich.)
1844 *The Sol-fa Tune Book* (5th edn).
1844 *The Norwich Guide to Sol-fa-ing* (2nd edn).
1845 *A Manual of the Norwich Sol-fa System, for teaching Singing in Schools and Classes or A Scheme for Rendering Psalmody Congregational* (3rd edn), Hamilton, Adams & Co, London, Jarrold & Sons, Norwich. (To be found in Norwich Central Library.)
1850 *The Tetrachordal System*. Manual containing a development of the tetrachordal system designed to facilitate the acquisition of music, by a return to first principles (4th edn), J. Alfred Novello, London, Jarrold & Sons, Norwich. (To be found at Norwich Central Library.)
1853 *The Sol-fa Tune Book* (6th edn).
1859 *The Norwich Sol-fa System Manual*. (Ms. at the Strangers' Hall Museum, Norwich.)
1860 *The Rise and Progress of the Notation of Music by Sol-fa letters*

from the year 1812 to 1860. (Ms. at the Strangers' Hall Museum, Norwich.)

1860   *The Sol-fa Harmonicon* with two Rotary Indexes. (Ms. at the Strangers' Hall Museum, Norwich.)

There is a significant change in the titles to the third and fourth editions of Sarah Glover's *Scheme* (1845 and 1850) which obviously reflects her changing attitude to it and her attempts to reach a wider market. It may also be significant that the fourth edition is published in London by the more well-known firm of Novello, the only one of her works to be so published.

Performances of Ethel Smyth's Music During Her Lifetime

In an appendix to the book, *Female Piping in Eden*, Ethel Smyth lists the total number of performances of her important choral works since 1893. These, she claimed, totalled sixteen,[1] and included seven performances of *The Mass in D*, two of *The Prison*, plus performances of *Two Short Choruses*, *Hey Nonny No* and *The Spring Canticle*.

Until 1914 it would be true to say that the opportunities for performance of her music in no way compared with that of composers like Parry, Stanford and Elgar, whose large-scale choral works were frequently performed at the Three Choirs Festival, The Birmingham Festival, The Norwich Festival and The Leeds Festival. When one examines in more detail the works performed it is noticeable, however, that these composers were producing new works for each performance: their output was prodigious.[2] The only large-scale choral work which Ethel Smyth could offer during this period was *The Mass in D* and it is obvious that the novelty of new works was certainly a major attraction to concert promoters and conductors. Holbrooke, in his book, *Contemporary British Composers* (1925) discusses the reasons why Ethel Smyth's music was not more frequently performed and suggests that its difficulty debarred it from amateur performance and that, being a woman, she belonged to no coterie or clique. There is some truth in these comments, but one should remember that Elgar belonged to no coterie and, like Ethel Smyth, had not the backing of the English Colleges of Music or the two older Universities. The fact surely is that whilst Parry, Stanford and Elgar plus many others devoted their energies largely to satisfying the demands of the provincial choral societies, Ethel Smyth poured her musical energies into opera. England has never been the home of opera in the same way as it has been in Italy or Germany: the English tradition is a choral tradition and to this very day it is difficult to get new operas performed in England. It was certainly even more hazardous an undertaking in the pre-1914 period during which time Ethel Smyth was trying to get her works performed.

The post-war years, particularly the 1920s, saw many performances of her works: in this period performances of her music compared favourably with many of her male contemporaries. Unfortunately, by this time, the struggles of the past had left their mark, and Ethel Smyth ascribed her lack of recognition as a composer to her being a female. It would seem that it had more to do with the kind of music she wrote and its inability to escape from a narrow and confining influence.

Notes

1 Checking through the performances at the Three Choirs Festivals one noted a performance of Ethel Smyth's *Mass*, conducted by the composer, in 1928, which does not appear in her list. Could there be other such omissions?
2 See Galloway (1910, pp. 91–98) for a summary of the works performed at these festivals.

Women Composers Referred to in the Text

Dates are given, where known, and teachers or institutions where taught.

Abrams, Harriet, 1760–1825, *ARNE*
Allitsen, Frances, 1849–1912, *Guildhall School of Music*
Bisset, Elizabeth born 1800
Boyce, Ethel, 1863–1936, *Royal Academy of Music*
Bright, Dora E., 1863–1951, *Royal Academy of Music*
Brissac, Jules (Mrs John Macfarren), 1824–1895, *Royal Academy of Music*
Carmichael, Mary G., 1851–1935, *Royal Academy of Music*
Chamberlayne, Elizabeth A., *PROUT*
Chaminade, Cécile, 1857–1944
Claribel (Mrs Charlotte Alington Barnard), 1830–1869
Clarke, Emilie
Cristabel (Florence Attenborough)
Dolores (Ellen Dickson), 1819–1878
Dufferin, Lady, 1807–1867
Ellicott, Rosaline F., 1857–1924, *Royal Academy of Music*
Flower, Eliza, 1803–1846
Gabriel, Virginia, 1825–1877, *MOLIQUE*
Hardelot, Guy de (Mrs Rhodes), 1858–1936, *Paris Conservatoire*
Harraden, Ethel
Heale, Helen, born 1855 *HULLAH*
Hill, Lady Arthur (Anne Fortescue Harrison), 1851–1944
Holmès, Augusta, 1847–1903, *FRANCK*
Lawrence, Emily, born 1854, *Royal Academy of Music*
Lehmann, Liza, 1862–1918, *CLARA SCHUMANN, JENNY LIND*
Lindsay, Miss M. (Mrs J. Worthington Bliss), 1827–1898
Macirone, Clara A. 1821–1914 *Royal Academy of Music*
Millard, Mrs Philip
Moody, Marie
Mounsey, Ann (Bartholomew), 1811–1891, *S. WESLEY, ATTWOOD*
Mounsey, Elizabeth, 1819–1905
Needham, Alicia 1872–1945, *Royal Academy of Music*
Norton, Hon. Mrs. Caroline, 1808–1877
Nunn, Elizabeth, 1861–1894
Orger, Caroline (Reinagle), 1818–1892
Prescott, Oliveria, 1842–1919, *Royal Academy of Music*
Sainton Dolby, Helen C., 1821–1885, *Royal Academy of Music*
de Sivrai, Jules (Jane Jackson), 1834–1907, *CLARA SCHUMANN*

Smith, Alice M. (Mrs Meadows White), 1839–1889, *Royal Academy of Music*
Smyth, Ethel, 1858–1944, *Leipzig Conservatorium*
Spottiswoode, Alicia A. (Lady John Douglas Scott), 1810–1900
Stirling, Elizabeth, 1819–1895, *Royal Academy of Music*
Stresa, Mrs (Florence Skinner)
Temple, Hope, 1859–1938, *MESSAGER*
Tennyson, Lady Emily
White, Maude Valérie, 1855–1937, *Royal Academy of Music*
Woodforde-Finden, Amy, 1860–1919
Wurm, Marie, 1860–1938, *CLARA SCHUMANN, SULLIVAN, STANFORD, BRIDGE*

General Bibliography

Acland, A. (1948), *Caroline Norton*, London: Constable.

Anon. (1830), *Memoirs of the Life of Madame Vestris, illustrated with numerous curious anecdotes*, London: privately printed.

Baker, E.C. and Hess, T.B. (1973), *Art and Sexual Politics*, New York: Collier Books.

Barnard, H.C. (1966), *Fénelon on Education*, Cambridge: Cambridge University Press.

Beauvoir, S. de (1949, reprinted 1972), *The Second Sex*, London: Penguin.

Beecham, Sir T. (1944, reprinted 1961), *A Mingled Chime*, London: Hutchinson & Arrow Books.

Beilby, Lord Bishop of London (1790), *A Charge delivered to the Clergy of the Diocese of London*, London: St. Paul's Church Yard.

Bell, A.O., (ed.) (1980), *The diary of Virginia Woolf, Volume 3*, London: Hogarth Press.

Benson, E.F. (u.d.), *Dodo*, London: Hodder & Stoughton.

Blunn, J.R. (1972), *Northern Accent*, Altrincham: John Sherratt & Son.

Bowers, J. and Tick, J. (ed.) (1986), *Women Making Music. The Western Art Tradition 1150–1950*, London: The Macmillan Press.

Bray, Mrs – see under classified bibliography of women writers.

Briggs, A. (1954, reprinted 1965), *Victorian People*, London: Pelican Books.

Brown, J.D. and Stratton, S.S. (1897), *British Musical Biography*, London: William Reeves.

Brown, P. (1814), *The History of Norwich*, Norwich: Bacon, Kinnebrook & Co.

Buxton, C. (1848), *Memoirs of Sir Thomas Fowell-Buxton*, London: John Murray.

Byrne, J.C. – see under classified bibliography of women writers.

Campbell, Lady A. – see under classified bibliography of women writers.

Citron, M.J. (1993), *Gender and the Musical Canon*, Cambridge: Cambridge University Press.

Chesterton, G.K. (1913), *The Victorian Age in Literature*, London: Oxford University Press.

Clayton, E.C. – see under classified bibliography of women writers.

Collis, L. (1984), *Impetuous Heart – the story of Ethel Smyth*, London: W. Kimber.

Cook, S.C. and Tsou, J.S. (ed.) (1994), *Cecilia Reclaimed. Feminist Perspectives on Gender and Music*, Urbano & Chicago: University of Illinois Press.

Corder, F. (1922), *A History of the Royal Academy of Music from 1822 to 1922*, London: F. Corder.

Cowden-Clarke, M. – see under classified bibliography of women writers.

Cox, Rev. J.B. (1872), *Musical Recollections of the last half century*, London: Bradbury, Evans & Co.

Crawford, A. et al. (eds) (1983), *The Europa Biographical Dictionary of British Women*, London: Europa Publications Ltd.

Crichton, R. (1987), *The Memoirs of Ethel Smyth*, Harmondsworth: Viking.

Cropper, M. (u.d.), *M. Wakefield*, Kendal: Cumbria Records Office.

Crow, D. (1971), *The Victorian Woman*, London: George Allen & Unwin Ltd.

Curwen, J. (1843), *Singing for Schools and Congregations*, London: J. Curwen.

——— (1848), *The Grammar of Vocal Music*, London: J. Curwen.

Curwen, J.S. (1882), *Memorials of John Curwen*, London: John Curwen & Sons.

Disher, M.W. (1955), *Victorian Song: from Dive to Drawing-room*, London: Phoenix House.

Donaldson, J. (1907), *Woman: Her position in Ancient Greece and Rome and among the Early Christians*, London: Longmans, Green & Co.

Dore, G. and Jerrold, B. (1872, reprinted 1971), *London*, London: David & Charles.

Drinker, S. (1948), *Music and Women*, New York: Coward-McCann.

Du Page, R.P. (1921), *Une musicienne Versailles – Augusta Holmès*, Paris: Fischbacher.

Eastlake, Lady – see under classified bibliography of women writers.

Einstein, A. (1949), *The Italian Madrigal*, Princeton: Princeton University Press.

Elgar, E., (ed. P. Young) (1968), *A Future for English Music*, London: Dennis Dobson.

Eliot, T.S. (1975), *Selected Prose of T.S. Eliot*, London: Faber & Faber.

Elkin, R. (1946), *Royal Philharmonic*, London: Rider & Co.

Fay, A. – see under classified bibliography of women writers.

Fuller-Maitland, J.A. (1902), *English Music in the Nineteenth Century*, London: Grant Richards.

Galloway, W.J. (1910), *Musical England*, London: Christophers.

Gerson, N.B. (1973), *George Sand*, London: Robert Hale & Co.

Glover, S. – see detailed list, App. 3.

Godsen, P.H.J.H. (1969), *How they were taught*, London: Blackwell.

Goldsmith, O. (1908), *Unacknowledged Essay: V, Parallel between Mrs Vincent and Miss Brent, Volume 7*, New York: Putnam & Sons.

Greer, G. (1971), *The Female Eunuch*, London: Paladin.

Grierson, E. (1959), *Storm Bird: The Strange Life of Georgina Weldon*, London: Chatto & Windus.

Grove, Sir C. (1908), *Dictionary of Music and Musicians*, London: Macmillan & Co.

Hackett, M. – see under classified bibliography of women writers.

Haddon, C. (1977), *Great Days and Jolly Days*, London: Hodder & Stoughton.

Haldane, C. (1957), *The Galley Slaves of Love. The story of Marie d'Agoult and Franz Liszt*, London: The Harville Press.

Haweis, Rev. H.R. (1875), *Music and Morals*, London: W.H. Allen.

Heriot, A. (1927, reprinted 1974), *The Castrati in Opera*, New York: Da Capo Press.

Hetherington, J. (1967), *Melba*, London: Faber & Faber.

Hixon, D.L. and Hennessee, D. (1975), *Women in Music: A Bibliography*, Methuen: The Scarecrow Press.

Hodgart, M.J.C. (1950), *The Ballads*, London: Hutchinson's University Library.

Holbrooke, J. (1925), *Contemporary British Composers*, London: Cecil Palmer.

Holland, A.K. (1948), *Henry Purcell*, London: Penguin Books.

Holst, I. (1938, 2nd ed. 1969), *Gustav Holst*, London: Oxford University Press.

Howes, F. (1966), *The English Musical Renaissance*, London: Secker & Warburg.

Hughes, F.J. – see under classified bibliography of women writers.

Hughes, G. (1962), *Composers of Operetta*, London: Macmillan & Co.

Hughes, M.V. (1978), *A London Girl of the 1880s*, London: Oxford University Press.

Hutchings, A. (1967), *Church Music in the Nineteenth Century*, London: Herbert Jenkins.

Jaeger, M. (1956), *Before Victoria*, London: Chatto & Windus.

Jekyll, W. (1907), *Jamaican Song and Story*, London: David Nutt.

Jezic, D.P. (1988), *Women Composers. The Lost Tradition Found*, New York: The Feminist Press at the City University of New York.

Kamm, J. (1965), *Hope Deferred*, London: Methuen & Co.

Kennedy, M. (1971), *The Story of the Royal Manchester College of Music*, Manchester: Manchester University Press.

Kerman, J. (1962), *The Elizabethan Madrigal*, New York: Galaxy Music Corporation.

Klein, H. (1903), *Thirty Years of Musical Life in London, 1870–1900*, London: William Heinemann.

Lamb, C. (1908), *Mrs Leicester's School and Other Writings in Prose and Verse*, London: Macmillan & Co.

Lang, P.H. (1941), *Music in Western Civilization*, New York: W.W. Norton & Co.

Lee, E. (1970), *Music of the People*, London: Barrie Books.

Lehmann, L. (1919), *The Life of Liza Lehmann by Herself*, London: T. Fisher Unwin Ltd.

Lutyens, E. (1972), *A Goldfish Bowl*, London: Cassell.

Mackenzie, Sir A.C. (1927), *A Musician's Narrative*, London: Cassell.

Mackerness, E.D. (1964), *A Social History of English Music*, London: Routledge & Kegan Paul.

May, R.F. – see under classified bibliography of women writers.

Marshall, E. – see under classified bibliography of women writers.

Martineau, H. (1832), *Illustrations of Political Economy*, London: Charles Fox.

Mason, L. (1854, reprinted 1967), *Musical Letters from Abroad*, New York: Da Capo Press.

McClary, S. (1991), *Feminine Endings. Music, Gender and Sexuality*, Minnesota: University of Minnesota Press.

Mitchell, J. (1975), *Psychoanalysis and Feminism*, London: Penguin Books.

Moers, E. (1978), *Literary Women*, London: The Women's Press.

Neilson, F. (1952), *My Life in Two Worlds*, Appleton, Wisconsin: Nelson Publishing Co.

Nettel, R. (1952), *The Englishman Makes Music*, London: Dennis Dobson.

Newmarch, R. – see under classified bibliography of women writers.

Newsom, J. (1948), *The Education of Girls*, London: Faber & Faber.

Northcote, S. (1942), *The Ballad in Music*, London: Oxford University Press.

Novello, C. – see under classified bibliography of women writers.

Palmer, R. (1974), *A Touch on the Times*, London: Penguin Education.

Pearsall, R. (1969), *The Worm in the Bud: The World of Victorian Sexuality*, London: Weidenfeld & Nicholson.

Pincherle, M. (1955), *Vivaldi*, New York: W.W. Norton & Co.

Pleasants, H. (1974), *The Great Opera Singers from the dawn of Opera to our own time*, London: Victor Gollanz.

Ponder, W. (1928), *Clara Butt*, London: Harrap & Co.

Pulling, C. (1952), *They Were Singing*, London: George A. Harrap.

Rainbow, B. (1967), *The Land Without Music*, London: Novello.

Raymond-Ritter, F. – see under classified bibliography of women writers.

Raynor, H. (1972), *A Social History of Music from the Middle Ages to Beethoven*, London: Barrie & Jenkins.

Reese, G. (1940), *Music in the Middle Ages*, New York: W.W. Norton & Co.

―――― (1959), *Music in the Renaissance*, New York: W.W. Norton & Co.

Ridgway, J. (1792), *Memoirs of Mrs Billington from her birth*, London: James Ridgway.

Rossi, A. (1973), *The Feminist Papers*, New York: Columbia University Press.

Rowbotham, S. (1972), *Women, Resistance & Revolution*, London: Penguin Press.

Rutland, H. (1972), *Trinity College of Music: the first hundred years*, London: Trinity College of Music.

Sadie, J.A. and Samuel, R. (eds) (1994), *The new Grove dictionary of women composers*, London: The Macmillan Press Ltd.

Santley, C. (1909), *Reminiscences of my Life*, London: Sir Isaac Pitman & Sons.

Scholes, P.A. (1947), *The Mirror of Music*, London: Oxford University Press.

Scott, D. (1989), *The Singing Bourgeois. Songs of the Victorian drawing room and parlour*, Milton Keynes: Open University Press.

Sheppard, E.S. – see under classified bibliography of women writers.

Shaw, G.B. (1932), *Music in London 1890–1894, 3 vols*, London: Constable & Co.

—— (1937), *London Music in 1888–1889*, London: Constable & Co.

Silbermann, A. (1963), *The Sociology of Music*, London: Routledge & Kegan Paul.

Simpson, H.F. (1910), *A Century of Ballads*, London: Mills & Boon.

Smyth, E. (1919), *Impressions that Remained, vols 1 & 2*, London: Longmans, Green & Co.

Smyth, E. (1921), *Streaks of Life*, London: Longmans, Green & Co.

—— (1927), *A Three-legged Tour of Greece*, London: William Heinemann.

—— (1928), *A Final Burning of Boats, Etc.*, London: Longmans, Green & Co.

—— (1933, revised 1934), *Female Pipings in Eden*, Edinburgh: Peter Davies.

—— (1935), *Beecham & Pharaoh*, London: Chapman & Hall.

—— (1936), *As Time Went On*, London: Longmans, Green & Co.

—— (1938), *Maurice Baring*, London: Heinemann.

—— (1939), *Inordinate (?) Affection*, London: The Cresset Press.

—— (1940), *What Happened Next*, London: Longmans, Green & Co.

Soldene, E. – see under classified bibliography of women writers.

Spencer-Curwen, Mrs J. (u.d.), *Psychology Applied to Music Teaching*, London: J. Curwen & Sons.

Sphor, L. (1878), *Autobiography*, London: Longmans, Reeves & Turner.

St. John, C. (1959), *Ethel Smyth*, London: Longmans, Green & Co.

Sterling-Mackinlay, M. (1906), *Antoinette Sterling and Other Celebrities*, London: Hutchinson & Co.

Thackeray, W.M. (1904), *Mr Brown's Letter to a Young Man about Town*, London: Macmillan & Co.

Thompson, F. (1939), *Lark Rise to Candleford*, London: Oxford University Press.

Tomalin, C. (1974), *The Life and Death of Mary Wollstonecraft*, London: Weidenfeld & Nicholson.

Tovey, D.F. (1937), *Essays in Musical Analysis, Vol. V*, London: Oxford University Press.

Townsend, P. – see under classified bibliography of women writers.

Treherne, P. (1923), *A Plaintiff in Person: The Life of Mrs Weldon*, London: Heinemann.

Turner, M.R. and Miall, A. (1972), *The Parlour Song Book*, London: Michael Joseph.

Turner, W.J. (1941), *English Music*, London: William Collins.

D'Urfey, T. (1691), *Love for Money or the Boarding School*, London: Abel Roper.

Vaughan Williams, R. (1963), *National Music and Other Essays*, London: Oxford University Press.

Waitzkin, L. (1903), *The Witch of Wych Street*, Cambridge, Mass: Harvard University Press.

Wakefield, M. – see under classified bibliography of women writers.

Walker, B. – see under classified bibliography of women writers.

Weldon, G. – see under classified bibliography of women writers.

White, M.V. (1914), *Friends and Memories*, London: Edward Arnold.
—— (1932), *My Indian Summer*, London: Grayson & Grayson.
Wollstonecraft, M. (1967), *A Vindication of the Rights of Women*, New York: W.W. Norton.
Woolf, V. (1929), *A Room of One's Own*, London: Hogarth Press.
—— (1959), *A Writer's Diary*, (ed. L. Woolf), London: Hogarth Press.
Young, G.M. (1936), *A Portrait of an Age*, London: Oxford University Press.
Young, K. (1967), *Music's Great Days in the Spas and Watering-Places*, London: Macmillan.
Young, P. (1967), *A History of British Music*, London: Ernest Benn.

Magazine articles

Abromeit, Kathleen (1989), 'Ethel Smyth: *The Wreckers* and Sir Thomas Beecham', *Musical Quarterly*, 73 (2).
Armitt, Mary (1845), 'Old English Fingering', *Musical Times*, March.
Armitt, Mary (1891), 'A Richmond Idyll', *Musical Times*, November.
Banfield, Stephen (1986), 'British opera in retrospect', *Musical Times* (1718), April.
Barnes, Jennifer (1990), 'Preparation for a production of Ethel Smyth's *Fête Galante*', *Royal College of Music Magazine*, 87, (1).
Broadwood, Lucy (1905), 'Collecting of English folk-songs', *Musical Times*, August.
Cowden-Clarke, Mary (1879), 'Festival of the Salzburg Mozart Institution', *Musical Times*, August.
Cowden-Clarke, Mary (1879), 'Music in Dresden', *Musical Times*, September.
Crichton, Ronald (1986), 'Ethel Smyth at the opera', *Opera*, 37, October.
Curwen, Annie (1899), 'Music in the concrete', *Child Life*, April.
Dale, Kathleen (1994), 'Dame Ethel Smyth', *Music & Letters*, XXV, (191).
—— (1949), 'Dame Smyth's prentice works', *Music & Letters*, XXX, (329).
Franca, John (1981), 'An Ethel Smyth discovery', *The Strad*, 91, February.
Goodwin, Noel (1989), '*Fête Galante*: Britten Theatre Royal College of Music', *Opera*, 40, September.
Hold, Trevor (1993), 'Ethel Smyth: Chamber music and songs vols. 1–3', *Musical Times*, 1779.
Johnson, Carl (1982), 'Ethel Smyth: the only woman composer to ever be heard at the Met', *American Music Teacher*, 31, (3).
Macgregor, Margaret (October 1932, January 1933), 'Amelia Opei', *Smith College Studies in Modern Languages, XIV*.
McNaught, W.G. (1900), 'Miss Wakefield', *Musical Times*, August.
Scott, Derek (1994), 'The sexual politics of Victorian musical aesthetics', *Journal of the Royal Musical Association*, 119, pt. 1.
Smith, Christopher (1982), 'Smyth's *Mate*', *Opera*, 33 (59).
Osborne, Charles (1983), '*The Wreckers*, Arts Centre University of Warwick', *Opera*, 37, May.

Wakefield, Mary (1884), 'Amateur music as it should be', *Musical Times*, March.
Wakefield, Mary (1888), 'Foundation stones of English music', *Murray's Magazine*, July–December. The various titles are:

Henry VIII to Elizabeth
Madrigal time
Henry Purcell
National melodies
Music competitions
Carols, serious and secular.
Wakefield, Mary (1896), 'A Medieval Singer and his Songs', *The Commonwealth*, August.
Wood, Elizabeth (1995), 'Performing rights: a sonography of women's suffrage', *The Musical Quarterly*, 79 (4).

Reference is also made to the following magazines/journals/newspapers:

Cosmopolitan	August 1873
The Educational Magazine	January 1841
The Girl's Own	September 1883, November 1884
The Independent Magazine	1842
Illustrated London News	25 May 1844, 20 August 1892, 10 September 1892
Music in Education	January 1974
The Musical Herald	March 1867, December 1874, February 1877, September 1889, December 1896, February 1900, November 1905, February 1910, July 1944
Punch	30 April 1853
The Sunday Times	12 July 1896
Tennyson Research Journal	November 1976
Tonic Sol-fa Jubilee Magazine	1892
Tonic Sol-fa Reporter	April 1855, July 1855, December 1869
Victorian Studies	1975, **XIX** (2)

Miscellaneous:

Minutes of the Committee of the Royal Academy of Music: 1828, 1830, 1831, 1833, 1834
Graves, Percival (u.d.), 'Script of three broadcasts on Liza Lehmann', London, *British Library*.

Other articles by Mary Wakefield, though not referred to in the text are:
Murray's Magazine (July 1890), 'A studio in Provence'.
Saturday Review (26 August 1893), 'Two North Country Festivals'.
The Commonwealth (April 1896), 'A Northern gala – Grasmere sports'.
Fortnightly Review (October 1896), 'Home arts in the Cumberland mountains'.
Fortnighty Review (April 1905), 'Memories of spring in Sicily'.
The Planet (2 March 1907, 29 June 1907), General articles on music.

Atkinson & Pollitt (u.d.) 'The management of competition festivals', (Kendall).

Theses

Copley, Edith (1991), 'A survey of the choral works of Ethel Smyth with an analysis of the *Mass in D*, University of Cincinnati.
Mollowitz, Kate (1933), 'Ueber die Musikerziehung bei Ann Glover und John Curwen', University of Konigsberg.
Rush, John (1971), 'The life and work of John Curwen', University of Reading.

Classified Bibliography of Nineteenth-Century Women Writers on Music

a) Biographical

Bray, Mrs. (1857), *Handel: his life, personal and professional with thoughts on sacred music*, London: Ward & Co.

Byrne, J.C. (1892), *Gossip of the century, (Vols 1 and 2)*, London: Ward & Downey.

Byrne, J.C. (1898), *Social hours with celebrities (Vols 3 and 4)* (ed. Busk, R.H.), London: Ward & Downey.

Clayton, E.C. (1863), *Queens of Song*, London: Smith, Elder & Co.

Cowden-Clarke, M. (1858), *World-noted Women*, New York: A. Appleton & Co.

Cowden-Clarke, M. (1864), *The Life and Labours of Vincent Novello*, London: Novello & Co.

May, F. (1905), *The Life of Johannes Brahms (Vols 1 and 2)*, London: Edward Arnold.

May, F. (1912), *The Girlhood of Clara Schumann*, London: Edward Arnold.

Marshall, E. (1900), *A Story of Handel's Day*, London: Seeley & Co. Ltd.

Newmarch, R. (1912), *Mary Wakefield – a memoir*, Kendal: Atkinson & Pollitt.

Townsend, P.D. (1884), *Joseph Haydn*, London: Sampson Law, Marston, Searle & Rivington.

Weldon, G. (u.d.), *Gounod and my orphanage in England*, London: Georgina Weldon.

Weldon, G. (1875), *Musical Reform*, London: Georgina Weldon.

Weldon, G. (1902), *Mémoires*, London: Georgina Weldon.

b) Autobiographical

Cowden-Clarke, M. (1896), *My Long Life*, London: T. Fisher Unwin Ltd.

Fay, A. (1896, reprinted 1926), *Music Study in Germany*, London: Macmillan & Co.

Lehmann, L. – see general bibliography.

Novello, C. (1910) (ed. Gigliucci, Contessa V.), *Clara Novello's Reminiscences*, London: Edward Arnold.

Smyth, E. – see general bibliography.

Soldene, E. (1897), *My Theatrical and Musical Recollections*, London: Downey & Co.

Walker, B. (1890), *My Musical Experiences*, London: Richard Bentley & Son.

White, M.V. – see general bibliography.

c) Music aesthetics and philosophy

Campbell, Lady A.S. (1886), *Rainbow-Music, or the Philosophy of Harmony in Colour-grouping*, London: Bernard Quaritch.

Eastlake, Lady (1852), *Music*, London: John Murray.

Hughes, F.J. (1883), *Harmonies of Tones and Colours developed by Evolution*, London: Marcus Ward & Co.

Raymond-Ritter, F. (1877), *Women as musicians – an art historical study*, London: William Reeves.

Wakefield, M.A. (1894), *Ruskin on Music*, London: George Allen.

d) Treatises

i) Theoretical.

Gunn, A. (1803), *An Introduction to Music*, Edinburgh: C. Stewart & Co.

Paige, K. (1881), *Exercises on General Elementary Music*, London: William Reeves.

Place, G. (1856), *A Catechism of Music for the use of young children*, London: T. Bosworth & Harrison.

Prescott, O. (1882), *Form, or Design in Music, Instrumental and Vocal*, London: Ascherberg & Co.

Prescott, O. (1903), *About Music*, London: Methuen & Co.

ii) Singing.

Heale, H. (1898), *Short Voice-training Exercises in two and three parts for singing classes*, London: Augener.

Lehmann, L. (1913), *Practical Hints for Students of Singing*, London: Enoch & Sons.

Novello, S. (1856), *Voice and Vocal Art*, London: J.A. Novello.

Novello, S. (1860), *Exercises for a Contralto Voice*, London: J.A. Novello.

Sainton-Dolby, H. (1872), *Tutor for English Singers*, London: Boosey & Co.

Weldon, G. (1872, revised 1882), *Hints on Pronounciation*, London: Georgina Weldon.

iii) Piano.

Glen, A. (1894), *How to Accompany*, London: Robert Cocks & Co.

Kirkmann, J. (1854), *A Piano Instructor for the Million*, London: Boosey & Sons.

Paige, K. (1883), *Daily Exercises for the Pianoforte*, London: Patent Paper Type Co.

Reinagle, C. (1855), *A Few Words on Pianoforte Playing with rules for fingering passages of frequent occurrence*, London: J.A. Novello.

Thomas, A. (1908), *Forty Short Artistic Studies on an original system of pianoforte touch in connection with emotional expression*, Brighton: National Training School of Music, Brighton.

e) Editing

Bate, J.D. (1886), *North India Tune Book*, London: Alexander & Shepheard.

Broadwood, L. (1890), *Sussex Songs*, London: Weber & Co.

Broadwood, L., Fuller-Maitland, J. (1893), *English Country Songs*, London: Leadenhall Press Ltd.

Broadwood, L., Fuller-Maitland, J. (1908), *English Traditional Songs and Carols*, London: Boosey & Co.

Gillington, A. (1907), *Eight Hampshire Folk-songs*, London: J. Curwen & Sons.

Gillington, A. (1910), *Old Christmas Carols of the Southern Counties*, London: J. Curwen & Sons.

Gillington, A. (1910), *Breton Singing Games*, London: J. Curwen & Sons.

Gomme, A.B. (1894), *Children's Singing Games*, London: D. Nutt.

Gomme, A.B., Sharp, C. (1909–1912), *Children's Singing Games*, London: Novello & Co.

Heale, H. (1887), *Class Singing School*, London: Augener.

Mason, M.H. (1877), *Nursery Rhymes and Country Songs*, London: Metzler & Co.

Mundella, E. (1890), *The Day School Hymn Book*, London: Novello & Co.

f) Translation

Listed are the name of the translator, the title of the work and, in brackets, the author.

Bache, C. (u.d.), *Descriptive Sketch of Beethoven's Ninth Symphony* (Wagner).

Carmichael, M.G. (1894), *Celebrated Pianists of the Past and Present* (Ehrlich).

Cowden-Clarke, M. (1854), *Modern Instrumentation and Orchestration* (Berlioz).

Cowden-Clarke, M. (1854), *Counterpoint and Fugue* (Cherubini).

Cowden-Clarke, M. (1854), *Treatise on Harmony* (Catel).

Novello, S. (1855), *Collected writings on thorough-bass* (Albrechtsberger).

Novello, S. (1857), *Succinct instruction for the guidance of singing schools* (Silcher).

Novello, S. (1857), *Eighty-one part-songs and choruses by Nageli and Pfeiffer* (Nageli).

Novello, S. (1862), *Method of learning the pianoforte* (Kalkbrenner).

Raymond-Ritter, F. (1877), *Letters on music to a lady* (Ehlert).

Raymond-Ritter, F. (1877–1880), *Music and Musicians* (Schumann).

Townsend, P. (1882), *Mozart* (Jahn).

Wallace, Lady M. (1869), *Reminiscences of Felix Mendelssohn* (Elise Polko).

Wallace, Lady M. (1877), *The Life of Mozart* (Nohl).

g) Miscellaneous

Hackett, M. (1813), *Letters and Evidences respecting the Ancient Collegiate School attached to St. Paul's Cathedral*, London: Nichols, Son & Bentley.

Hackett, M. (1816), *Correspondence, Legal Proceedings, and Evidences respecting the Ancient Collegiate School attached to St. Paul's Cathedral*, London: Nichols, Son & Bentley.

Hackett, M. (1824), *Brief Account of Cathedral and Collegiate Schools with an abstract of their Statutes and Endowments*, London: Nichols, Son & Bentley.

Hackett, M. (1832), *Correspondence and Evidence respecting the Ancient Collegiate School attached to St. Paul's Cathedral*, London: Nichols, Son & Bentley.

Sheppard, E.S. (1853), *Charles Auchester*, London: Ward, Lock, Bowden & Co.

Index of names

Of female artists, composers, teachers and writers involved with music who are referred to in the text.